DATE		ATTENDANCE			UMPIRES							

DODGERS	POS.	1	2	3	4	5	6	7	8	9	10	11	12
30-WILLS	6	17		X	03		43						
19-GILLIAM	5	8			8		X	5-3					
3-W. DAVIS	8	85			F4			03					
41-JOHNSON	7	X	F7		X	5 / 6	B̄	•					
6-FAIRLY	9		8			514	63						
5-LEFEBVRE	4		8			K	—	X	12				
28-PARKER	3		X	63		13			13				
10-TORBORG	2			53		X	8		7				
32-KOUFAX	1			13		K			A				
		0	0	0	0	0	0	0	0				
		0	0	0	0	0	0	1	6				

SANDY KOUFAX

Also by Jane Leavy

Squeeze Play *(novel)*

SANDY KOUFAX

A Lefty's Legacy

JANE LEAVY

HarperCollins*Publishers*

HarperCollins books may be purchased for educational, business, or sales promotional use. For information, please write: Special Markets Department, HarperCollins Publishers Inc., 10 East 53rd Street, New York, NY 10022.

Scorecard appearing on the endpapers courtesy of the
Los Angeles Dodgers

FIRST EDITION

Designed by Elias Haslanger

Printed on acid-free paper

Library of Congress Cataloging-in-Publication Data

Leavy, Jane.
    Sandy Koufax : a lefty's legacy / by Jane Leavy.—1st ed.
      p. cm.
    ISBN 0-06-019533-9
      1. Koufax, Sandy, 1935– 2. Baseball players—United States—
Biography. I. Title.
    GV865.K67 L43 2002
    796.357'092—dc21
    [B]   2002068722

02 03 04 05 06 WB/RRD   18 19 20

For Nick and Emma

Another time,
I devised a left-hander
Even more gifted
Than Whitey Ford: a Dodger.
People were amazed by him.
Once, when he was young,
He refused to pitch on Yom Kippur.

—from "The Night Game," by Robert Pinsky

Contents

Preface

THE POET AND THE PITCHER

I DIDN'T GO TO THE Library of Congress searching for Sandy Koufax.

I went for a poetry reading, in support of a friend. Also, there was the promise of free food. Sportswriters will go anywhere for free food.

I was just back from Fantasy Camp in Vero Beach, Florida, winter home of the Los Angeles Dodgers, where I first met Koufax and several of his former teammates. Clem Labine, an estimable pitcher in his own right, had tutored me in the physics of the Koufax curveball, explaining how he held the ball without his thumb, rolling it off his uncommonly long fingers with such velocity and spin that when the ball met the wind, the air cried.

I was attempting to demonstrate the proper grip to my friend Jane Shore, a poet who had not yet recovered from seeing Mike Mussina beaned on the mound at Camden Yards. An unexpected enthusiast exclaimed, "Sandy Koufax? I *devised* Sandy Koufax."

Jane introduced me to Robert Pinsky, poet laureate of the United

States. I was too unlettered to get his allusion and Pinsky was too polite to make a point of it. He turned to a student clutching a copy of his collected works and, borrowing the volume, opened it to page 86. "The Night Game" is a poem about sex and imagination, green grass and stadium lights that turn night into day. It is about the act of creation and new love, possibility. Koufax is not so much its subject as its solution. "The solution to an emotion," Pinsky said.

Once, when he was young, Pinsky saw Sandy Koufax pitch at Ebbets Field. He doesn't remember much about the game. Just that it was night, that he sat along the third base line, that he knew who Koufax was. It was probably 1955, Sandy's rookie year. Pinsky remembers the green of the grass and blue satin shimmering against the white flannel of Koufax's shirt, and how the fabric wrinkled with exertion. He does not remember who won; whether Koufax started or relieved.

Years later when Pinsky was teaching writing at the University of California at Berkeley, someone sent him a poster of Koufax pitching: a study in kinetic sculpture, midway through his delivery, coiled and balanced on his back leg, his foot the only point of contact with the earth.

Pinsky hung the poster on his office door. In the arc and force of the pitcher's motion, Pinsky saw everything he wanted his students to know about writing: balance and concentration; a supremely synchronized effort; the transfer of energy toward a single, elusive goal.

Pinsky is a sturdy man with a square jaw, a poet whose father was a catcher for the Jewish Aces, a New Jersey barnstorming team. Surrounded by his fans, people who don't confuse the poetry of baseball with iambic pentameter, he raised his arm above a tray of canapés, attempting to replicate the impossible angle of bone and ball just prior to release. "You can't really do it," he sighed, lowering his arm. "It was like a catapult. Elegance followed by violence."

I never saw Sandy Koufax pitch. My father, who grew up on Coogan's Bluff rooting for the New York Giants, made me what I am today, a Yankee fan, by refusing to take me to Ebbets Field before the Dodgers left Brooklyn. I was probably the only Jewish kid in New York who didn't root for Koufax. I rooted for the gentiles in the Bronx instead—a fate sealed by the proximity of my grandmother's apartment to the House That Ruth Built. I watched the world series from the second floor ballroom of the Concourse Plaza Hotel during High Holiday services. I went to synagogue to pray the Yankees wouldn't have to face Sandy Koufax.

Though I was a devoted subscriber to *Life* magazine, I don't remember seeing the August 1963 issue with him on the cover. It is an iconic, Norman Rockwell treatment. At age ten, I somehow failed to notice his importance. I was a Yankee fan first, a Jew second. I was assimilated. I did not feel compelled by Judaism to place him above baseball.

Twenty years later, I was covering the U.S. Open tennis matches for the *Washington Post* on Yom Kippur. It was the day the Korean airliner was shot down over Soviet airspace. Deadlines were tight. I remember feeling pressured and something else, a discomfort in my own skin. I remember thinking, "Sandy Koufax didn't pitch on Yom Kippur." I have not worked on the High Holidays since. Sandy Koufax had made himself at home in my soul.

In this I am not alone.

In Vero Beach, Florida, I met John Gentillon, a regular at Dodger Fantasy camp, who lived next door to him for a while in California. At a family reunion one day, forty of his tipsiest relatives, most of them female, spotted Koufax watering his trees and barreled down the hillside "like a herd of elephants, screeching, Sand*ee*!" Gentillon was mortified. Koufax signed an autograph for each of them.

In the suburbs of New York, I found David Saks, a camper at Camp Chi-Wan-Da in 1953, who has been having recurring dreams about his bunk counselor, Sandy Koufax, ever since. In his dreams he gets to ask Koufax what so many others have wondered: "How did you become that great? How did that happen?"

In Manhattan, I met a woman named Shirley at the seventy-second anniversary gala of the Jewish Community House of Bensonhurst, where Koufax played on the 1951 National Jewish Welfare Board championship basketball team. A fleshy arm attached to a big voice and a firm grip took me by the wrist. "You would like, maybe, to create a Jewish memory?" I assured her I had plenty. "So why are you here?" Shirley said, disappointed. I explained my purpose, finding people who had known Koufax in Brooklyn. In an instant, she was dragging me across the ballroom, dodging vats of kosher dill pickles and mounds of chopped liver, bellowing at the top of her considerable lungs: "Anybody here know Sand*ee*?"

Everything stopped. Mel Goldfeder, the event chairman, stepped forward. While he couldn't claim to know Koufax, they had spoken when Koufax telephoned his regrets. Goldfeder still hadn't gotten over it. "He called *me* sir!"

I have met Koufax collectors and Koufax "completionists." In Washington, I was introduced to Michael Levett, whose youthful devotion to Koufax led to an adult passion for collecting the baseball card of every Jewish major-leaguer. (He has 128 of the 148 he covets.) In Philadelphia, I discovered Phil Paul, whose ambition is to acquire a ticket stub from each of Koufax's 165 victories. So far, he's got 107, including all four no-hitters, the world series games, the record strikeout performances, and two one-hitters. Stubs cost him anywhere from twenty to forty dollars. A full ticket is double the price. "My Holy Grail, the one game I really need is his first win, August twenty-seventh, nineteen fifty-five," Paul said. "There were only ten thousand people at Ebbets Field." Paying customers that night: 7,204.

On a mountaintop in Southern California, I met Buzzie Bavasi, former general manager of the Dodgers, in his study overlooking the Pacific. He's retired from baseball, but not from storytelling. "In all my years in baseball, I never saved a thing," he said. "About two years ago, I decided to get autographed balls from friends of mine, people I knew in the Hall of Fame. So I got twenty-two of them." Among them: Ted Williams, Joe DiMaggio, Stan Musial, Willie Mays, and Hank Aaron. "Somebody broke in here. What do you think they took? One ball. Sandy's. I never laughed so much in my life."

A few hundred miles north, in a subdivision of Cape Cod townhouses in the outwash sprawl east of Los Angeles, I met Pete Bonfils, a former Dodger batboy, longtime batting practice pitcher, and present-day Koufax aficionado. In his study, he has a custom-made, glass-

encased coffee table, eight feet square, built to house 132 batting practice balls. In his hard drive, he has a three-page catalogue of Koufax
memorabilia he has assembled over the last thirty years: magazine covers and newspaper headlines, baseball scorecards and autographed
glossies, a brick from Ebbets Field, a porcelain Koufax beer stein, a
1965 issue Volpe tumbler ("That's a hundred-dollar glass right there—
it's never been used"), a Koufax photo tattoo, a 33 1/3 RPM recording of
the "Last Inning, Sandy Koufax Perfect Game" ("Actual reproduction,
as narrated by Vince Scully"), a Koufax money clip/nail file/pen knife, an
autographed ticket stub from game one of the 1963 World Series, a
1981 "Official Minor League Photo Fact Card" of the Albuquerque
Dukes with pitching coach Sandy Koufax in red and yellow team colors,
every extant Koufax biography, juvenile and adult, forty-two Topps
Koufax baseball cards, and a picture of Pete and his hero on the field at
Dodger Stadium the day he was named batboy in 1969.

Pete also has a mean, pink scar on his left shoulder, acquired in the
process of trying to become Sandy Koufax. Growing up in Pasadena,
Pete, a lefty, imagined himself as Koufax every time he took the mound.
Eventually, the game surpassed his talent. He never got further than Class
A ball. But he never outgrew his devotion to Koufax. "There seems to
be a story on every guy. Ted Williams can be rude. Willie Mays too. These
guys sell their souls. Koufax could sell his soul. He could make millions
of dollars. He could do anything he wants. I don't want to say he's Jesus
Christ walking on water but he has such an aura. He, like, glows."

W	L	PCT	ERA	G	GS	CG	IP	H	BB	SO	ShO
165	87	.655	2.76	397	314	137	2324.1	1754	817	2396	40

Sandy Koufax pitched twelve seasons in the major leagues: six of
them indifferent, six of belated brilliance. Five consecutive years, from
1962 through 1966, he led the National League in earned run average.
(He is the only pitcher ever to do that.) Four times he led the National
League in strikeouts. Three times, he won at least twenty-five games.
Ninety-seven times, he struck out ten or more batters. He is one of five

pitchers in major league history who pitched at least one thousand innings with more career strikeouts than innings pitched. His last year, pitching with a crippled, arthritic arm, he won twenty-seven games and completed as many. And he never missed a start. Then, abruptly, he was gone. "He was a meteor streaking across the heavens," his friend and former roommate, Dick Tracewski, said.

Thirty-six years have passed since he last threw a pitch in competition, yet you see him on the menu at Gallagher's Steak House in New York, on the wall mural celebrating the history of the Jews outside Cantor's Deli in Los Angeles, on a six-dollar stamp issued by St. Vincent and the Grenadines, on the canvases of the renowned Jewish painter R. J. Kitaj, and on the library shelves at the Washington Hebrew Congregation in Washington, D.C. The paperback biography, a quickie clip job published in 1968, was so well thumbed librarians had to put it between hard covers. It remains the most asked for book in the synagogue's children's collection.

It was his childhood friend Fred Wilpon, co-owner of the New York Mets, who helped me understand why. Growing up with Sandy in the Brooklyn neighborhood of Bensonhurst, Wilpon was the star Koufax became. Sitting in his office high above New York's Fifth Avenue nearly fifty years later, Wilpon challenged me to find "the defining differences" that mark Koufax's career. And, he confided, in what sounded like an afterthought but felt like a benediction, "I think Sandy would never want to be remembered only by what he accomplished on the field. He may not admit it but he also stood for values that he thought were important."

What began as a search for a telephone number, an address, a way to apprise Koufax of my interest, soon became a search for those defining differences, and for the man within the myth. Of course, I also wanted to find him, which I did, finally, through Wilpon and Donald Fehr, executive director of the Major League Baseball Players Association. I wasn't home when Sandy called. The message he left aspired to tartness. "Hi, Ms. Leavy, this is Sandy, uh, Koufax." The pause told me something I would come to know about the man: formality does not become him.

"I don't really have any interest in this project," he continued. "But I'll call you back."

Yeah, sure, right, I thought.

The next day the phone rang. His voice is as smooth as his archetypal delivery. No hint of Brooklyn in the inflection. He had a well-taken—though erroneous—objection. He didn't see how a person, me, could agree to write a book about another person, him, without informing the subject of her plan. In fact, I told him, I had yet to sign a contract because I hadn't been able to contact him. Reaching him had taken four months.

"Everybody has my telephone number," he protested. "I haven't changed it in twelve years."

"Yeah, well, not me."

"You want it?" he said.

I reached for a pen. And started talking. I talked for close to an hour, afraid that if I shut up, he'd hang up. Or worse, say no, as he had to so many other aspiring authors. So I kept talking, explaining the premise for this book.

Sports in the modern incarnation is a jungle—the name Jim Rome has given to his call-in radio show out of "SoCal" where "clones" wait on hold for hours in order to trade "takes" and "smack" in a guttural and debased competition for air time. It is impossible to imagine Koufax in the jungle. In virtually every way that matters, ethically and economically, medically and journalistically, he offers a way to measure where we've been, what we've come to, what we've lost. Just as he provided me, the grandchild of Jewish immigrants, with an unlikely barometer of my own assimilation into mainstream American culture, so he affords much-needed perspective on an industry in which a shortstop is paid $252 million, more than the gross national product of ten nations.

A case in point. The first call I made, when I began reporting, was to the Major League Baseball Players Alumni Association, looking for old ballplayers who had a key at-bat, a good swing, a good story to tell. I was connected to Dan Foster, who considered my request, and then said: "Here's what I want you to do. Write a letter to each of these individuals. Place his name in the center of a white envelope. Place your

return address in the upper left-hand corner and a stamp in the upper
right-hand corner. We will fill in the address. That way, if they choose to
respond they can."

Koufax laughed when I told him the story. He got it. He remembers
when you didn't need FBI clearance to talk to a ballplayer and baseball
was what you did until you grew up. The guys he played with pumped
gas in the off-season. Duke Snider didn't carry an attaché case. He delivered the mail.

Koufax spans two distinct eras in baseball and in America. He epit-
omizes a time as distant as my childhood when presidents were believed
and pitchers went nine innings; when $4,000 was a bonus; when the
words "team" and "mates" could be used separately or in conjunction
but always without irony; when a member of the 1955 World Champion
Brooklyn Dodgers would go straight from Yankee Stadium to Columbia
University after the seventh game of the world series. Admittedly,
Koufax hadn't played much that year. He was a bonus baby kept on the
roster only because the rules demanded it. Still, it is unimaginable to
think of any of today's multimillionaire benchwarmers showing up for
class. I'm not sure which is more remarkable: that he was enrolled in
school or that he asked the professor's permission to leave early so he
could attend the team party.

Koufax is the sixties before the sixties became the sixties. He is
celebrity before celebrity became an entitlement. He is hound's-tooth, a
crisp white shirt, and a skinny black tie held in place by a discreet gold
tie tack. This is how he appears in that August 2, 1963, issue of *Life*,
vastly handsome and inaccessible. It is a cover story that promises much
and delivers nothing by today's intrusive standards. No details, no reve-
lations, except this: He built his own hi-fi! How easily satisfied we were.

Koufax defined and distinguished himself by what he did on the
baseball field and by what he refused to do. He challenged batters and
stereotypes. On the evening of September 9, 1965, he pitched a perfect
game against the Chicago Cubs. Less than a month later, he achieved
another kind of perfection by refusing to pitch the opening game of the
world series because it fell on the holiest day of the Jewish year.

As a modern athlete, he stands resolutely with one spike in the "bonus-baby" fifties and the other on the cusp of the "free-agent" seventies. His joint holdout with Don Drysdale in 1966 was an unprecedented act of solidarity, a revolutionary act, received as heresy in a time of national rebellion. The insular world of baseball has never been the same.

After that season, he quit. He could still pitch but he could no longer straighten his left arm. He could not envision a whole life without being whole. Quitting was an act of imagination and emancipation. It required the ability to conceive of an existence as full and as important as the one he had so publicly led.

No other baseball immortal in memory retired so young, so well, or so completely. He may be the last athlete who declined to cash in on his fame. He has refused to cannibalize himself, to live off his past. He remains unavailable, unassailable, and, as Pete Bonfils points out, unsullied.

This won't be so much a biography, I told Koufax, as a social history of baseball, using his career as a way to measure how much has changed. My aim, I said, is to limn the trajectory of his career and in so doing re-create that time in baseball and America when change was imminent, when a well-placed tie tack held it all at bay.

"And, by the way," I told him, "you should call Phil." A mutual friend, Phil Collier, was feeling poorly and I thought he ought to know. I also thought I was the biggest schmuck on the planet. Four months it takes to reach the man and now I'm lecturing him about how to be a friend. The next day, there was a message on the answering machine. "Jane, this is Sandy. I called Phil. Thank you."

So began this improbable journey. The search for Koufax has taken me from Bensonhurst to Beverly Hills, from the cathedrals of baseball to my rabbi's study. I have interviewed over four hundred people: players and coaches; teammates and opponents (high school, college, and major league); friends, fans, and others—Koufax has a lot of distant cousins he's never met, roommates he never roomed with, and high school friends he doesn't remember. Such is the price of fame.

I have spoken with humpties and Hall of Famers, baseball scouts and baseball executives, gentiles and Jews. Opinion was ecumenical. I gave up counting the number of times I was told, "You won't find anyone to say a bad word about him," and started wondering what it meant that so many people assumed that's what I was after. "Gentle" is the word used most often to describe him.

Those who know him well were invariably wary, often seeking his permission before agreeing to talk to me. Sitting in the visitors' dugout at Camden Yards in Baltimore, pitcher Orel Hershiser said, "I cherish my friendship with Sandy. You'd probably have an easier time doing this after he was dead." Undoubtedly, Koufax's preference. Running into my friend Dave Kindred, the sportswriter, at the Final Four a while back, he asked, "You haven't been able to talk her out of it yet either, huh?"

As word of this project spread, I was besieged by requests for his time and attention. It was my first intimation of what it must be like to be Sandy Koufax. Some messages were passed along, others deflected. I became a de facto and awkward conduit to him. Don Newcombe, his former teammate, asked me to ask Sandy for an autograph for his nephew. Such is the respect for Koufax among his peers that even those who know him are reluctant to intrude. Koufax chafes at this perception but not at such requests. An autographed picture was immediately dispatched.

Sometimes, it felt as if he were stalking me. I had surgery and just before the anesthesiologist told me to start counting backward from one hundred, he said, "Sandy's my cousin. My mother used to walk him in his carriage on Bay Parkway." A New Year's Eve guest volunteered she was his girlfriend's best friend in high school. A beatific stay at a Tuscan inn was interrupted by a knock at the door. Ouismane, the polylinguistic Somali concierge, delivered a fax from home on a silver tray: the first page of *Sports Illustrated*'s millennium tribute to its favorite athlete, Sandy Koufax. "'The Left Arm of God,'" Ouismane exclaimed, reading over my shoulder. Imagine elevating an athlete to the Holy Trinity. "You Americans! I will never understand you!"

We live in an era where privacy is suspect and the distinction between what is private and what is secret has been lost. Privacy as an act of integrity is a conceptual has-been. Koufax is a private man in the old-fashioned sense of the word. He says he would like to leave this world without a trace, which given his accomplishments is an impossibility. He told his friend Tom Villante at a funeral not too long ago: "It'll be thirty days before they know I'm gone."

He has no need to be noticed. Joe DiMaggio, to whom Koufax is so often compared, marketed his privacy; Koufax cherishes his. On the field, athletes are coached to "stay within themselves." Yet, an individual who chooses to do so, to keep an inner life inner, is deemed reclusive, enigmatic, aloof. "That whole reclusive, ghostly Howard Hughes thing is bullshit," his friend Joe Hazan says emphatically.

An enigma defies understanding. Koufax defies nothing, except perhaps the expectations of a debased, media-driven age. Nor does he defy understanding; he just doesn't particularly need to be understood, an anachronistic impulse in our "tell all" culture. In an age of promiscuous self-promotion, a woman dressed as the "Cat in the Hat" who stands outside the *Today Show* studio with a poster announcing "I am having breast cancer surgery tomorrow" is thought normal. A man who opts out of his celebrity, declining to prolong or exploit his allotted fifteen minutes, is thought odd. There must be something wrong. Something hidden.

Out of such reserve, apocrypha grow. He's lived in New Zealand, Nova Scotia, and Australia. (False.) He raised horses in North Carolina. (False; there were two horses in the barn, and he never tried to ride either of them.) Comedian Buddy Hackett was his childhood baby-sitter. (False; it was Buddy's sister.) He was the first athlete to use ice as an analgesic. (False; it was Drysdale.) He tried out for the Maccabiah Games in basketball. (False.) He struck out the heart of the Dodgers order in batting practice prior to a 1981 World Series game. (False; he says Pedro Guerrero took him deep.) He did not love to play the game. (False.)

With his reticence, Sandy Koufax asks a pertinent fin de siècle question: How, ethically, do you write about someone who would prefer not to be written about, a public person who has chosen to lead a private life but whose public deeds demand consideration? A person who grants you access to his friends and maybe even a little bit of his soul and then says, "This book has to be yours, not mine."

From the beginning, Koufax made it clear he did not want this book to be written. But, if it was going to be done, he wanted it to be done right. To that end, he agreed to verify matters of personal biography and gave friends the go-ahead to be interviewed as long as it was clear that the book is "based on what others said, not on what I'm saying." I agreed, at his request, not to interview his closest living relatives: the son and daughter of his late sister, Edie. I chose not call his ex-wives, ex-girl-friends, or the woman with whom he currently shares his life. You don't need to know everything to write the truth. You just need to know enough. He refers to this project whimsically and ruefully as "an unau-thorized biography by a neat lady." He also calls me a CPA—"a certified pain in the ass."

I can't pretend not to know him; nor do I pretend to know him better than I do. I have seen him in public venues, such as baseball's celebra-tion of the Team of the Century, where, he noted wryly, the placard in front of him misspelled his name. And on the golf course at Bob Gibson's annual charity tournament where the press of humanity wanting a piece of him momentarily trapped him in a Port-O-Johnny. With one exception (see page 266), I have quoted him only when the words were spoken at public events or in previously recorded interviews and conversations.

I've seen him in private settings where I experienced the kindness of which so many people spoke and his sense of humor. When he inquired about the health of my mother-in-law after surgery that required implanting a pig valve in her heart, I told him: "Well, now she's trayf." The Yiddish word for unclean food. "All mother-in-laws are trayf," he replied.

Early one inhospitable February morning, soon after I began work-ing on the book, I found myself at the Budget Rent-A-Car counter in the airport at Melbourne, Florida, at 1:00 A.M. A viciously pert attendant refused to rent me a car because my D.C. driver's license had expired in flight. There wasn't a living soul I knew within three hours of Melbourne (not to mention a cab or a limo) except Sandy Koufax. Slumped by the

Budget counter, I asked myself the existential question: Could I call him? Would he come?

I decided I could and he would. Then I remembered he was out of town. So I heedlessly hitchhiked down I-95, heading south toward Dodgertown, thinking, Is this sonofabitch really worth it? To which he later, cheerfully, replied, "You get a resounding no from me."

Among those who respectfully disagree is Herb Cohen, the Sage of Bensonhurst, author of *You Can Negotiate Anything*. Herbie is Larry King's close friend, not Sandy's. Their lives were peripheral to each other's: Lafayette High School, Bay Parkway, the "J." But Herbie knows things. "I watch fish," Herbie told me one day, puckering his lips. "The thing about fish is they don't know they're in the water. Their vision is always blurry. Don't let Sandy dissuade you from his significance."

In Robert Pinsky's poem, Koufax stands in opposition to my childhood hero, Whitey Ford, whom he beat twice in the 1963 World Series. Whitey and the Yankees were anathema to Pinsky. They were the establishment, people who got all A's. One early fifties night in Monmouth, New Jersey, when Whitey was pitching for the U.S. Army and Pinsky was still very young, he waited for an autograph. When the moment came, the boy ventured forward with his request. "Not now, kid," the pitcher replied.

Big mistake: you never know who's going to grow up to be poet laureate. Whitey's fate was sealed; in the poet's mind he would always be Sandy's foil. So, although I didn't go to the Library of Congress in search of Sandy Koufax, that's where I found him or, at least, the defining differences Fred Wilpon urged me to consider. As Pinsky put it, "His triumph surpassed mere success."

I called Sandy the next morning to tell him what the poet had said. There was quiet on the other end of the line. After a moment or two, he asked with a delivery every bit as smooth as his windup, "Do you think he'd like a ball?"

The package arrived a couple of weeks later, accompanied by a note: "Whitey's really a good guy."

Ford subsequently redeemed himself in Pinsky's estimation with a plaintive, if belated, explanation for his youthful rudeness: "Soldiers don't give autographs." (And in mine by asking for a copy of Pinsky's poem. "He wrote nice about Sandy?" Whitey said. "I'd like to see that.")

Now, every night before he goes to bed, Pinsky thinks about Sandy Koufax. He sets the alarm on the security system of his home and considers his valuables: a signed first edition of Robert Frost's first book of poetry, *A Boy's Will*, and a signed Sandy Koufax baseball. On the sweet spot it says, "There was never a better night game."

Except, perhaps, one.

Chapter 1

WARMING UP

THREE DECADES AFTER he threw his last pitch, Sandy Koufax was back in uniform at Dodgertown, a rare occurrence given his belief that baseball uniforms do not flatter those of a certain age. This is where he made his debut in the spring of 1955 and Vero Beach is where he has chosen to make his after-baseball home—an odd choice for a man said not to like the game and the attention it brings him. Mornings when he's in town, he works out in the training room. The clubhouse guys gave him a key. He brings the bagels.

On this particular day in February 1997, he was at Dodgertown for a seminar on sports medicine. He had been recruited by Frank Jobe, the Dodgers' team physician, to teach an audience of biomechanical experts how to throw a ball. He couldn't very well say no: he was on Jobe's operating table at the time. He had torn his rotator cuff falling down the stairs. The Boys of Summers Past are not immune to senior moments.

Thinking of Koufax as clumsy is as disconcerting as the sight of the familiar "32" confined to this minimalist stage: sitting behind a bunting-draped table in a multipurpose room at what is now known as the Conference Center at Dodgertown. He looked thinner than in memory, thirty pounds less than his playing weight, the legacy of an afterlife as a marathoner. The old baggy uniforms always made him look less imposing than he was. His hair was thinner too, but silver, not gray. He had the appearance of a man aging as well as one possibly can, somehow managing to look graceful in uniform while perched beside a droopy fern.

In 1955, Dodgertown was a baseball plantation with diamonds that disappeared into the orange groves on the horizon. No one could have envisioned then the industry that baseball would become; the science that throwing would become; or the pitcher Koufax would become. A pitcher so sublime, people remember always the first time they saw him—among them fellow lecturers Duke Snider and Dave Wallace. What Wallace, a baseball man, recalls most is leaving the stadium convinced: "The ball comes out of his hand different from anybody else's."

His virtuosity was a synthesis of physiognomy and physical imagination. He didn't just dominate hitters or games. He dominated the ball. He could make it do things: rise, break, sing. Gene Mauch, the old Phillies skipper, was once asked if Koufax was the best lefty he ever saw. Mauch replied: "The best righty, too." As Billy Williams, the Hall of Famer, put it: "There was a different tone when people talked about Sandy Koufax."

Hank Aaron was his toughest out: "You talk about the Gibsons and the Drysdales and the Spahns. And as good as those guys were, Koufax was a step ahead of them. No matter who he pitched against, he could always be a little bit better. If somebody pitched a one-hitter, he could pitch a no-hitter."

John Roseboro was his favorite receiver: "I think God came down and tapped him on the shoulder and said, 'Boy, I'm gonna make you a pitcher.' God only made one of him."

He was an artist who inspired ballplayers to reach beyond their usual idiom for metaphor and simile. They called him the game's Cary Grant and Fred Astaire and compared him to the *Mona Lisa* and the *David*. "He looked like Michelangelo," Ernie Banks said. "Pitching, walking, whatever he did was kind of in rhythm with life, *stylish*." Sometimes one analogy did not suffice. As Koufax's teammate, the noted art historian Lou Johnson, said, "He was Michelangelo and Picasso rolled into one."

Absent the radar guns and computer-generated technology of the late twentieth century, which turned acts of grace into biomechanical models, he was admired rather than analyzed. His fastball remains elegantly understated, unmeasurable, unknowable. His curveball lives on in grainy television footage and in the memory of the unfortunates who tried to hit it. There are those, romantics and catchers, content to leave it at that—Roseboro among them: "That SOB was unusual. There's never been another like him and I don't think there ever will be. Trying to explain how he throws, how he got his control, how he thinks—he was just un-*fucking*-usual. Who gives a shit *how* he threw it?"

Koufax cared. Long after he retired, he became a roving pitching coach in the Dodgers' minor league system and a stealth advisor to an ardent cadre of pitchers, coaches, and managers who quote him like a shaman—*Sandy says!*—and then get in line for his autograph just like everyone else. He didn't want them to do what he said because Sandy Koufax said, "Do it." He wanted them to understand *why* it worked.

He had come to see his body as a system for the delivery of stored energy, intuiting the principles of physics inherent in the pitching motion. This realization not only put him ahead of batters, it put him ahead of science. It would take decades for the gurus of biotech medicine to catch up. Later, when he had the time, he visited their labs and delved into their textbooks seeking proofs for what he knew empirically to be true. He learned to break down the pitching motion into its component parts and to put the science of motion into accessible language. He improvised drills using a bag of balls and a chain-link fence, giving impromptu clinics in the parking lot of Bobby's Restaurant in Vero Beach. He held whole pitching staffs in thrall with his knowledge—sitting, as John Franco of the Mets put it, "bright-eyed at his feet in the middle of the locker room like little boy scouts."

His face changes when he talks about pitching. His eyes light up, his grammar comes alive, the past tense yielding to the present. The tightness in his voice often noticed in the presence of reporters disappears. As he spoke to the doctors and physical therapists arrayed before him in Dodger jerseys in a conference room at Dodgertown, his voice was as light as his fastball. Before long his hands began to move, first tentatively, then more broadly, arms spread wide, as if to envelop his subject and his audience.

"Everybody who performs an athletic event of any kind is a system of levers," he began. "You can't alter what the bones do. If you can make the bones work, the injuries to the soft tissue will be a lot less. It's when guys are in a bad position and now they try to make the muscles do something to compensate for the bad position that they injure themselves."

Rising, he turned to an easel and drew a simple figure: >. Then he added a series of lines fanning out from the upper arm so that > became /. His drawings are famous. They circulate through baseball's underground, accompanied by the whispered awe usually reserved for great art. Truth to tell: Koufax may have painted the corners but he's no Matisse. His audience had no clue what they were looking at. "This is usually my quiz," he said, apologetically. "But in the interest of time I'll give you the answer."

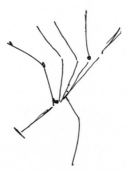

A pitcher from the beginning of his motion through his delivery, using his body as a catapult.

"While it may look ridiculous, that's a pitcher from the start of his windup to the finish when he releases the ball. What's happening is the hips get out front and you create some energy by leaving the upper part of your body behind."

Using his Magic Marker, he directed their attention to the second to last of the fanned lines. "The most critical point is right about here. The front leg is charged with stopping the torso. When the torso stops, the arm catches. You've now multiplied the force factor. So the arm now develops more speed than it had when it was simply moving with the body. It's the law of the flail. It's somewhere between six and eight to one, I don't remember; I have it at home.

"In the Middle Ages when they first had catapults, they had the single-arm catapult. It's a simple ratio: the length of the catapult to the speed. Then some guy—I don't know who the hell it was—said, 'Hey, how about one with two shorter arms?' They threw that stone six times as far. He's thinking: Hey, we're throwing rocks on these guys and they can't reach us. So basically that's what happens with the body. It's a two-armed catapult. You try to get the front half out as far as you can. All power pitchers do that. When the front leg stops, the upper body catches, the arm straightens, and you see a straight line. Basically, you try to work as much as you can with leverage and weight and energy rather than having to use the force of the muscles to perform those actions that just letting your body get in the right position will take care of. You get the work done by leverage and weight rather than force. You gotta do what the bones do."

"Form follows function," Louis Henri Sullivan wrote in 1896. He was referring to architecture, but he might as well have been talking about Koufax. He embodied the principle. His form, evolved over twelve major league seasons, was ideally suited to its function. First he perfected it. Then he learned to repeat it. Finally, he came to understand and articulate the physical laws implied in what he did.

His delivery was the kinetic equivalent of E. B. White's "clear, crystal stream" of the English language: honed, pared down, essential. Every pitch landed like a punch line. He flowed. There were no glitches or hitches; no Brooklyn shrugs. Photographers and painters, with their ability to freeze a moment in a stop-action sequence of images, could isolate elements of his delivery—the high leg kick, the grotesque torque of his elbow, the pinched contortion of his eyes at the instant before release. These are powerful images. They are also misleading. A motion doesn't stop. It is a continuum.

Today, biomechanical researchers like Jobe's colleague, Dr. Marilyn Pink, use computer-enhanced telemetry to analyze a pitcher's motion. When she performed a "qualitative visual analysis" of Koufax's form in her lab at Centinela Hospital in Los Angeles, she discovered what batters already knew: He was biomechanically perfect. "There was absolutely not a wasted piece of energy there," Pink concluded. "He knew exactly what was extraneous and what was needed."

The beauty of his delivery was a function of his mechanics and his mechanics were a function of obeying the laws of nature. Every pitch came over the top. He didn't drop down. He didn't come sidearm. He didn't fool around. His fluidity lulled minds and dulled reflexes. *Let the body put you to sleep and let the arm get you out*, he would say. No matter how many times a batter saw it, the ball's arrival at home plate always came as a shock. It was a humbling, disorienting sensation. In the immortal words of Willie Stargell, trying to hit Koufax was like "trying to drink coffee with a fork." Hitters talk about it all the time and invariably in the same words. The ball presented itself as an offering. *It was right there. I was right on it.* And, then, nope, good-bye, it was gone.

Andy Etchebarren, the Baltimore catcher who was the last batter ever to face him, quickly assessed the problem. "See, you need a certain amount of time for the eye to see what it sees and to tell the brain what it needs to be told and then your hands gotta move. And that is all taking place in less than a second. With Koufax, your eyes couldn't tell your brain to react in time."

Many hitters revert to the present tense in an effort to describe the experience of facing him. It's almost as if they are frozen in the long-ago moment just as they were frozen at the plate. "Koufax had the purest delivery," said Tim McCarver, the former catcher better known as a TV announcer to a new generation of baseball fans. "There's no deception in trying to pick the ball up. That's what made Koufax Koufax. It was like one muscle throwing the ball.

"With Koufax the left arm goes up and everything's connected, a flowing unit coming toward you. The curveball was biting down and the fastball was exploding up. You had to look up and down, up and down—it was a very difficult thing for a hitter to adjust to."

Talk to guys who faced him and they all say pretty much the same thing: "You know, he only had two pitches." Of course, as Willie Mays points out, "He threw them very well." And he threw them from the same place, the same angle, the same motion. You didn't know which was which until one went up and the other went down. The curve mesmerized and seduced; the fastball inspired awe and onomatopoeia: *Ptoom. Psssst. Whchooo. Woooo. Wsssszzzzzzt.* Or, as Ralph Branca put it with rhetorical flourish: "How did Koufax pitch? Whoosh. *Whoosh. WHOOSH!*" He never believed in a change of pace. If he needed to change speeds, he figured he'd just throw harder.

"He didn't have to think too much," Jim Bouton concluded after watching him disarm the Bronx Bombers in the 1963 World Series. "He just had to decide whether to throw his overpowering, overwhelming fastball or his off-the-table curveball. Of course, either one would have been fine. The fact that he threw both with the same grace and the same beautiful delivery was hypnotizing. Nobody knew how fast he was. I spoke to him once or twice. His style of speaking and his manner was the same as his pitching motion: all of a piece, seamless and smooth. It looked like one of those jumbo jets coming in for a landing. They look so huge and graceful that they look really slow but of course they're coming in as fast as any other plane."

Koufax's fastball inspired scientific debate, pitting the empiricism of the batting eye against scientific principle. The laws of physics and logic dictate that an object hurtling through space must lose height and momentum. Anyone can make a Whiffle ball rise, sure. But a man standing on a fifteen-inch-high mound of dirt throwing a five-ounce horsehide sphere downhill? "Rise, my butt," Roseboro, the skeptic, says.

Hitters scoff at science. Their expert testimony is unanimous.

Stan Musial: "Rose up just before it got to the plate."

Willie Mays: "I don't know how much it rose, it just rose. Ain't got time to try and sit there and count how high it goes. You just know it went up—very quickly."

Hank Aaron: "It did *something*, you know?"

Pitchers, coaches, and umpires concur.

Carl Erskine: "It reaccelerated. It came again."

Dave Wallace: "Fifteen feet from home plate where the grass ends and the dirt begins, it got an afterburner in its ass."

Doug Harvey: "I don't know why or how. In thirty-one years, I've never seen anybody else that could do that. Nolan Ryan's ball did not do it. Jim Maloney's ball did not do it. I'm talking hard throwers—Gibson, Seaver. Nobody's ball did what Koufax's ball did."

It was enough to make you question your sanity, if not your eyesight. During the 1965 World Series, Koufax threw five consecutive fastballs past Tony Oliva—a dead fastball hitter. After the series, Oliva went straight to the eye doctor. "The doctor said, 'Nothing is wrong with your eyes, Tony, you have the best eyes on the club,'" Oliva recalled. "Everybody on the club just laughed."

A ball in flight is subject to three forces: gravity, which accelerates movement downward; drag, which impedes forward motion; and lift. Lift is created by backspin, which vies with gravity for control over the trajectory of the ball. According to science, gravity always wins, causing a ball to drop three feet over the distance of sixty feet six inches. Physicists insist that the hop on Koufax's fastball was an optical illusion created by the expectation that it would drop more than it did. "Physics is full of shit," said another expert on the subject, Jim Bunning, a Hall of Fame pitcher who graduated to the United States Senate. "Physics also said you can't throw a curveball. And I guarantee you his ball when he threw a curve did very *un*physical things."

If Koufax's fastball defined him in the popular imagination, his curveball distinguished him in the minds of major league hitters. They had a whole vocabulary to describe his curve and what it did to them. They called it an overhand drop. (*Started at twelve, finished at six.*) They called it a yellow hammer. They called it a biter and they called it a bitch. Mostly, they called it unfair. It started a foot over your head and headed south in a hurry. Hitters swore it broke two feet. From the letters to the knees. From the table to the floor. From heaven to God's green earth. They said it fell out of the sky.

Guys would swing at it like they were chopping wood and end up hitting only the plate. Juan Marichal once broke his bat in half that way. It fooled batters, umpires, and sometimes his own catcher. The first time Jimmy Campanis, Al's kid, caught Koufax, he stood up to catch the ball and it hit him in the knee.

Some came to regard his curveball as an act of God, a force of nature. "A *mystic* waterfall," Jimmy Wynn called it. Mystic? Surely he meant misty. "Either one," the Toy Cannon replied. "It makes your eyes water when you see it coming. And when you miss it or you take it for a strike, you walk back to the dugout and see guys hiding their mouths. You know they want to laugh at you, just saying to themselves, Thank you, Jimmy. I'm glad it was you, not me."

An average major league curveball rotates perhaps twelve or thirteen times on its journey to home plate. Pitcher Al Leiter swears you can count the revolutions on Koufax's curve by slowing old footage to a crawl. He also swears: "It's up to fourteen or fifteen!" Which Leiter's old pitching coach, Wallace, says is a little high.

When it was right, you could hear it coming. "It sounded like a little tornado," said Orlando Cepeda. "*Bzzzzzzz.* And it looked like a high fastball. Then it dropped—BOOM—in front of you. So fast and so noisy, it scared you."

To understand how Koufax did what he did, it is necessary to see a ball in his hand. When Wallace tossed him one, it disappeared in his grasp. Wrapping the ball, players call it. Before middle age set in he could hold six balls in his hand. Or a friend's infant grandson. A women's size six and a half glove fits comfortably—in his palm. As former Dodger Rick Monday says, "When Sandy Koufax holds a baseball there's no question who's in control."

Koufax held the ball aloft to show the proper grip on the curveball: between the middle and ring fingers with his middle finger resting inside the long seam of the ball. His thumb, index finger, and even his ring finger were largely superfluous. He threw his curve off his middle finger, karate-chopping the air, pulling down on the seams with uncommon force and friction, thus generating unprecedented spin. "When you push back up, you've got to bend your wrist, hook it, so your hand is almost inside your arm," he explained. "You can't throw it as hard. You can't spin it as fast pushing up as you can pulling back down."

Pulling down also places less stress on soft tissue and prevents the ball from popping up into view. In photos, you can see his thumb sticking straight up as if hitching a ride.

Watching from the back of the room, Duke Snider hooted, "And we're supposed to hit it, right?" Snider tried only once, his last season in the majors when he was playing out the string with the Giants in hateful Candlestick Park. He was trying to stay warm at the end of the dugout when manager Alvin Dark summoned him to pinch-hit for Willie McCovey, who had pulled a muscle swinging at a 3-and-1 pitch. "I said, 'Alvin, are you out of your mind? I strike out quite often.'

"He says, 'He might walk you.'

"I said, 'I never thought of that.' I went up and Sandy was laughing so hard he walked me. I said, 'Thank you, Sandy.'"

The hardest thing in sports is no single act, it is the replication of that act in an endless vacuum of infinite space. That is the ultimate discipline. In biomechanical terms, what made Koufax perfect was the ability to repeat a motion. Pitch after pitch. Batter after batter. Game after game.

His control—so admired and so hard won—was a corollary to his body control. "As much as you can do to get the variables out of the delivery, the easier it is to repeat," he explained. "That's the key to a repeated golf swing, or pitching motion or batting swing. Hitters have the variable of not knowing where the ball is going to be. The pitcher wants to do exactly the same thing every time. He just wants to do it in a slightly different direction each time."

To call this *a* motion is misleading. A pitcher's delivery, windup to follow-through, synthesizes a thousand separate physical acts, many of which occur simultaneously and all of which take place in approximately 3.68 seconds. Koufax learned to isolate and replicate the most crucial of them. "He thought it all through before science," Pink said. "Now science has caught up with him and the data supports what he has known all along. He figured out some of the basic keys to throwing harder, faster, and more accurately *early* in the pitch. If you get them down, you can't help but deliver the ball properly. How many arms has he saved? As many people as want to listen."

Koufax rarely speaks publicly about pitching. Jobe and his associates have tried to persuade him to collaborate on a pitching video, and taped this discussion for instructional use. His acolytes within baseball are noteworthy and numerous: Alan Ashby, Tim Belcher, Kevin Brown, John Franco, Orel Hershiser, Tim Leary, Al Leiter, Chan Ho Park, Kenny Rogers, Nolan Ryan, Dave Stewart, Don Sutton, Bob Welch. "This isn't a philosophy," says former major league manager Kevin Kennedy, another Koufax disciple. "It's the way the body works."

Or, as Koufax has been known to say, *Mechanics is what's natural.*

"For every action there is an equal and opposite reaction," Koufax said, reminding his audience of Newton's law of motion. When, in the course of delivering a pitch, a man applies force to the dirt in front of the mound, an equal but opposite force is applied by the ground to the pitcher. A stream of elastic energy is carried upward through the large muscles of the lower body and dispersed through the shoulder, the elbow, and the hand. A kinetic chain, it's called.

Think of a line of skaters whipping across a patch of ice. Each one represents a portion of a pitcher's body—thigh, trunk, shoulder, arm. Their linked hands are joints and connective tissue. Each link in the chain is dependent on the others for speed and stability. They all rely on the anchor for security. If he wobbles, the chain breaks down. The skaters go nowhere—or go flying. But when they move in unison, like a set of interconnected levers, energy builds. That accumulated energy is transferred from skater to skater until it reaches the last man on line, who travels fastest and carries most of the force.

The efficiency of Koufax's motion generated greater than usual force. The anatomical advantages inherent in his impossibly long arms and fingers enhanced that efficiency. Maximized efficiency also meant maximized stress. Each pitch was an act of violence. Ironically, by making his body into the perfect catapult, he may have hastened the built-in obsolescence of his elbow.

In baseball, a Great Arm is admired, massaged, milked, deified, and amortized. It is deferred to and referred to as if a thing apart. In fact, like the last skater on the imaginary line, it is a dependent. The back leg is the controlling authority, in Koufax's view, "the single most important thing in pitching."

As the batter dug in at the plate, Koufax wedged his back foot into the pitching rubber, inclining his ankle toward home. The angle was crucial. It created its own momentum, insisting that his body move forward in space. It was the source of the energy he was about to release.

It remains a subject of esoteric debate in biomechanical circles whether a pitch begins with a push or a controlled fall off the pitching rubber. Koufax pushed. Flat feet can't push. Most pitchers go into their windup with their back foot flat against the rubber, a passive approach. So ingrained is this orthodoxy, it took Hershiser three months practicing nothing else to get it right. Koufax finally told him to take the middle spike out of his shoe so he could wedge his foot into the rubber.

The difference is as subtle as it is essential. By aligning muscle *with* bone, stress is minimized, force is maximized, and leverage is increased. "If your foot is at the angle you want it to be, your force is straight up that leg bone," he said. "If you start in that position, there's a lot more that you can do with the back leg a lot quicker. You're already in a position to push. In fact, it automatically pushes your hips forward."

His front leg came up. The right knee, as it rose, seemed to touch his elbow. His toe extended like a dancer on point. For an instant, he seemed in equipoise, his back leg a pedestal. It was his only point of contact with the earth. Every other part of his body was flying.

The angle also precludes what Koufax calls "an erratic and flexible base." Joints are inherently unreliable, not to mention breakable, requiring timing and attention. Inclining his foot as he did eliminated his ankle as a variable while accelerating his forward motion.

His upper body turned as a unit like a matador pirouetting away from a charging bull, the ball and his left hand tucked inside his glove. Then his hands parted and his left shoulder dipped, his arm dangling below his knee, the ball obscured from view From the batter's perspective, he looked almost simian. From the photographer's well, it seemed he reached so far back his hand actually touched the mound.

Anyone who has ever handed something to a whining child in the backseat understands the peril of reaching back with only your arm. Koufax kept his arm in line with his shoulder blade, reducing the pressure on his rotator cuff. In medical jargon: "On the scapular plane," thirty degrees forward of lateral. "Just the way we teach it now," Jobe said.

One leg reached toward home, the other extended behind him, forming an inverted V with his hips at its apex. They were his infrastructure, flying buttresses supporting his upper body.

Some athletes describe an out-of-body experience at peak performance, a freedom from the bonds of physical activity. Koufax never lost consciousness of where his body was, particularly the lower half. He knew that if his hips went where they were supposed to go the rest of him would surely follow. "You gotta lead with your hips," he always tells young pitchers.

As he planted his foot on the downward slope of the mound, his back knee grazed the ground. His torso arched, his legs splayed. From certain angles, it almost looked as if he were straddling the hill.

His stride was long and exact (it should be about 70 to 80 percent of a pitcher's height), which made him fussy about his pants. If they were too tight, they impeded his stride and Nobe Kawano, the Dodgers' accommodating clubhouse man, would scurry for new ones, waiting as Koufax tried on pair after pair, going through his pitching motion in each of them.

"You have to be low," he said, simulating with his hand the motion of a plane taking flight. "If you look at pictures of Tom Seaver, Nolan Ryan, myself, the back leg is on the ground. If you ever had a Whiffle ball and tried to make it do that, you know you've got to get down as low as you can and make the ball spin backward. You have to get your center of gravity low so that when you're throwing the ball, you're throwing it straight out, rather than down. You can't defy gravity."

His eyes never left the target. Oh, he'd look over at first base if by chance anyone got that far. Otherwise, his gaze stayed level, blazing a path for the flight of the ball.

He never threw downhill. Gravity would take care of that. He told himself, "Throw through the target, not to it." And that target was always on the other end of a level plane. What made him different from other pitchers, biomechanical experts would later conclude, was his ability to conceive of and stay on that plane longer than anyone else.

No matter where the target was, three or four inches off the outside of the plate or brushing the inside corner, his release point was always the same. Only the direction varied.

"You see a lot of pitchers trying to change direction with just the hand or arm," Koufax said. "It doesn't work. You have to do what the bones do. You want to shoot it over there, you point over there. Like a bow and arrow."

Inside his glove, his hand stayed on top of the ball until the last possible instant before rotating it into position to deliver the desired pitch. His fingers were his compass, the seams a topographical map, pointing the way home.

The ball nestled in a V between his fingers. That V was his sight—a sharpshooter's guide. "All the time I'm pitching I see this," he said, splaying his fingers. "When I pick the ball out of the glove and here, and here, and here, all the time I look at this. The only time I stop seeing it is as I release the ball."

Now the arm came forward like a whip, hurtling the ball in its assault on home plate. The power generated by his lower body traveled upward and exploded through his fingertips. The catapult had done its job. The transfer of energy was complete.

"It's KISS," he told the doctors with that familiar Brooklyn shrug. "Keep It Simple, Stupid."

Of course, it isn't simple. The experts had lots of questions, some of which couldn't be answered with a Magic Marker. They were having trouble visualizing that thing he did with his foot on the pitching rubber. He got up from behind the table and placed himself on an imaginary pitching mound, asking them to envision a hundred-pound weight at his foot and the best way to go about moving it. He swung his left leg out to the side, as if to push the object with a scissor kick. "There's no way I'm going to do it this way," he said.

Then he tipped his left foot inward and pushed the imaginary weight again. "I'm going to turn my foot and push as hard as I can this way," he said. "If my foot is in this position, the minute I pick my right foot up, I'm gone. I can't *not* do it."

His hands were cupped at his waist as if in prayer, his feet splayed in that familiar bowed angle. His weight shifted from back to front, the momentum of his body carrying him toward home. The years faded and all that remained was the blank, white movie screen behind him. It was easy to project onto it a different scene—say the corrugated pavilion in deep center field at Dodger Stadium. It didn't take much imagination at all to see him on the mound, warming up again.

Chapter 2

THE PREGAME SHOW

S UNSET ON SEPTEMBER 9, 1965, was at 7:08 P.M. The lights were on at Dodger Stadium, obliterating the last vestiges of smog and smoke lingering over Watts some ten miles away. It was that last moment before darkness compromises the light. But the absent sun still asserted its control over the ebbing day.

Sandy Koufax, the Dodgers' starting pitcher, knew he was in the gloaming of his baseball career. He had not won a game in three weeks. Not since black Los Angeles had exploded in rage. Not since he watched in horror as San Francisco Giants pitcher Juan Marichal bludgeoned John Roseboro with a baseball bat. Not since he had confided in his friend Phil Collier, the beat reporter for the *San Diego Union*, that the next season would be his last.

Traumatic arthritis in his left elbow required him to douse his body with Capsolin, a hot sauce derived from red hot chili peppers, before every game. Trainers used tongue depressors to apply it, smearing him with the stuff the way you'd spread mustard on a Dodger Dog. Bill Buhler, the head trainer, wore surgical gloves for this procedure; otherwise his wife wouldn't let him put his hands beneath the sheets when he got into bed.

All season, Koufax had been taking Butazolidine pills and cortisone shots. Empirin with codeine was a staple of his pregame diet. Afterward, he bathed his arm in a tub of ice water cold enough to chill three postgame beers left behind by the trainers. When the bottles were empty, the treatment was done. But the inevitable erosion of time, bone, and cartilage had not yet compromised his ability. He could still throw the tantalizing curve that broke like a waterfall. And he could still blow.

There were times, many times, when he would come into the dugout before the game mindful of the Dodgers' paltry offense and tell his teammates: "Just get me one. All I need is one." No one thought he was bragging. Other times, he would emerge from the tunnel kvetching, "I can't get loose. I ain't got shit." They'd watch him dangle from the dugout roof trying to stretch, the only time he ever looked ungainly, and laugh: "*It's in the bag. Big Boy's got it tonight.*"

This was not one of those times. It was just another Thursday night in September: an improbable confluence of lives, careers, dreams, and fates. There were no bullpen portents or predictions, only the usual great expectations. The Dodgers had lost their last two games to the hated, league-leading Giants to fall a half game behind in second place. A scheduling quirk had brought the dismal, last place Chicago Cubs to Los Angeles for a one-game visit. The U.S. Weather Bureau had predicted light to moderate smog and a game-time temperature in the seventies. The ball wouldn't carry; it never did at night. By the late innings, batting helmets and bullpen chairs would acquire a fine residue of condensation, as dampness settled into the basin of Chavez Ravine. It was a forecast almost as providential as the scheduled pitching matchup.

Koufax (21–7) vs. Hendley (2–2)

Elsewhere in the continental United States, the outlook was not so fair. A killer hurricane named Betsy had forced 250,000 people from their

coastal homes, postponing a chess match between Soviet Vasily Smislov
and American wunderkind Bobby Fischer. On the comics page, Lucy,
from the Peanuts crew, was already cursing the darkness. The morning
paper also brought news of the 650th American casualty in Vietnam,
where 108,000 U.S. troops were now engaged in combat. In Dallas, Jack
Ruby told a press conference that people in high places were suppressing
facts about the Kennedy assassination. In Boston, a headline proclaimed:
"Negro Children Invade White Schools." In San Francisco, Marichal was
making his first start at Candlestick Park since his suspension for the
attack on Roseboro. In New York, Major League Baseball announced
that the first game of the world series would be played on October 6,
Yom Kippur, the holiest day of the Jewish calendar.

Help, the Beatles' new color movie, had been held over at Los
Angeles theaters for a second smash week. Schoolboys preparing to
return to Orange County classrooms were warned that Beatle-bobs
would not be tolerated in public schools. Dorothy Dandridge was found
dead in her West Hollywood apartment. Three weeks after the worst
racial rioting in U.S. history, the *Los Angeles Times* reported "Two Fires
Flare in Burned Riot Area Buildings." A one-paragraph item buried
deep inside the news hole explained:

> Firemen quickly extinguished two blazes which began seven
> minutes apart Wednesday in burned-out buildings in the
> south Los Angeles riot area. Officials said both may have
> been set by Molotov cocktails. The first fire was reported at
> 3:07 P.M. in the ruins of a commercial building at Vernon and
> Central Aves. The other started at 3:14 P.M. in the abandoned
> theater at Vernon and Broadway.

Ten miles away, at Dodger Stadium, Koufax was preparing to try to
win his twenty-second game. Emotionally and geographically, Dodger
Stadium is as far as you can get from Brooklyn and still be in the continental United States. It is gaudy in its expanse, luxurious in its spa-
ciousness. Nestled in the Elysian Hills, with the purple San Gabriel

Mountains standing sentinel to the north, it feels at once intimate and expansive. The nooks and crannies of urban constraint do not pertain. The trolley car dodgers of the forgotten borough, who gave the franchise its name, are a distant and severed memory. Mass transportation? Forget it. Parking we got: twenty-one terraced lots, vast, undulating swaths of concrete circling the ravine which the Los Angeles city fathers had ceded to Walter O'Malley in order to lure him out of Brooklyn.

He created a cheerful place, often called the most beautiful stadium in baseball, dotted with eucalyptus and acacia, palm trees and rose bushes, its fixtures and appointments painted the color of swimming pools as seen from the sky. It was not just state of the art, it was a state of mind, a $22 million steel-and-concrete symbol of the continental shift in American culture. The sun still rose in the east. But that's about all. Dodger Stadium spoke to the ascendancy of the West. It was the place to be, and to be seen, especially if Koufax was pitching.

A half hour before the first pitch, Milton Berle spotted home plate umpire Ed Vargo by the backstop. Vargo was schmoozing with some tonsured Brothers from the Christian Brothers Winery. "Hey, Eddie, quit worrying about the Catholics," Berle bellowed. "The Big Jew's pitching tonight." Uncle Miltie, always with his finger on the pulse of America, claimed authorship of the line: "Koufax is the greatest Jewish athlete since Samson." Or maybe it was Georgie Jessel. His teammates called him "Super Jew." "That, or God," Stan Williams said.

A decade earlier, when Koufax became a Dodger, there was no deification. Nor was there major league baseball in California. No red-eyes. No West Coast swings. So much had changed in America, in baseball, in Sandy Koufax's life. Even staid, WASPy *Time* magazine had taken notice. A cover story was in the works. Koufax was baseball's biggest name and biggest draw, filling ten thousand additional seats every time he pitched. He was buzz before there was a word for it. Dodger attendance had already surpassed two million after only sixty-five home games, prompting one old-time Brooklyn fan to crow, "You know what they counted when he pitched? How many were turned away."

On September 9, there were only 29,139 paying customers in the stands, a small crowd by his standards. The city was still smoldering from the violence of August. Among the spectators were season ticket holders who had been permitted to exchange their August 14 seats for a later date because of the riots. O'Malley was in the owner's box; general manager Buzzie Bavasi was not with him. He was in Tulsa, Oklahoma, scouting a minor league pitching prospect named Don Sutton who was making his first trip west of the Mississippi. Richard Hume, a young attorney working in the office of J. William Hayes, Koufax's lawyer and advisor, was sitting in seats Koufax had left for him, a blank scorecard on his lap. Gary Adams, best friend of the Cubs' rookie catcher Chris Krug, was sitting twenty rows up behind first base. Tommy Davis, the disabled Dodger outfielder, was roaming the stands. Bill DeLury, a Brooklyn guy who worked his way up in the organization and came west with the team, took a club-level seat along the third base line. Bill Buhler was in his customary spot in the dugout, a 16-mm Bell and Howell camera in his lap. Vin Scully settled himself before the microphone in the broadcast booth, preparing to call the game for KFI radio.

There was no local television coverage of home games for the same reason there were no water fountains at the fan-friendly stadium when it first opened in 1962. O'Malley wanted people to come to the ballpark and spend. The folks at home had a choice. They could watch Buddy Hackett, the comedian who grew up next door to Koufax, starring in a one-hour TV special: "Once Upon a Tractor." Or they could listen to Vin Scully and Jerry Doggett on KFI.

Kevin Kennedy chose KFI. He was eleven years old and living in the west San Fernando Valley. He was supposed to be asleep in bed, but he was a Dodger fan. So he hid his transistor radio under his pillow and put the ear plug in his ear and hoped his parents wouldn't come in to check on him. Dave Smith, a seventeen-year-old living in Escondido, thirty miles north of San Diego, made a different choice. And it wasn't an easy one. His high school sweetheart was leaving for college in the morning. Dave chose the girl but left the radio on in his bedroom and a new reel of tape in the tape recorder by his bed.

Radio broadcasts were not routinely taped for posterity. Scully's words, carried by the night air and fifty thousand watts clear channel, floated across the ballpark into the greater Los Angeles Basin. In some neighborhoods, you could walk down the block without missing a ball or a strike. People brought radios to the ballpark too. A cacophony of transistors filled the empty seats, making the crowd seem larger than it was. Sometimes, a pitcher would hear laughter echoing from the stands and know that Scully had said something funny. "You didn't need a PA announcer," Adams said. "You didn't even need to see. You could hear Vin Scully's voice all over the ballpark."

Don Drysdale and Claude Osteen were listening in the clubhouse, lying side by side on training tables while trainer Wayne Anderson assuaged late-season aches and pains. Maury Wills, the agent provocateur of the base paths, was nursing his sore legs while his wife nursed their two-day-old baby girl one thousand miles north in Spokane, Washington. He hadn't seen the child, their sixth. Leave the team during a crucial series with the Giants, in the middle of the pennant race? Unthinkable.

Jim Lefebvre, the ex–Dodger batboy, who hadn't expected to be playing in the majors this soon, was preparing to start his 136th game at second base. In the home opener, he faced Warren Spahn, the old lefty who was beginning his twenty-first and last major league season. Lefebvre had a lot of family in the stands. He figured he'd show the old man a thing or two. Three strikeouts and one fly ball later, he was back in the locker room, hanging his head, when he felt a tap on his shoulder.

"Kid," Koufax said, "if you can't take it, get out of here. We don't want people in here that feel sorry for themselves. You've earned the right to wear this uniform. You busted your rear end. You're a Dodger. Dodgers don't hang their heads. They don't feel sorry for themselves and they don't point fingers." That was the day Lefebvre said he truly became a Dodger, the day the rookie grew up.

The public didn't see the Koufax his teammates knew, the clubhouse leader who nurtured rookies and scrubs, honing them into veterans so they would be strong up the middle when he needed them to be. They didn't see the clubhouse instigator who would grab your head in one hand, like a melon, and not let go, one because it was funny and two because he could. They didn't see his generosity. Koufax, a bachelor, was Doggett's guest on the postgame show every time he pitched and a collector of countless new electrical appliances. Blenders and can openers were especially popular gifts. Jeff Torborg, the young catcher, was newly married and setting up housekeeping with his bride, the former Miss New Jersey. One day, in the locker room, Koufax handed him a blender. "Here," he said, "you can use this more than me." Torborg made his wife promise never to get rid of it—even if it stopped blending, mixing, chopping, *and* pureeing.

Torborg sat at his locker going over the Cubs' lineup in his mind. There was no pregame meeting, no statistical analysis to review. No matter what the scouting reports said, Koufax would pitch his game. He believed in cultivating his fastball, working it the way a farmer works the land. Little by little, he would expand the strike zone, training the umpire to see its dimensions his way. By game's end, he'd get that strike call on the outside corner. He told Torborg, "Sit in the middle of the plate and if I start hitting your glove, then we'll move to the corners."

The Cubs were operating under an unusual system of rotating coaches; there was no manager. Lou Klein, the head coach, had written a lineup with two sure Hall of Famers and five rookies, two of whom were playing in their first major league game. Byron Browne, the left fielder, had flown in from Indianapolis earlier that afternoon. As the plane descended through the smog, he pressed himself to the window, not wanting to miss any part of his life's biggest day. What he saw was more than just the usual West Coast haze. "The place was burning!" he told teammates later. "It looked like someone dropped a bomb on L.A."

He was met at the airport by Yosh Kawano, the Cubs' clubhouse man, whose brother, Nobe, occupied the same position with the Dodgers. Yosh told him he was in the starting lineup. "I said, 'Well, who's pitching?' He said, 'Don't worry about it.' I get to the hotel. Billy Williams says, 'Leave your bags, we're going to the ballpark.' I said, 'Who's pitching?' He said, 'Oh, don't worry about it.' I said, 'Okay.'"

At the ballpark, he noticed the quiet, internal preparation of his new teammates, which he attributed to experience, a calm at variance with his own emotions. Dodger Stadium made the requisite impression. "Randolph Scott was there and I think Doris Day. Guys said there were a lot of stars in the stands. The only stars I knew were the Dodgers."

Then he heard Johnny Ramsey announce the starting lineups: "And tonight, pitching for the Dodgers, Sandy Koufax." *Jesus, Sandy Koufax.* "Welcome to the big leagues, Brownie," he mumbled to himself.

Krug, the rookie catcher, was grizzled by comparison. He was called up in May. Still, he was so green he wandered around the infield smelling the grass so he would remember the scent if he got sent down. Also wandering was Uncle Miltie. Krug thought Berle looked upset because no one was paying attention to him. So they chatted until he had to go inside to get in uniform.

Ed Bailey, the old catcher from Strawberry Plains, Tennessee, was happy to spend the evening in the bullpen. "That's as close as I want to be when *he's* throwing," he said. Bailey was in the lineup when Koufax no-hit the Giants in 1963. It was a perfect game until Koufax walked him on a 3 and 2 pitch in the eighth. Bailey came over to the Cubs in May in a three-for-two deal that sent two fine-print guys named Bertell and Gabrielson to San Francisco in exchange for three guys who had seen better days: Bailey, Harvey Kuenn, the 1959 American League batting champ, and starting pitcher Bob Hendley.

Hendley was a journeyman just back from an unpleasant tour of the minors. He was a big old country boy from Macon, Georgia, whose voice rose and fell like the languid countryside in which he was raised. He hadn't slept much the night before. He hadn't slept much at all since that road trip from Salt Lake to Oklahoma City in a plane so small they had to refuel in Denver. Six A.M., they went to the hangar. Sat there for hours. People started peeling off their shirts it was so hot. Then, as they take off in Denver, a big gust of wind comes up and the wing almost hits the ground. In Oklahoma City, it's a hundred degrees. People are throwing up, it's so hot. Who gets to pitch? Hendley. He's thinking he'll never make it through the first inning. He struck out twelve and lost

2–1. He told the manager, "I'll pay my way, I'm not getting on that plane again."

His teammates coaxed him into it. This was his second start since being called up from Triple A. Hard to say which was worse: facing Koufax or another crop duster. Pacing the sumptuous major league quarters, he told himself, "I've been gone and I don't want to go back."

Al Spangler, the utility man, was trying to make himself useful by demonstrating how Koufax tipped his pitches in the stretch position. Veterans, like Joey Amalfitano, nodded. *Sure, kid.* Everybody had Koufax's pitches. And it didn't fucking matter. Like Willie Mays said, "I knew every pitch he was going to throw and I still couldn't hit him."

Kenny Holtzman, the young lefty from St. Louis, came in from throwing batting practice. Some of the guys wanted to face a left-hander before seeing Koufax. He'd only been in the big leagues a couple of days. He knew he had been selected because there was no way he was going to get into the game. At this point in his young career, simulating greatness was all that was expected of him. He took the job seriously. Throwing batting practice is an act of self-abnegation. You want to make the hitters look good, feel good. Holtzman was eager to please. But he was young and he threw hard and he wasn't sure what to expect. It wasn't this: *The Cubs couldn't touch him. In batting practice. When he was just laying it in there.* He sat down at his locker and thought, God, if they have that much trouble with me, what the hell are they going to do with Koufax?

Chapter 3

WHEN SANDY TOUCHED THE SKY

Coach "Red" Rabinowitz bellied up to his dining room table in Cedarhurst, Long Island, beneath the flight path to John F. Kennedy International Airport. When Koufax was captain of his basketball team at Lafayette High School in 1953, the airport was still called Idlewild. Jet plane service in the continental U.S. was still five years away. A person could hear himself think. On a warm June evening nearly fifty years later, Rabinowitz was having trouble concentrating on the remarks he was preparing for Lafayette's Diamond Anniversary Award Presentation. The alumni committee had decided to honor the coaches of Lafayette, past and present, and Frank Rabinowitz had a lifetime of things he wanted to say. "They said two minutes. They couldn't make it five?"

His dining table was piled high with scrapbooks, yellowing images of boys in slick white uniforms, boys who are now aging men if life has been kind. Arthur Greenfeld, known as "Trip" because he was one of triplets—he died in 1999. And "Big Job" Burt Abramowitz, Asher Jagoda and Sid Yalowitz, Jerry Doren and skinny Sandy Koufax. Their coach, Red Rabinowitz, was a football guy coaching basketball at a school better known for its gridiron exploits. First thing, he bought his boys some decent uniforms so they wouldn't have to walk home from practice soaking wet in moth-eaten woolens that added ten pounds to their frames. Got 'em gym bags too. He reached under the table for one, wondering whether to mention it in his speech. One thing, though, he wasn't going to talk about Sandy. He was firm about that. "Every kid to me was the same."

Rabinowitz keeps a napkin Koufax autographed at a 1974 reunion in a Ziploc bag inside his dresser. "My wife brings it out for me every once in a while," he said, smoothing the cloth, stained with age and stale coffee. "Sandy loved the kids who played basketball and he loved his coach. My wife says she doesn't recognize me when I start talking like this. I become young and strong, y'see?"

The next evening several hundred Lafayette alums gathered on the campus of Kingsborough Community College. There were lots of guys with big *Saturday Night Fever* hair and lots of guys without socks in from California. Gary David Goldberg, who produced the television show *Brooklyn Bridge,* was there, along with Senator Barbara Boxer, whose husband graduated from Lafayette. Herbie Cohen flew in from Washington. Some of Sandy's guys were there too: Asher Dann (né Jagoda), Bruce Glatman, Jimmy Massifero, and Freddie Wilpon. Larry King, class of 1951, was the emcee.

Koufax was a presence in absentia, his name whispered in hushed asides. As in, "He never comes to these things." Not since that 1974 dinner when King, known in the neighborhood as Larry Zeiger, made a big fuss over him. Arthur Greenfeld witnessed Koufax's embarrassment. "You want an autograph too, Trip?" Koufax asked glumly. "Only if it's on the bottom of a check," Trip replied.

Despite King's best efforts, the program at Kingsborough Community College ran long. Every one of the honored coaches had a lifetime of things to say. "The class of '47 has just passed away," King announced an hour and a half into the proceedings, thanking his urologist "for making it possible for me to sit here tonight." An old Danny Kaye line.

Rabinowitz, being among the most senior coaches, was also among the last to speak. He spoke and he spoke, holding up the maroon gym bag, until finally a voice rang out in the hall: "C'mon, Frank, enough already." Rabinowitz has a face the shape and patina of a well-traveled bowling ball. He summoned his chin from his chest and growled, "I'm not leaving till I have my say."

At which point Bruce Glatman and Asher Dann headed for the lobby. "We didn't go to our own graduation," Glatman said. "Why do we gotta go to this?"

"Can we get a drink?" Dann replied.

And then they started trading stories, which is the reason why people fly in from California for things like this. The first story they tell is the one about the bus stop. In Brooklyn, and at social functions celebrating Brooklyn (many of which take place outside of Brooklyn and all of which are known as "functions"), they always tell the bus stop story. It goes like this. They were hanging by the corner of 86th and Bay Parkway the way they always did—Herbie, Brucie, Bucko, Nick De Cicco, and Sam De Luca, the football player. Koufax was there, too, hanging back beneath an awning when Bucko decided to show everyone how strong he was.

In those days, the city had no bus shelters. Bus stop signs were held in place by concrete stanchions, a challenge to otherwise unoccupied minds and bodies. "Bucko lifted it up like six times," Glatman said. "Nick De Cicco, another famous guy, he then lifted it like seven times. So people started egging on poor Koufax."

"He didn't want to do it," Cohen said. "But everyone was bothering him. So he did. It looked like Koufax could do twelve but he did it eight. One more than De Cicco. That's Koufax. He didn't want to show off. He just wanted to do it. Then he put it down. He didn't bang it down, slam it down. He just put it down and went back toward the awning into the shadow, into a darkness. Around our corner, having these characteristics, humility, integrity, and not being willing to brag, he stood out."

Time plays havoc with memory. Or, as Herbie says, "Recollection is the manipulation of memory." Maybe the story's true. It ought to be. It has the feel of prophecy. Or maybe, as Koufax has been known to point out, "Kids just want to make heroes of their friends."

They also want to believe, at a remove, in the ability to see the future. They want to believe not just in heroes but in the ability to recognize the makings of one. Koufax was an unlikely choice. In a world of *tummlers* and self-promoters, he was modest, shy, polite, wholesome even, preferring shadows to limelight. Senior year in high school, he volunteered for the Cafeteria Squad. His ambition, as stated beneath his picture in the June 1953 *Lafayette Legend* yearbook, was "TO BE SUCCESSFUL AND MAKE MY FAMILY PROUD OF ME."

"The most regular guy." That's how Sid Young (né Yalowitz) describes him. All his buddies agree, he hasn't changed at all. He's consistent with a time and a place, and with himself. It is his peculiar fate to aspire to be the one thing his talent and fame did not permit: regular. Jerry Della Femina (Class of '54) is big in the advertising business now so you should forgive the hyperbole. What appears enigmatic to others about the present-day Koufax makes perfect sense to him. "It's very male, very much that neighborhood," Della Femina said. "Men from that part of Brooklyn don't talk. He's symbolic of all the people who turned out well from that neighborhood. They all have that quality and they all got it from their fathers. It was right after the thirties. Their systems were shocked by the Depression. They passed that shock onto their children. It's a way of being in yourself. Sandy isn't a recluse—to the rest of the world, maybe. Put him in Brooklyn, he's everyone. He's my father, my uncle. He's everybody I knew."

Born in the Depression, three years before Kristallnacht, Koufax spent much of his childhood among the potato fields of eastern Long Island. Though Brooklyn claims him as its own, he did not become Sandy Koufax until he left the borough. He was born to Evelyn and Jack Braun on December 30, 1935. His genetic father left the family, divorcing his mother when Koufax was three years old. Eventually, Jack Braun remarried and quit paying alimony. His relationship with his son all but ended with the payments.

Mother and son lived with her parents in an apartment in an attached row house. Evelyn was a working woman, a certified public accountant. Her son spent most of his time with his grandparents, Max and Dora. "Butch" Hackett, later known as Buddy, the rotund comedian, lived next door. Dora would yell down from the apartment window to Hackett, "Get off my stoop and go bother someone else, you meshuggener." When that didn't work, she poured water on his head.

Max Lichtenstein was a plumber and a socialist who dabbled in real estate. He loved classical music and Yiddish theater and imbued his grandson with his values and culture. On Saturday mornings, he took Sandy swimming in the surf at Coney Island. Unlike his grandfather, Koufax was a quiet insurrectionist, the sort of boy for whom not doing his homework was an act of defiance. But, in many ways, he remains his grandfather's son.

Koufax was nine when his mother married Irving Koufax, a neighborhood lawyer with a modest practice and a highly developed sense of honor. When Evelyn remarried, her son acquired a new father, a new last name, and an older sister, Edie, Irving's daughter from a previous marriage. Though he was never legally adopted, Koufax would write in his 1966 autobiography: "When I speak of my father, I speak of Irving Koufax, for he has been to me everything a father could be."

Irving Koufax moved his family to Rockville Centre, Long Island, nineteen miles and light-years away from Brooklyn. A move that presaged the great urban diaspora soon to follow. It was the beginning of the subdivision of America into shirtwaists and gray fedoras. Irving and Evelyn took the Long Island Railroad to work in the city each day. One day, the train they were scheduled to take was in a deadly, head-on collision. Sandy and Edie huddled together listening to radio bulletins about dead bodies and emergency calls for bags of plasma. It turned out their parents had missed the train. They had also had enough of commuting. The family moved back to Brooklyn in June 1949, the day Sandy graduated from ninth grade.

In those days, Brooklyn was not just the most heavily populated borough of New York City, it was seventy-five square miles of contiguous hamlets, each one a hometown. Bensonhurst was the hamlet in which

The Honeymooners, Ralph and Alice, lived and where the Koufaxes settled. It was a neighborhood of lower-middle-class Italians and Jews. Parents were just as likely to read *Il Progresso* and the *Jewish Daily Forward* as the *Daily News* and the *New York Post*. It was the era of waxed fruit, plastic-covered furniture, and plaster Madonnas on front lawns, of egg creams, celery tonic, and cream soda, of corner stores and concrete stoops. Streetlight poles admonished, "Post no bills," and nobody did. Cab-drivers were sages and an NYC medallion was a lifetime annuity. Spring began not with the equinox but with the annual preseason exhibition series between the Yankees and the Dodgers. Kids went to sleep in their baseball uniforms so they'd be ready to play ball in the morning.

Everyone played: stickball, punchball, square ball, Gi-Gi ball. The streets and playgrounds were multicultural before there was a word for it. Diversity was a fact, not a goal. Political correctness was preached only by Mao Tse-tung. Italians were guineas. Jews were born with silver spoons in their mouths. Nobody took offense. "My baseball coach wanted me to come out," Glatman said, explaining how he became a player. "He said, 'I need another Jew to persecute.'"

Baseball, specifically the Dodgers, was a religion. Many of the play-ers lived in the borough's neighborhoods. The sounds of the game suffused the streets, the crack of the bat ricocheting from one apartment radio to the next. "My wife would go shopping and go across the street and someone would holler, 'Hey, the Dodgers got runners on first and second,'" Duke Snider said. "Everybody would have their radio on. She'd go into Bernard Altman in downtown Brooklyn on Flatbush Avenue. There would be a radio on the speaker system. They loved us and we loved them. It was very special."

Catholic kids like Joe Torre and his older brother, Frank, went to early Sunday mass wearing their spikes so they could go straight to the ball field. Orthodox Jewish boys in the many neighborhood yeshivas worshiped Jackie Robinson. Among Koufax and his friends, Judaism was often more cultural than practiced. Many of them, including Koufax, were not bar mitzvahed. "It's not that he was religious, none of us were," said Gloria Marshak Weissberg, a classmate at Lafayette.

"It was the way we grew up. You're Jewish but you don't hold it up. Everyone would go to Temple on the High Holidays and hang out. Friday-night services? Nobody went. You were Jewish because you were born Jewish. Because you were from Brooklyn. The schools closed on the holidays because the teachers were all Jewish. You were Jewish by osmosis. You grew up in a *shtetl*."

The Lafayette crowd hung out at the Famous Cafeteria, lingering over a bottomless cup of coffee, at Marine Park, the Parade Grounds, and on the boardwalk at Coney Island just a couple of miles away. For kicks, they memorized the Hit Parade and Dodger batting averages and debated which was better ice cream, Carvel or Sealtest. There was no television. When there was nothing else to do, Herbie Cohen says, "We watched the wall." They formed clubs with important-sounding names—the Warriors, the Legends, the Seraphs—and paid off building superintendents so they could use unoccupied basement apartments for clubhouses, "borrowing" furniture from whomever and wherever they could. Joe McCarthy was less a presence in their lives than Holden Caulfield. J. D. Salinger's seminal teenage novel, decrying the phonies of the adult world, was published in 1951. Two years later, Hugh Hefner unveiled the first issue of a new magazine named *Playboy*. "Whatever the 1950s became under Ike, it hadn't gotten there yet," said Richard Kaufman (Class of '52). "The chaste fifties hadn't begun. We were still in the postwar boom period. We were having a helluva good time."

This was Brooklyn before urban blight, before baseball flight. It was a time of unbridled American optimism. We could win a war, stop Hitler, integrate the major leagues. Anybody could grow up to be president or a starting pitcher for the Brooklyn Dodgers, even Sandy Koufax. "Bensonhurst was a place of hope, where accidents could become adventures," Cohen said. "It was pregnant with possibility. What was conceivable was achievable. There was a feeling that in America you could transform yourself. We were the children of the high projections of our parents."

It was a can-do culture and there were plenty of people ready to help, teaching boys how to pitch, catch, wrestle, debate, behave. At

Ebbets Field, Happy Felton presided over the Knothole Gang, bringing neighborhood kids onto the field to meet real baseball players. And he wouldn't hesitate to lecture them, as he did one young man caught on newsreel footage saying hi to his dad. "Take your hat off when you talk to your father, son," Hap said sternly, yanking the cap from the boy's cowlicked head.

Boys were boys and girls (in Peter Pan collars) did what was expected of them. When they didn't, it was news. "A girl appeared in the press box at the Polo Grounds," a *Brooklyn Eagle* columnist huffed. Thank God, she was only a messenger.

It was to this world, this corner, this optimism, that Koufax returned at the beginning of tenth grade. Wilpon quickly became his closest friend. They slept at each other's apartments, ate dinner with each other's parents, confided teenage despairs and dreams. It was a carefree time filled with salami sandwiches and whole milk and sandlot baseball. They didn't worry about body fat percentages or what they'd be when they grew up.

They were the children and grandchildren of immigrants who came to America believing the streets were paved with gold. They were lower-middle-class Jews, sons of the working class, renters, humble enough in their economic standing to be awed by the first brick facade on the block. A mobster's home, Wilpon recalled, it blew up one afternoon while they were out playing ball. One thing they knew: Nine to five held no appeal at all. "Brooklyn had an enormous effect on Sandy's background and thinking," Wilpon said. "And in many cases, what he did not want. Sandy and I didn't want to be straphangers and go on the subway every day. I think the Brooklyn experience permeated his life."

It's in his Brooklyn shrug, that characteristic bit of body language which says everything about who you are while saying nothing at all. "The difference between Brooklyn then and maybe places like Brooklyn now is that when someone does something well, scholar or athlete or actress, people tend to pull them down," Wilpon said. "Just the opposite in Brooklyn in those years. People were there for each other. People tried to build you up: We're proud of you. That's what I mean by the

Brooklyn thing. Sandy wasn't a typical Brooklyn guy, but the Brooklyn thing was inside him."

As Koufax says, "It holds my youth."

Before it became a subject for coffee-table books, a locus for nostalgia, Brooklyn was just a place—a place to hang out and a place to want out of. Eventually the Bums left and so did most of the guys from the corner. Some changed their names, moved to California, and made money. Herb Cohen moved to Washington and became a best-selling author. John Sprizzo became a federal judge. Vito Farinola became Vic Damone. Wilpon became the owner of the New York Mets. And Sandy Koufax became the most unlikely pitcher in the history of major league baseball. But wherever they went, whatever they became, they took Brooklyn with them. As Sid Young says, "Being from Brooklyn is a full-time job."

Koufax was known as a quiet kid, always with the basketball. "A closemouthed kid" is how he described himself in his autobiography, noting that his mother requested an early copy "so she could find out something about me." He preferred dribbling a ball to talking about himself. He preferred basketball to everything. He liked to fix things (spaghetti and radios). He put ketchup on everything he ate, the sort of inane biographical detail that follows the famous to the obituary file. He was "a happy, healthy, dirty-faced kid," his sister Edie told *The Sporting News*.

Angelo Plaia, his general science teacher, who still calls him Sanford (a 90 student with excellent manners), said, "I had a lot of students. Nobody knew Sandy Koufax was going to be Sandy Koufax, not even Sandy Koufax. Isn't it funny I remember him?"

Gloria Marshak was a member of a girls club called the Seraphs—angels in Hebrew—who hung out with the boys from the Lafayette basketball team. Her best friend, known as Bootsie, was Koufax's girlfriend for a while. She vividly recalls them sitting apart in a corner of the clubhouse. "I ask myself why I remember him," she said. "The other guys were so noisy. They *tummeled,* they danced. He radiated a presence. Even as a child he had that. His shyness filled the room."

Quietness distinguished him, a stillness and self-sufficiency at odds with the motion he was otherwise constantly in. "He was outside the chaos," Cohen said. "Even if he never pitched, he'd be mentioned. It's like he *knew* things. In the Jewish tradition, there is a luftmensch—a person with the capability to see things that more accustomed eyes miss. When you're different you think. Unbelonging makes you free."

For Koufax and his crew, sports was not so much an act of conforming as defying. It was not just a vehicle for assimilation, it was a way of saying no to the immigrant mentality their forebears had brought with them to Ellis Island—what Irving Howe, in *World of Our Fathers*, called "the suspicion of the physical, fear of hurt," and "anxiety over the sheer pointlessness of play."

Herb Cohen's sister, Renee, remembers her brother's gang as a bunch of bums. "We were children of immigrants. The goal was a girl should be a teacher, a boy should be a doctor. You had to get an education. These guys were rebels. I was the goody-two-shoes. I ratted on Herbie. His notebooks all had batting averages on them. They were American kids and they were not going to follow the line. They were not going to sit down and be the perfect students. It was a form of rebellion."

Gloria Marshak agrees: "None of these boys worked hard at class. Their ambitions were to become famous, all of them." They lived for sports and gave each other exalted names. Richie Kaufman, the 164-pound Lafayette linebacker and future economist, was known as "Rug"—for rugged. Burt Abramowitz, the starting forward on the basketball team, was "Big Job." Koufax was "the Animal." "He was a fierce competitor, contrary to his demeanor, which is very soft and easygoing," Wilpon said.

His hardworking parents were not invested in their son's physical prowess except when it came to football. His mother, a sensible woman with a good set of shoulders (Dodger scouts would note these later in assessing his physique), rebuffed the entreaties of Lafayette's football coaches. Richie's brother, Larry, the assistant coach, who later wrote a sports column for the *New York Post* under the name Larry Merchant, remembers Koufax as the kid who could throw a football the length of the field. Wilpon remembers him as the kid who could catch anything.

In 1951, a coaches' strike shut down scholastic sports at public schools across the city. Koufax and his buddies spent their time that year at the Jewish Community House of Bensonhurst. They led the "J" house basketball team to the Jewish Welfare Board championship. The team picture still hangs by the door to the gym, where water pipes clank and radiators hiss and the perpetually optimistic score (Home O— Visitor O) is posted on the old scoreboard. The J's mission is still to "ennoble Jewish youth." But today the language heard in the halls is more likely Russian than English, thanks to the influx of Soviet émigrés in the neighborhood.

Milt Gold was director of athletics when Koufax competed there. One day, he told Wilpon: "If I had one year with Sandy I could train him to be an Olympic athlete in anything other than speed sports." Wilpon didn't need to be convinced. Koufax had him pinned to a wrestling mat. "This guy was a world-class athlete at age seventeen," Wilpon said.

This Richie Kaufman does not dispute. Back from college, he made the mistake of bragging that he had made the varsity wrestling team. Next thing he knew Koufax was all over him. "That kid was so wiry, all skin and bone, no fat anywhere," Kaufman said. "We wrestled and wrestled. I wrestled him to a draw but to me it was a defeat. Little did I know it was a moral victory. I had a roaring headache for the rest of the day."

Koufax was six feet two and built. He had dark hair, dark eyes, and God-given muscle definition. "Everything Sandy Koufax ate turned to muscle," said Eliot Greenfeld, Trip's brother. "When we were in high school a bunch of guys came up to visit us from Washington. So these guys are walking out on the boardwalk. They pointed to a guy running down the beach. 'Look at that guy, he's built like a Greek god.' We looked. It was Koufax. He was sixteeen years old then."

"Nobody knew how strong Sandy was," Buzzie Bavasi said. "Great upper body. Got it from his mother. Lovely woman."

Great lower body too. In a pickup basketball game at the YMCA, Cohen said, "he split his gym shorts, his thighs were so big. Cheap shorts."

Mike Napoli was Big Man in the neighborhood—a catcher signed by the Dodgers out of Lafayette in 1951 for a bonus of $10,000. Not bad considering his parents earned maybe $3,200 a year. The Torre brothers, Frank and Joe, both of whom would become major-leaguers, played sandlot ball, and the Aspromonte boys, Kenny, Bobby, and Sonny, played too. They lived across the street from the high school—it was their home not so far away from home. Tommy Davis played basketball for Boys High. Joe Pignatano, aka "Piggy," trained as a TV repairman at Westinghouse Vocational before he signed on as a catcher with the Dodgers. "You grew up in the streets," Frank Torre said. "If you didn't adjust you wouldn't survive. People who grew up in other neighborhoods, even though they were maybe more talented, didn't have the luxury, the pleasure of having the fun we did as kids. Hell, we gathered whoever was around in the morning. We'd go to the park and play some kind of a ballgame. If we only had three people, you had a pitcher, a backstop, and a right fielder. You figured out a game to play. If you didn't have a ball, you'd wrap up paper with a rubber band. There was always some improvisation."

Later, when, improbably, so many of them from the neighborhood became major-leaguers, it was like they never left home. They roomed together, fished together, got drunk together, and eventually grew old together. One evening in Milwaukee after a particularly egregious day at the plate against Koufax, Joe Torre, then a young catcher for the Braves, was consoling himself at a hotel bar. A waitress came over with an invitation to join Koufax at his table. "I told her to tell him, 'He's got to come to me 'cause I went to him all day,'" Torre said. "We sat and had a couple of drinks and got a little blistered."

When, in 1999, Torre was diagnosed with prostate cancer, Koufax showed up at Yankee spring training camp asking to see the manager. Don Zimmer, the old Dodger working as Torre's bench coach, was sitting in the clubhouse when he arrived. "He comes to the clubhouse door," Zim said. "There's a cop out there. The cop comes to me and says, 'A guy says he's a friend of yours and wants to see you.' I said, 'Who is that?' He said, 'Sandy Koufax.' I said, 'You're kidding.' Koufax would have been satisfied to talk to me in the driveway. He spent forty-five minutes talking pitching with the Yankee coaches. Talked more than all the years I played with him total."

Then he went to see Torre, demanding to know, "What is it with these Brooklyn catchers?" Piggy had received the same unwelcome diagnosis that spring. "He called me, he found me, knowing how much it meant to . . ." Torre paused, seeking refuge in an impersonal grammatical construction endemic to Brooklyn, ". . . the person."

When he was growing up, baseball was neither Koufax's dream nor his passion. His dream was to play for the New York Knicks. Wilpon was the sandlot star for whom a major league career was confidently predicted, the boy with all the tools, a polished pitcher at age sixteen who piqued every scout's interest. Koufax was a tagalong. Sometimes he kept Wilpon company when he was summoned to Ebbets Field to throw batting practice. The Dodgers made Wilpon an offer; he does not remember how much. "Everybody got an offer," he says.

Koufax wasn't good enough to play on Wilpon's sandlot team. Wilpon pitched for the exalted Falcons and Blue Jays, who competed in state and national tournaments. Koufax caught for the Tomahawks in "Pop" Secol's Ice Cream League; they already had a pitcher—the guy became a surgeon. Anyone on the receiving end of a Koufax snowball knew he had an arm but no one thought to ask him to pitch, certainly not Charlie Sheerin, Lafayette's baseball coach, briefly a major-leaguer. Plenty of guys will tell you now they faced Koufax when, but his old buddies know better: "Yeah, well, he musta done it from first base." He was so impotent at the plate one coach had a guy with a broken leg pinch-hit for him. They sawed off Walt Laurie's cast and told him to get a bat. "Sandy couldn't hit a cow in the ass with a bag of rice at five feet," said Dom Fristachi, who played with Wilpon. "In his senior year I think he got, like, one hit." Walter O'Malley and Jackie Robinson were present at the annual Ice Cream League banquet when Koufax received the award for Best Overall Basketball Player.

Koufax didn't play much basketball either until his family returned to Brooklyn, where every open space was a court, or a half court, and every fire escape ladder was a potential basket. Others practiced shooting; Koufax practiced the anonymous, contentious skill of rebounding. The first time Arthur Greenfeld encountered him on the court Koufax didn't get a single rebound. "I had him completely boxed out," Greenfeld said. "He said to me afterward, 'Why can't I get a rebound?' I said, 'You're not getting position.' A month later, I couldn't get a rebound from him."

He scoured the borough in search of The Big Game, which invariably took place at Brighton Beach, where playground legends, college stars, and pros gathered to hone their games, and the game basketball would become. Back then, no one knew from vertical leap. Vertical was for sky-scrapers. But Koufax had wattage in his legs, hands large enough to palm the ball, and he didn't shy away from contact. On the playground, play-ers asked: *You sure this boy is white?* "He was just a skinny Jewish kid in a bandanna who challenged our small little prejudices," Della Femina said.

Soon his name began to appear in the fine print of the *Brooklyn Eagle* sports pages, usually misspelled. *Caufax. Kaufox. Kofax.* "He was an incredibly smooth basketball player," said Alan Dershowitz, another neighborhood kid who made good—as a legal authority and author of *I, Dershowitz* fame. "He would fake a jumper, drive the baseline, come under the boards and reverse and dunk. We weren't used to that."

In Koufax's senior year, Rabinowitz named him captain of the bas-ketball team. The editors of the *Lafayette Legend* named him to the Society for the Prevention of the Accumulation of Wallflowers in Speakeasies (S.P.A.W.S.) They also voted him "Best Boy Athlete," confi-dently predicting stardom in professional basketball. As they walked to New Utrecht High School for the last game of the year, "Big Job" told him, " 'Let's make a pact in blood that the first one of us to make a mil-lion dollars has to give the other half.' He looked at me like—'What are you, some kind of nut?' In an attempt to cut off the stupid conversa-tion, he said, 'Okay, it's a deal.' So now if you calculate the interest on five hundred thousand dollars at five percent annually he probably owes me fifty to a hundred million."

In 1953, the National Basketball Association was a dark planet in the cosmology of professional sports. College ball was what mattered and

Brooklyn was in mourning for the city game. The point-shaving scandal at City College was all anyone talked about on the coveted court at Seth Low Junior High. They knew those guys and had competed against many of them. Nat Holman's boys broke more hearts than rules with the Big Fix but they also opened the door to the NBA. Seeking to capitalize on the void left by the scandal that came to be known as the Dump, the New York Knicks embarked on a marketing strategy that included scrimmaging against local high school teams in clinics sponsored by the Police Athletic League. The players didn't mind. It was an extra twenty-five bucks. And so a match was made with the "Frenchies" of Lafayette.

It was Friday night, about 8:00 P.M., when the Knicks arrived at the Bath Street gym. They were led by Harry "The Horse" Gallatin. And Harry was a horse: a big midwestern farmer's boy who could fill up the middle and rebound like a sonofabitch. He was Koufax's favorite player.

The gym was full, the cheerleaders in full pom-pomed confection, a blur of maroon and white leading the crowd in the Lafayette cheer. Della Femina was there, Dershowitz and Kaufman, too. During warmups, the big boys—Gallatin, Al McGuire, Carl Braun—showed off their moves while the high-schoolers formed layup lines. Then Gallatin decided to try a couple of dunks. Unlike most horses, Harry required a running start. "Harry dribbles in and tries to dunk," Rabinowitz recalled. "He misses. Harry tries again and misses again. I says, 'Harry, would you like to see somebody dunk the ball?' Very casual-like. He says, 'You have somebody who can dunk?' I said, 'Sandy, come over here.'

"In those days, there was no such thing as a dunk. Sandy didn't even know he was doing it. He'd take these long strides and hang around in the air. He didn't jump and come down, see. He'd stay in the air and hang around a little bit."

Next thing, Al McGuire's got Koufax by the elbow, dragging him across the court, saying to Gallatin, "I've got a kid right here who can show you how to do it." And he did. Rabinowitz couldn't help himself. "I says, 'Harry, you want to see him do it again?'"

Gallatin had seen enough. "Who are you?" he asked. "Sandy Koufax," the kid replied. Gallatin gave him an autograph; Koufax gave him his name and address. Then it was time to scrimmage. "He embarrassed the Knicks for the first ten minutes, totally outplaying them," Della Femina recalled.

Gallatin had the unenviable task of guarding him. "Generally, we clowned around," Gallatin said. "We even let a few of the kids beat us. But then after the kid started making fools of us, we thought, Hey, we better do something here. We just wanted to have fun. Koufax didn't want to have fun."

Next thing Della Femina recalls, "McGuire went up and Gallatin went up, and there was a Koufax sandwich. Last I remember, he was limping off the court with that 'I'm going to beat you' look. Very few are that quiet and that competitive. There was something there. You could smell success."

Thus, on February 10, 1953, Koufax made headlines for the first time—and they spelled his name right. "Lafayette Cager Wowed Gallatin," the *New York Post* proclaimed. Gene Roswell's story was a gusher, the lead paragraph a fifty-eight-word run-on sentence beginning and ending with Koufax.

> When the Knicks scrimmaged against Lafayette during a missionary preseason basketball clinic at the Bath Beach school, pro center Harry Gallatin was so impressed by the spring and coordination of a rangy youngster named Sandy Koufax, who actually outjumped him several times, that he told Frenchie Coach Frank Rabinowitz: "We'll be coming back for this kid some day."

Fifty years later, grown men who were present that night contemplate eroding memories and tell themselves, "Gee, I *think* I remember Sandy playing the Knicks."

Here it is, straight from the Horse's mouth: "It happened. Koufax wanted to show us up and he did."

Chapter 4

THE FIRST INNING

Game time was 8:00 p.m. Ed Vargo dusted off home plate. Groundskeepers refreshed the baselines with a powder of ground Georgia marble. The dugouts filled with the usual chatter and clatter of ash on ash. The starting lineups were announced. The umpires were introduced. Koufax walked to the mound. As always, he was accorded a greeting worthy of a maestro. "There was applause," Scully said. "Not cheers, applause."

So confident were the Dodgers when he pitched that Jerry Doggett, Scully's longtime broadcast partner, once successfully importuned him to prerecord a postgame interview. It was getaway day. Koufax reluctantly agreed. Anything for the team.

John Werhas, the young Dodger utility infielder, studied the body language in opposing dugouts whenever Koufax appeared on the field. Everything stopped. Everyone looked. And not just scrubs like himself. Mr. Cub, Ernie Banks, the most cheerful man in baseball, watched that big Number 32 walking out to the mound and thought, It's like being in the ballpark with Jesus.

In all the accolades, there was an inference of aloofness that seemed above it all. By September 1965, it was commonplace to see in Koufax's public demeanor an elegant but somber omnipotence—a touch of grimness perhaps, accompanied by an occasional grimace at a bad call. People saw him on the cover of *Life* magazine, tugging with purpose on the bill of his cap, looking up from beneath dark eyebrows at the headline: "The Mostest Pitcher." They saw no wasted motion or emotion. They saw the look of a smoldering prophet. "The way his eyes seemed to go way back in his head," as Torborg put it. "Almost like they were burning."

Few saw the obvious: how much he loved to play the game. Bob Hendley saw it. From his vantage point at the far end of the Cubs dugout (and the other end of the pitching spectrum) he was able to see what so many others missed. He saw Koufax smile. It was a big smile. He thought Koufax had a playful way about him. "Like he was saying, 'This is where I am, this is where I belong. I'm untouchable.' And not just in the baseball sense."

The smile, Hendley believed, wasn't so much a premonition as a statement of character and perspective. He saw in it the sheer joy of being able to compete at your best, an opportunity he had never been afforded. Hendley scared nobody. He inspired confidence only in the opposing team. Checking the lineup card in the Dodger dugout, Dick Tracewski was delighted to see Hendley's name penciled into the ninth place in the batting order. When you come to the ballpark and Bob Hendley is pitching, he thought, it's nice to be here.

Hendley was probably the only man in the ballpark who knew his lifetime record against Koufax was 2 and 0. In four tries, Koufax had yet to beat him. The Dodgers looked at the matchup and saw opportunity. Hendley looked at it and saw how much he and Koufax had in common: two lefties with bad elbows living on borrowed time. Mine, he thought, maybe worse 'n his. He knew how easy it would have been for them to inherit each other's destiny. There was a time the newspapers said Hendley might be the next Warren Spahn. He could flat out bring it. He figured he'd pitch until he was fifty years old. He learned the hard way never to presume where ligaments and sinew are concerned.

At 8:03 P.M., Vargo yelled, "Play ball." Koufax stepped to the pitching rubber; Torborg went into his crouch; trainer Bill Buhler moved into position behind the backstop, the forbidden area just behind the home plate gate deemed off-limits by the fire marshals. He had to be discreet. An unctuous usher patrolled this select section of ballpark real estate and was always on the lookout for trespassers. From this strategic outpost, he had a perfect view over Torborg's shoulder of Koufax's delivery. He hadn't won since beating the Pirates 1–0 in ten innings on August 14, his longest dry spell since joining the starting rotation in 1961. ("Sandy to Try Again," the morning paper moaned.) No doubt, the coaching staff was hoping Buhler's camera would detect some kinetic flaw to explain why Koufax was making his sixth attempt to win his twenty-second game.

For Torborg, working one of Koufax's games was an on-the-job tutorial. On days when he wasn't pitching, Koufax—he called him "The Great Sandy Koufax!"—would hit fungoes to the young catcher so that he could acclimate himself to pop-ups behind the plate at Dodger Stadium. Koufax could be tough, too. Earlier in the season, he chewed Torborg out on the mound at Forbes Field in Pittsburgh. Torborg's father had come down from Jersey for the game. He could see the back of his son's neck pinking up and wondered what in hell was going on. Torborg had an arm. He'd gun that ball back to Koufax on the mound, popping up from his crouch after every pitch. Finally, that night in Pittsburgh, Koufax summoned the hyperkinetic young catcher to the mound and said, "Would you stop throwin' so hard? You're throwing it harder than I am. Would you please sit down? I like the picture of the catcher being quiet behind the plate, staying down, so everything I see is low."

Chastened, Torborg replied, "Well, sure, I can do that." But it was hard. Staying within himself wasn't within his personality. So as he settled into his crouch on September 9, Torborg reminded himself to stay down and not to throw the ball back so goddamn hard.

There's a special place in heaven reserved for guys who face Koufax in their first major league at-bat. It's like losing your virginity to the prom queen. Donald Wayne Young, a .267 hitter touted as a defensive outfielder in the Texas League, was in the unenviable position of batting leadoff against Koufax in his first major league game. He took the first pitch to get acclimated—a curve that bounced in the dirt. "Ball one," Vargo said.

Young was a late-season call-up on the worst team in the majors. He was also overmatched, overwhelmed, and overanxious. He popped out on the second pitch. Richard Hume, the young lawyer sitting in a field box Koufax had arranged for him, picked up a three-cent pencil and marked his scorecard: P4. He wasn't sure why. He had never kept score at a ballgame before.

Glenn Beckert, the second batter, stepped to the plate and took a deep breath, reminding himself of the hitter's mantra: *You gotta get to him early*. This was true of all power pitchers but particularly of Koufax. You had to get to him before muscle memory and fatalism kicked in. You were contending with not just his stuff but his aura. You ever try making contact with an aura?

"Beck" was also a rookie. He had not yet absorbed the obdurate futility peculiar to the Cubs and those who root for them. And, Koufax didn't seem to have his best stuff. Unlike other pitchers who changed speeds and arm angles, Koufax threw only two pitches and he threw them the same way. It didn't take long to know whether he was sharp. When he wasn't, the fastball sailed too high and the curve dropped gently into the strike zone instead of biting through it.

The second pitch to Beckert was one of those curves, rolling in on him like the tide. He swung with the urgency that comes from knowing you don't get many such chances and hurled himself down the first base line. Koufax had jammed him with the pitch, and the resulting line drive eluded Jim Gilliam at third base. Beckert knew he had hit it decent. Enough for a double anyway, he thought.

Torborg leapt from his crouch with a guttural epithet, "Umyaaauuooh!" From where he stood, it looked as if the ball had hit the baseline. Beckert had a better view. As he rounded first, he saw the ball "going down the line with the chalk on the wrong side." Foul by no more than the width of the ball. Oh shit, he thought, as he returned to the plate. Now he's got me two strikes, not a place you want to be.

Beckert struck out rarely. But Koufax got him looking at another overly round curve. Beckert wasn't dejected by this turn of events. In fact, as he headed back to the dugout he was optimistic about the future, specifically the next eight innings. There's hope, he thought.

As Billy Williams settled into the batter's box, Beckert's roommate, Ron Santo, ventured into the on-deck circle. "Hey, Rooms," Santo said. "What kind of fastball does he have?"

"So-so," Beck replied.

Williams also struck out looking at an oversized curve to retire the side. They're big, Torborg thought. Too big. They would fool some of the people some of the time but not for nine innings. "He's struggling," Torborg murmured to himself, as he headed to the dugout. "Struggling for Sandy."

Chapter 5

THE ACCIDENTAL PITCHER

IN THE HIGHLY CALIBRATED WORLD of modern athletics, a talent like Sandy Koufax would be harvested, cultivated, and enhanced. His muscle twitch fibers would be counted, his vertical leap measured, his fastball—and perhaps even his snowballs—timed. He would be coddled, wooed, and ruined. His parents would be assailed by men with beepers and stopwatches who can measure everything but serendipity.

It was Milt Laurie, who delivered papers for the *New York Journal-American*, who first saw the potential in Koufax's left arm. And he saw it in the most prosaic way, during infield practice, when Koufax was a senior playing first base for his high school team, just whipping the ball around the horn. Laurie's sons, Wally and Larry, also played for Lafayette. At their father's behest, they recruited Koufax to pitch for his sandlot team.

Milt had been a prospect once, signed by the Boston Braves. Just before spring training, his newspaper delivery truck skidded on a wet

New York City street, flipping over and crushing his right side. He saw in Koufax the hopes and ambitions of his own thwarted major league career. Perhaps that is why he saw what no one else did.

Later, in the reconstructed history of his fame, headline writers proclaimed Koufax a "Boro Sandlot Star." In truth, his dispassion was such that his parents didn't even know he played baseball until his father happened by the field one day. Milt sometimes kept him overnight in order to make sure he got to the field on time. Later, there were some hard feelings. Walt didn't think Koufax credited his dad enough. Sonny Aspromonte, whose brothers Bob and Ken went on to the major leagues, mentioned it to Koufax one day around the batting cage in Houston. Next thing Sonny reads in the newspaper is a quote from Koufax: "My sandlot manager, Milt Laurie, was the first to recognize my ability."

Milt's team, the Parkviews, competed in the Coney Island Sports League. Wally, Koufax's first catcher, remembers one kid coming up to the plate in the fog and leaving in a thicker one after the umpire called a strike on a pitch he hadn't seen—walking away from the plate, never to return. Another kid Koufax hit in the throat. He turned blue. Koufax turned white. "He was a caring kid." Wally said. "You know, he had feelings."

Dick Auletta, whose father, Pat, founded the league, played outfield for the Parkviews. "One time when Koufax pitched, the entire infield and outfield sat down," he said. "He only walked people or struck them out. He was one strike away from his first no-hitter when the third baseman yells out, 'C'mon, Sandy, get the no-hitter!' Sandy didn't even know he had one. He burned it in there. And Lu Lu DePace, the umpire, goes, 'Strike three!' The batter says, 'Where was it?' And Lu Lu replies, 'I don't know, but it sounded like a strike.'" Not the last time an umpire would employ such logic.

Nah, Wally says, it wasn't that way at all. Dolly King was behind the plate. And when the game was over, King turned to him and said, "You were the only thing between me and the hospital."

In his spare time, Milt took Koufax over to Lafayette to work on his control. The Aspromonte family lived across the street. One chill fall afternoon Sonny, the oldest, was watching the New York football Giants on television. At halftime, he went outside to get a breath of fresh air. "I heard the mitt cracking," he said. "I said, 'This kid is throwing too hard.' I went inside and got a jacket. I said, 'I gotta see this kid throw.' In November. In the cold.

"I say to the catcher, 'What the hell is going on?' The guy says, 'My father's working on his delivery.' It was Wally and Milt Laurie. I stand up there. I give him a target. I made believe I had a bat. Wow, he looks good. I figured I'd look for the kid the next year on a sandlot team. What happens? He goes to the Univeristy of Cincinnati. He tries out for baseball and the rest is history. I said, 'What's his name?' 'Koufax.' Oh, Koufax."

Koufax arrived at the University of Cincinnati in the fall of 1953 without an athletic scholarship of any kind. He was a walk-on for the freshman basketball team, a complete unknown to coach Ed Jucker. "He just showed up," Jucker said. "I didn't know him from anything. I told the head coach, 'We might have something here.' I always wondered why he came. Maybe he liked the way we played, how we cut our hair. I still don't know."

Koufax was awarded a partial scholarship after Jucker saw him practice. Walter Alston, who was about to be named manager of the Dodgers, was in the stands the night Koufax had his best game, against Miami of Ohio. He had enrolled in the school of liberal arts with the idea he might transfer to the school of architecture. He liked Cincinnati because it had a work-study program—eight weeks of school, then eight weeks of work. A scholar he wasn't. He lived off-campus in a fraternity popular with Jews and other Easterners. His roommate was Norman "Left-ky" Lefkowitz, a guard on the basketball team, another New York kid. "When I think back it's hard to say I knew him. He was sort of quiet, into himself. We should have had a lot in common. He was very bright. I remember before a test, instead of studying, he was reading *Battle Cry*. You're too young to remember that. I said, 'Sandy, why aren't you studying?' He said, 'Oh, I gotta finish this.' He was smart enough to be able to pass without studying."

Having a good time was more important. For that the college boys went across the river to the Kentucky towns of Covington and Newport where the ladies were a little faster and the bars a lot looser about who got served. Ed Rothenberg, another teammate, was with Koufax one day when "a pretty waitress, maybe thirty years old, started massaging his arm while taking the order. She said, 'My God, Sandy, are you this hard all over?' He smiled sheepishly. He was not the type who bragged or talked about women. He'd just go off by himself, across the river."

During spring break, the baseball team, also under Jucker's supervision, made a road trip to New Orleans and Florida, which sounded a whole lot better than April in Bensonhurst. Tony Trabert, the tennis player, another Cincinnati kid, was playing an exhibition match against Ham Richardson of Tulane. In order to justify the cost of the trip, the athletic department arranged a schedule for the baseball team. "It was near the end of the season and Jucker was finding it hard to find players," Lefkowitz said. "Sandy said, 'I think I'll go out for it. I played a little in high school.'"

Koufax went to his coach and said: "I can pitch."

"Don't bother me now, kid," Jucker replied. "When the season's over, I'll come over and watch you throw."

Baseball try-outs at the University of Cincinnati were held indoors in the old gym, the Schmidlaff. It was a dank place that earned its nickname, "The Band Box." The air was heavy, the space was tight, and the light even worse thanks to dark wood paneling above the tiled walls. The gym was just large enough to accommodate the distance between the mound and home plate—with perhaps two and a half feet behind the pitcher and the catcher. Jucker couldn't find anyone willing to catch Koufax. "Anybody who tried, the ball would go right by them," he said. "I can still hear that noise, I can hear it right now, as the ball hit the wood. Bang! *Bang!*"

Don Nesbitt, another pitcher who tried out that day, witnessed the result in the shower: "Anyone who tried to catch him, they were just a series of bruises all over their backs, their behinds, the backs of their legs from the ball hitting the floor and tile wall and bouncing back."

Nesbitt refused even to play catch with him, hiding in the locker room until Koufax found somebody else to throw with. Two catchers, Bill Hall and Joe Miller, quit the team rather than deal with him. "Then," Jucker said, "this big country kid stepped forward and said, 'I think I can do it.'"

Danny Gilbert settled optimistically into a crouch. Gilbert was a farm boy from Minford, Ohio, onetime home of Roy Rogers. He had met Koufax at the try-outs for the freshman basketball team. They spent a little time together, riding the roller coaster at Coney Island— Cincinnati's version of the original.

The first pitch he saw from Koufax was the real thing. "Oh, my gosh," Gilbert said. "You ever take a sledgehammer and hit a knot in a piece of wood? You know how it bounces back? That's how it felt."

They made the 1954 varsity squad and Gilbert started padding his glove, which he kept for the next fifty years. After graduating, Gilbert returned to Minford and became what he was supposed to be—a high school teacher and a guidance counselor. Koufax became what no one expected him to be. When Koufax returned to campus for the first time in February 2000 to attend a dinner honoring Jucker, it was his old battery mate, Danny Gilbert, who picked him up at the airport. He had tossed the old mitt in the trunk, just in case Sandy wanted to throw.

The spring of 1954 was Koufax's only season of intercollegiate baseball. Koufax was 3 and 1 with a 2.81 ERA. He had fifty-one strikeouts in thirty-two innings—and thirty walks. "With other pitchers, I'd work inside, outside, up and down," Gilbert said. "With Sandy, we were working just to get it over the plate. When he got it over the plate, it was Katie bar the door."

The first scout to approach him was Bill Zinser, a bird dog for the Dodgers, who was also the only person ever to accuse Koufax of being a good hitter. The glowing report he sent to the front office promptly got lost in the paperwork at 215 Montague Street in downtown Brooklyn.

Bill Zinser Scouting Report
May 15, 1954

Arm	A+	Running Speed	O+
Fielding	A−	Accuracy	A−
Hitting	A−	Power	A−

Very good prospect, also a very good hitter
Has averaged 16 strikeouts per game this season
Aptitude—very good
Aggressiveness—Outstanding
Definite Prospect?—Yes

Physical description, Tall—muscular—quick reflexes, well
   coordinated
Other remarks: Going to U. of Cincinnati on Scholarship—
   not interested in pro ball until he graduates.
Also plays 1st because of hitting ability.

The big game that spring was against Xavier, Cincinnati's cross-town rival. Xavier was Catholic. Cincinnati was "diversified," said Jim Bunning, the future Hall of Famer who was then coaching Xavier's freshman basketball team. Rothenberg would recall that more than the usual elbows and insults were traded during the annual basketball matchup that winter. Koufax was looking forward to pitching against Xavier in the spring.

The night before the game he sprained his ankle, falling down the stairs at his fraternity. He didn't tell his coach. Buzz Boyle, a scout for the Cincinnati Reds, was at the game, as were Koufax's basketball buddies, "Left-ky" and Rothenberg, both of whom remember the catcalls directed at him from the Xavier bench. "I couldn't believe the nerve of those guys, making these Jewish cracks—big nose, sheeny, kike," Rothenberg said. "He totally ignored it. I was getting angry. He acted like he didn't even hear it. Afterward I said, 'Sandy, how do you take this shit?' He said, 'Ed, the only way I can deal with this is to beat 'em.'"

He didn't. The winning pitcher that day was Irvin "Hank" Schmidt, the number-three man in Xavier's pitching rotation. He was a former Marine with a menacing, sidearm delivery. Late in the game, he made the mistake of backing Koufax off the plate. "He kind of glared at me like, 'You didn't have to do that, I'm not going to hit the ball,'" Schmidt said. "I thought it was funny. I didn't realize I was leadoff man the next inning. When he wound up, I started thinking about it. And I just started backing out of the batter's box. Right where my knees were was where the fastball came. Otherwise, I might not be walking today."

Koufax lasted eight innings, giving up nine hits, including a 400-foot home run to a left-handed batter that landed on a hillside beyond the playing field. He lost the game and his temper, calling the umpire a sonofabitch over several disputed calls. "He'll never make it" was Boyle's glum assessment.

At the end of freshman year, Koufax went back to Brooklyn and a job as a camp counselor in the Catskills, where his mother kept the books. He'd been going to Camp Chi-Wan-Da since he was three. As a counselor, he made a lasting impression on one young boy, David Saks, who has been having recurring dreams about Koufax ever since. The campers loved the dirty jokes Koufax told and the softball games he organized. Saks will never forget the first words he heard Koufax utter: "I don't give a shit what you guys do."

Some weekends, Wally Laurie came up to the Catskills to work out with him. Other times, Koufax went home to pitch for the Parkviews. "Milt sent Wally up to camp in his *Journal American* delivery truck," Dick Auletta remembers. "He'd bring him down, pitch, shower, sleep over, and take him back. And his folks knew nothing about it. The way we heard it, they weren't too keen on baseball."

Scouts began coming around. The momentum of his improbable baseball career was gathering force. The Yankees, with their customary ethnic sensitivity, sent a Jewish scout to court him, offending his family and precluding any possibility of a future in pinstripes. When he went to the Polo Grounds to try out for the Giants, he forgot his baseball glove. Frank Shellenback, the pitching coach, took him to the locker room to borrow one. Johnny Antonelli, a lefty pitcher, was summoned to the clubhouse door. "He said, 'Can I please borrow your glove?' I remember he called me Mr. Antonelli.' First time I'd been called that in a clubhouse, and ever since too."

Using Antonelli's glove, Koufax went out and threw several pitches over the catcher's head. So much for the Giants. Ed McCarrick, a scout for the Pittsburgh Pirates, was his most ardent suitor. At his urging, Branch Rickey, then general manager of the Pirates, sent his son Branch Jr. and his most trusted aide, Clyde Sukeforth, to have a look. When Rickey was still running the Dodgers and searching for the right man to break the color bar, he sent Sukey to see Jackie Robinson. When Robinson played his first game in 1947, Sukey was his manager (filling in for the suspended Leo Durocher). When the bullpen phone rang on that fateful October day in 1951, Sukey was the coach who recommended bringing in Ralph Branca to face Bobby Thomson. Three years later, Sukey was back in Brooklyn eyeballing Koufax through the wisps of fog hovering over Dyker Field.

Sukey would remember that Sunday morning with a clarity he brought to little else in the fall of 2000. In his last days, his vision was gone and his hearing was going. It was the dawn of a new millennium and Sukey was almost a century old. Callers were discouraged. Those who persevered were admonished to speak loudly and to use simple sentences. His granddaughter said, by way of introduction, "He may think you're Sandy's wife."

Sukeforth was just back from the hospital for cataract surgery. But, oh, he remembered scouting Koufax, remembered it in the present tense. "This boy is unbelievable," he said, his voice as strong as the memory. "I'm as high on him as anybody. Everybody regards him as the best prospect."

He spoke highly of "the boy's habits and disposition," dismissing as inconsequential the wildness "you expect from a boy like that" and the fact that Koufax got clobbered in a sandlot game later that day. "How hard did he throw?" Sukey said. "Harder than anybody else we had. He has what you look for in qualities. I mean the good Lord was good to him."

Sukeforth quickly arranged for an audition before Mr. Rickey Sr. Grover "Deacon" Jones, another prospect, and Koufax took a midnight sleeper to Pittsburgh out of Penn Station. They lay in the dark talking about their prospects and trying to be cool about them. Not that Koufax had to work at it. "Cool," Jones said. "That's just how he is."

Dick Groat was at Forbes Field when Koufax arrived the next morning. Like Koufax, Groat had begun his athletic career as a basketball player, a star at Duke University. "We always parked in left field and came in through the gate, past the visiting bullpen," Groat said. "As I walked through the gate I saw all the Pittsburgh brass—Branch Rickey Sr., Clyde Sukeforth, Rex Ballen, George Sisler, Fred Haney, the manager— and there's a young boy throwing, great body, a marvelous delivery."

Mr. Rickey was excited. Groat could tell by the vigorous way he chewed on his unlit cigar and grabbed at his hat. Sam Narron, the bullpen coach, was catching. "They finally brought our third-string catcher in to catch him," Groat said. "They sent one of the kids to the locker room to say, 'You better get out here or he's gonna kill Sam.'"

In fact, he broke Narron's thumb. When the workout was over, Sukey quoted Rickey as saying, "'This is the greatest arm I've ever seen.' Mr. Rickey was in love with him. You don't see talent like that."

Koufax made a second trip to Pittsburgh with his parents expecting to sign a contract, but they left town without the anticipated offer or an explanation. Apparently, Branch Rickey Jr. remembered seeing Koufax get shellacked at Dyker Field and discouraged his father from signing him. John Galbraith, the Pirates owner, refused to budge from his initial offer of $15,000. Later, after selling off their New Orleans farm team, the Pirates came back to Koufax with a promise to better any offer by $5,000. But by then Al Campanis had seen God.

Many claimed credit for alerting the Dodger scout to this "Kovacs" kid. Jimmy Murphy, the high school columnist for the *Brooklyn Eagle,* was often mentioned. Pat Auletta wasn't. Pat was a mover and shaker in the sandlot world and owner of a sporting goods store across the street from Nathan's Famous in Coney Island. His sons, Dick and Ken, the author, remember their father urging Campanis, "You gotta come see this kid."

Bob Marino, who played third base and outfield, savors the memory of Campanis showing up at Lafayette High School in a black Caddy convertible with the top down, wearing a great black cape. Biggest car he'd ever seen. Koufax made as much of an impression on Campanis as Campanis did on Marino. He drove Koufax and his father home in the Caddy and scheduled a try-out. "First time he saw him throw, he invited him to Ebbets Field," Al's son, Jimmy, said.

After Koufax was signed, the Dodgers donated the satin uniforms once worn for night games to the Parkviews as a gesture of thanks. Auletta wore Duke Snider's uniform proudly though with some difficulty. The sleeves dangled below his knuckles. But the symbolism outweighed the inconvenience. "One of us made it," he said. "And with dignity and class."

For several years thereafter, until the team moved out of Brooklyn (and until the clubhouse guys explained major league etiquette to him), Koufax continued to buy his spikes and gloves at Pat Auletta's store.

In September, just before returning to school, Koufax pitched off the mound in Ebbets Field for the first time. Nobody in the organization made the connection with the University of Cincinnati fireballer who'd been invited to visit Brooklyn by their bird dog, Bill Zinser, earlier in the spring. Vin Scully, the young Dodger broadcaster who had taken over the catbird seat from Red Barber, was in the locker room when Koufax arrived. "There was this fellow getting dressed into a baseball uniform," Scully said. "And the thing that I noticed right away—he was stripped to the waist at the time—he was fully tanned, which made me think he didn't play much baseball. Because certainly in those days, ballplayers had what you'd call a truck driver's tan. The arms would be burned but the chest would be white. Sandy was completely tan.

"The second thing I found unusual as I looked at him was his back. It was extremely broad. And if I remember again, he had this large muscle on the right side of the back which I believe he inherited from his mother." "Wide back strong" is how Dodger trainers described him.

Dave Anderson, later a Pulitzer Prize–winning sports columnist for the *New York Times*, was a cub reporter for the *Eagle*, looking for an angle on a rainy day. "They told Sandy, 'Stick around and when the field dries we'll have you throw,'" Anderson recalled.

As manager Walter Alston and scouting director Fresco Thompson watched from the owner's box, Campanis assumed a hitter's stance at the plate. "He actually liked to stand in to get the feeling of the batter," Anderson said. "Koufax started to steam the fastball in on him. Al Campanis said—and I'll never forget this—'The hair on my arms rose, and the only other time that happened was the first time I saw the Sistine Chapel.'" ("On my neck, too," he told his son, Jimmy.)

Rube Walker, the catcher, said, "Whatever he wants, give it to him. I wouldn't let him get out of the clubhouse."

Al Campanis Scouting Report
September 17, 1954

Fast ball	A+	Good velocity and life	77
Curve	A+	Breaks sharply	72
Change (F.B.)	A−	A bit too fast	60
Control	A−		60
Definite Prospect?	Yes		

Remarks: Athletic build, good musculature.
Good poise and actions—smoother delivery—many clubs interested. Two are willing to make him a bonus player. Lad appears to possess confidence in himself. He has the tools. Whether or not to make him a bonus player is the question.

In 1954, "whatever he wants" was a relative term. The minimum major league salary was $6,000, club owners recently having rejected an attempt to raise it to $7,200. They had also vetoed a proposal to raise the pension for a ten-year veteran from $100 to $400 a month. A new bonus system was in place requiring any player signed for more than $4,000 to be kept on the major league roster for two years. General manager Buzzie Bavasi would make the final decision.

Campanis took Koufax home to Long Island to meet his family, introducing him as a future Hall of Famer. "It's written all over him," Al said. He visited Koufax's parents at home, took them to the Latin Quarter, pleading the case for the home team. Eventually, the families became social friends. "My dad pushed Buzzie real heavy to keep him," Jimmy Campanis said. "Buzzie had to make a decision to give him all that money and to keep him on the roster. Buzzie said, 'Okay, Al, if you believe he's going to be a superstar, I'll agree with you.'"

Irving Koufax negotiated on behalf of his son. He asked for $20,000—$6,000 for the first year's salary and a bonus of $14,000—the cost of a four-year college education. Bavasi remembered: "I called Arthur Dede and said, 'Mr. Koufax wants fourteen thousand dollars—give it to him.' When he was walking out of my office, Ed McCarrick of the Pirates came by and said, 'Mr. Rickey told me to give you five thousand dollars more than the Dodgers offered.' And his father said, 'I can't do that. We've already shook hands on it.'"

Koufax returned to Cincinnati with a major league contract in his back pocket. Jucker, who was a bird dog for the hometown Reds, tried to interest Birdie Tebbetts in giving Koufax a look but the manager refused. Jucker never spoke to him again. He sent him a couple of players, however.

Koufax had one more appointment to keep, a pro forma try-out with the Milwaukee Braves. He slept through it. He'd been up late the night before and when he got to his hotel he fell asleep so soundly he didn't hear repeated knocks on the door. A bellhop was dispatched to remove the door from its hinges. When he was awake enough to pitch, the Braves liked what they saw and offered him $30,000, which Koufax declined, honoring his handshake deal with the Dodgers.

The *New York Times* reported the transaction on December 14, the day after the Dodgers traded Preacher Roe and Billy Cox to Baltimore in order to clear space on the major league roster. Sports columnist Jimmy Cannon went to the Koufax home and reported that the youngster seemed unfazed by this unlikely turn of events. On January 7, 1955, Irving Koufax sent Bavasi a letter confirming the deal. Preserved behind glass in the Dodger Museum at Chavez Ravine, it is a model of courtliness. You can still see the impassioned punctuation—emphatic periods and commas—impressed upon the page with leverage and feeling.

> Dear "Buzzie,"
>
> I sincerely appreciate your gracious letter of the 4th instant.
>
> To me it has always been a matter of deep satisfaction to be able to feel that I have earned the good will and respect of any person with whom I have had any contact. To have it confirmed was all the more heartwarming. Sandy doesn't say much because he feels that he has yet to prove himself, but I know that he is proud to be a "Dodger" and that he will not throw this opportunity away. I earnestly hope that in time he will measure up to all of your expectations and fully justify the faith shown in him.
>
> With all my good wishes for a great season for the Club and you personally for a successful and prosperous year, I am.
>
> Very Sincerely,
> Irving Koufax
>
> P.S. I need hardly say that every Koufax, big and little, of close or remote degree of relationship and wheresoever situate, is now an earnest "Dodger" rooter and will follow the fortunes of the club with utmost interest.

Chapter 6

THE SECOND INNING

JOEY AMALFITANO WAS COMING DOWN the tunnel from the Cubs clubhouse when he heard the sound of the ball crashing into Torborg's glove, *pow!* He'd taken his time showering, listening to the first inning on the radio while getting dressed. He was a reserve, a clutch pinch hitter. He had thrown some batting practice. He knew his number wouldn't be called anytime soon.

Like Koufax, Amalfitano was signed as a bonus baby, but their careers had gone in different directions. Koufax was invaluable. Amalfitano made himself invaluable. As he entered the dugout, Ron Santo was putting his bat back in the rack and looking for Glenn Beckert, who was hiding from him at the other end of the bench. Santo had gone to the plate mindful of Beckert's assessment of Koufax's stuff. *We got him where we want him tonight. He's not throwing that good.*

Santo loved Dodger Stadium almost as much as Wrigley Field in Chicago. It was a new park, only four years old, but already it had a sense of occasion. He had been preparing for this at-bat since getting on the team bus earlier in the afternoon. Getting ready for Koufax meant coaching muscle fibers to react in the absence of the usual stimuli. Others allowed you to see the labor in their work. Koufax only allowed you to see it when it was done: in the way his hat needed straightening after every pitch. It looked like he was tipping his cap after each delivery.

Like most of his colleagues, Santo wasn't disconcerted by Koufax's speed. On the contrary. He wasn't one of those guys who made you toss and turn at night. Unlike Drysdale, he was dominating as opposed to intimidating. His control was expected and presumed. He was one of the few opposing pitchers who actually said hello on the field. Santo figured it was because "he knew he was going to get you out."

I go to the plate and I'm looking fastball. And I see this first fastball. Whish. I take a look at it, I want to see the ball, you know, the velocity. And I haven't moved my hands. The next pitch, whish. Fastball. And I haven't moved my hands. I haven't made a move to swing. Now I haven't seen the curveball yet. And you're oh and two and you feel like you're completely naked because you got no chance. What does he do? Whish. Fastball.

He walked back to the dugout thinking, I must not have seen the ball or I'd have swung at least at one of them. In fact, he *had* swung, popping out to Torborg, who silently thanked Koufax for all those practice fungoes as he settled under the towering foul ball.

Santo's confusion wasn't unusual. Koufax had that effect on a lot of hitters: scrambling sense, reflex, and memory. Ernie Banks, the next batter, had faced Koufax every year since 1955. In his opinion, Koufax was not only the best pitcher in baseball but the smartest. Banks figured he must have graduated from Harvard or Yale with a degree in economics. Koufax could outthink you with just a fastball and a curve. He struck out on a forkball.

Byron Browne walked to the plate for his first major league at-bat. He was twenty-two years old. Most of the summer he'd spent in Class

A ball in Wenatchee, Washington, a prospect with minimal prospects. He'd been with the Triple A club for all of a week when he was called up. The night before, in Indianapolis, he hit two home runs off a long, tall pitcher named Dave DeBusschere, who also played a little basketball. Twenty-four hours later, he was facing Koufax, "a little-assed rookie trying to pick my jaw up off the floor."

As he stepped into the batter's box, Browne considered the light. It was hazy and dim, minor league light. Maybe it was from those fires he had seen from the sky. Billy Williams had mentioned something at the team hotel about there being some riots. Browne didn't know any of the details. That 22,000 people had rioted in the streets less than three weeks earlier. That 1,032 people had been injured and three times that many arrested. That the National Guard had been called in. That thirty-four people had died with the rallying cry on their lips: "Burn, baby, burn." That on the evening of August 14, the last time Koufax won a game, the scoreboard at Dodger Stadium posted bulletins listing the freeway exits that were closed due to rioting. He was a ballplayer. And when you're a ballplayer facing Koufax in your first major league at-bat, you're not thinking about anything except the scouting report that Williams had given him: "Lay off the fastball high, try to work him in the count, look for the slow curve."

Everybody knew what to look for. Gene Mauch, the Phillies' manager, would stand on the dugout steps and whistle every time Koufax threw a curve, not so much because he thought it would help his hitter—he knew it wouldn't—but in hopes of distracting him. One time, Koufax stepped off the mound and growled, "Get a bat."

Lots of people could call Koufax's pitches in the stretch. Banks watched the position of his elbows. Willie Mays watched the thumb on his glove. Some players wouldn't share such information even with teammates for fear of retribution. Joey A. was not that way. "When he opens his glove like an umbrella, he's throwing the curve," he told his teammates. "When he holds it tight, he's throwing a fastball."

Amalfitano figured it was a function of the size of his fingers; he had to open the glove wider to get a grip on the curve. Roseboro said as much: "As they say in the ghetto, 'Shit, he's got great big fucking hands,' which is what you need to throw that curveball."

It was a curve unlike any Torborg had ever seen. By season's end, he was splitting the catching with Roseboro. No matter what, he always offered to warm up the pitchers. He figured Rosie had earned the right not to do it. Catching Koufax in the pregame silence of an empty stadium, Torborg would listen for the sound of the seams biting the air. *Thk, thk, thk.* The ball spun so fast and broke so sharply that he had to learn a whole new way to catch it, sliding up toward the batter and reaching immodestly under his legs to grab the ball before it dropped out of the strike zone. Torborg thought, If the mound were any higher, the darned thing would go on back to him.

Lots of people questioned his hearing, even Roseboro. But not Browne. After listening to a curve for strike one, he wondered why Williams had told him to look for it. *You keep looking and it's still not there.* The second pitch was a fastball aimed at his belt. By the time he swung at it, the ball was at his armpit. Strike two. Now he understood. *When he gets your eyes up to that level, he comes back with the curve.*

And that's just what Koufax did. But this one didn't paralyze, embarrass, or deceive. It hung like a full moon on a cloudless night over the outside corner of the plate. Browne went out and got it, driving it toward Willie Davis, who was playing shallow in center field. Like a Punch and Judy hitter, Browne thought indignantly. He didn't know that Davis played everyone shallow.

It was the first hard-hit ball of the evening. Wow, he thought. I got a hit off Sandy Koufax! The roar of the crowd told him otherwise. He figured Davis must have made a great catch. Torborg saw nothing exceptional in the play. Neither did the official scorer. He marked his scorecard L8, baseball's notation for a line drive to center field. No exclamation point was deemed necessary.

Chapter 7

THE GREENHORN

Tommy Lasorda stood on the mound of Field One at Dodgertown, the same artfully crafted perch of dirt and sand from which Sandy Koufax launched his first pitch as a pro in the spring of 1955. Aside from being left-handed and lifelong Dodgers, the two have little in common. Lasorda embraces celebrity, Koufax eschews it. Lasorda is voluble and Italian. Koufax is reserved and Jewish.

As manager of the Dodgers, Lasorda filled his office with stars and their trappings. As manager emeritus, in an era of corporate ownership, Lasorda was adjusting to a reduced role with the Dodgers, serving as a goodwill ambassador without portfolio. In the spring of 1999, he was a manager without anything to manage, an executive without an office. He was not in a good mood. He did not want to talk about Sandy Koufax.

"What happened?" he grumbled. "What happened with what? He took my spot. What do I have to do? I won twenty games the year before."

It was the spring of 1955, and Lasorda, a career minor-leaguer, was hoping to go north with the team. Koufax was a nineteen-year-old bonus baby who threw the ball like a streak of lightning but didn't know where to go after batting practice. Because of the bonus rule under which Koufax was signed, the Dodgers had to keep him on the major league roster. Because of Koufax, Lasorda had to go back to Montreal. Or take the job driving a beer truck that general manager Buzzie Bavasi thoughtfully arranged as an alternative. Nearly fifty years later, Lasorda was still feeling grumpy about it.

Cajoled by Tommy Hawkins, Dodger vice president for communications, and having nothing better to do than throw batting practice to the son of a former player, Lasorda slowly warmed to the tale of their intertwined fate. He likes to cast himself as a *zelig* in the Koufax saga. He was there when Koufax tried out at Ebbets Field, when Koufax played winter ball in Puerto Rico, when Koufax needed someone to throw to the night before his second no-hitter, when Koufax needed tickets before the seventh game of the 1965 World Series. Once he got going on the subject, Lasorda didn't stop, failing to notice that one of the people to whom he was speaking had doubled over in acute pain with stomach cramps.

"One day, the general manager calls me into the office," Lasorda said. "I said, 'What, one of my relatives die or something?' He says, 'Nope, I'm sending you down to Triple A.' Had to keep Koufax on the roster. He said, 'The rules of baseball say if a player receives over a four-thousand-dollar limit, he must stay on the roster two years.'

"He says, 'Who would *you* send down?'

"I said, without blinking an eye, 'Koufax—he can't hit the side of a barn at sixty feet.'"

Lasorda paused before delivering his gleefully polished punch line: "It took one of the greatest left-handers in history to get me off the Brooklyn team."

The year, 1955, would prove seminal for both the Dodgers and the country. Graham Greene published *The Quiet American*, his prescient novel about a faraway place called Vietnam. A black woman named Rosa Parks refused to give up her seat on a bus in Montgomery, Alabama. The development of the oral polio vaccine was announced. The Kramdens of Bensonhurst got a half-hour network TV slot. President Dwight D.

Eisenhower held the first televised presidential news conference, bringing the presidency into American living rooms. Everyone liked Ike. And anyone who didn't could turn the channel with the newest electronic gadget, a remote control TV clicker.

The Dodgers were desperate to change their luck. Vanquished by Joe DiMaggio's Yankees in 1941, 1947, and 1949; slain by Bobby Thomson's "shot heard round the world" in 1951; humbled by the Yankees again in 1952 and 1953, the Boys of Summer were growing old waiting till next year. Walter Alston was back for his second year as manager, charged with the responsibility of turning the perennial "Bums" into champions. It was a veteran club, not all of whom were enamored of their manager, a conservative midwesterner with prodigious strength and considerable inexperience. Not all of them saw the merits of allocating a roster spot to a pitcher who had pitched exactly four college games. As Duke Snider put it, "We had lost so many pennants by one game, the world series by one game, that it was tough to take a chance on someone going out there and throwing strikes unless they've proven that they can."

Ownership, however, regarded the signing of a Jewish ballplayer the way others regarded the coming of the Messiah. The Dodgers were so desperate for a Jewish presence, given the demographics of Brooklyn, that Bavasi had hired Lee Scott as traveling secretary under the mistaken impression that he was one of the Chosen People. Bavasi was disappointed when Scott showed up one Ash Wednesday with traces of his faith on his brow. Jewish ballplayers were even more scarce than lefties. Harry Eisenstat, Sid Gordon, and Cal Abrams were all gone: traded, retired, flamed out. Koufax was a marketing godsend. "Why Flock Signed Sandy Koufax!" trumpeted the *Brooklyn Eagle*. "Jewish Southpaw from Boro a Natural for Ebbets Field."

Walter O'Malley told reporter Dave Anderson: "We hope he'll be as great as Hank Greenberg or Sid Gordon. But we don't want to be accused of discriminating against the Irish."

Long after O'Malley moved the Dodgers out of Brooklyn, he confided to Roger Kahn, author of the seminal history of the franchise, *The Boys of Summer*, "I'm in Brooklyn. I'd have given my right arm for a

Jewish star—I'm talking about a *big* Jewish star. Maybe I'd still be in Brooklyn. I come out here and I can fill the ballpark with nine fucking Chinamen and what do I get? Koufax."

Despite the marketing potential of the young lefty's faith, he was an unknown quantity to baseball, and baseball was an unknown quantity to him. A preseason story in the *Eagle* boasted: "Dodger Roster Lists Four Super Rookies." Koufax wasn't one of them. A spring training story in the *New York Times* referred to him as "the bonus right-hander."

He reported a week early, joining Joe Black and Roy Campanella in Miami, where they were working out on their own. "We got a young bonus kid, Sandy *Koo*-something, wants to join us," Campy told Black after hearing from Bavasi.

"Okay, we'll see," Black replied.

In 1955, Miami was still very much a segregated city. *Brown v. Board of Education*, the Supreme Court decision declaring an end to the era of separate but equal, was less than a year old. The black players stayed at the Lord Calvert: the place to be among the black elite. "If you were at the Lord Calvert, you were *down*," Black said before his death in May 2002. "That's where Dorothy Dandridge stayed, and Nat King Cole."

Irving Rudd, the Dodgers' director of promotions, got Koufax a room at a whites-only hotel—and some ink in the local papers. Rudd always introduced himself as "I. Rudd, press agent." Not for him the grubby moniker "p.r." man. He was a master in the performance art of the publicity stunt. He put Koufax in the lobby of the hotel with Jimmy Durante and called in the photographers. *Fireballing young lefty teaches Durante how to pitch!* That was the angle. "Oh, he was excited," Rudd recalled shortly before his death. "After all, where does a kid from Brooklyn get to meet a guy like Durante? But it wasn't ha-cha-cha-cha."

Who knew that ten years later Durante would be singing Koufax's praises: "Sandy, dandy, Sandy!"

The week in Miami was formative, forging relationships and precedents that would last his entire career. He visited his teammates at the Lord Calvert and, in Black's recollection, admired the view: "He was saying, 'Man, look at that girl around the swimming pool. This isn't bad.' Sandy was right at home."

He also received his first award as a major leaguer—a key to the City of Miami Beach. The mayor's aide had to scurry to find another key for the anonymous rookie the big leaguers had in tow. "They took us all there in a little car caravan," Black said. "We went out on the steps and they gave us keys to the city. Then boom, as soon as we got our keys, back over to the Lord Calvert. They put us back in the cars and we didn't see each other again until we got to the ballpark, yeah."

At the ballpark, Campy was in charge. There were no weight machines, no stretching regimens, no facilities to speak of. "Campy says, 'Okay, we're going to run,'" Black remembered. "Sandy's running and Sandy be saying, 'What the hell, is this a track meet?' I said, 'Nah, the theory is if your legs are strong, your arm's strong.' We're running, see, and I'd talk to him, joking, 'I thought you were a baseball player.' He said, 'I'm a basketball player.' I said, 'Really?' He said, 'Yeah, baseball is just a game to me.'"

He liked baseball fine, he liked pitching even better, but he thought it was presumptuous to call himself a ballplayer. If the Dodgers were willing to take a chance on him, why not? He could always use the bonus money to go back to college.

On March 1, 1955, forty-two players, including twenty-one pitchers, reported to Dodgertown for the official opening of spring training. There were three boys from Bensonhurst: Sandy Koufax, Joe Pignatano, and Mike Napoli. Koufax was the only bonus baby and the only Jew. Karl Spooner was the pitching phenom in camp, having pitched two shutouts with twenty-seven strikeouts at the end of 1954. Spooner had a great arm and liked to show it off. On occasion, he took the Brooklyn boys fishing with him—you can see them in an old snapshot from Napoli's scrapbook in their plaid shirts with their feet dangling from a ragged pier. Spooner hurled the catch back into the Indian River with cherry bombs stuck in their craws. Laughed like hell when the damn things blew up.

Dodgertown is still baseball's most famous spring address, but it bears little resemblance to the abandoned naval air station Branch Rickey leased from the government in 1949. There is nothing in the denatured architecture or the landscape to connect the place now advertised as "The Conference Center at Dodgertown" to its past except the quaint use of military idiom. Being caught off base in 1955 was a violation of curfew as well as a base-running error.

There were no eagle-eyed autograph hunters or kids thrusting squares of toilet paper in Duke Snider's face demanding: "Sign." There was no gift shop in which to purchase a uniformed Dodger troll for $9, an authentic Ebbets Field Beer Stein for $125, or a Jackie Robinson Limited Edition Bear (55/1,000) for $480. There was no Sandy Koufax Room either, in which chapel services are held every Sunday morning. The military infrastructure long ago gave way to "villas"—generic motel-style accommodations—with addresses like 191 Sandy Koufax Way. Today's Dodgers rent lavish villas by the seaside. A sculptured alligator wallowing in Bermuda grass is the only reminder of the bog and tangle this was when Koufax arrived for his first spring training.

In 1955, Dodgertown was American primitive: The fragrance of orange blossoms mingled with the smell of old wool blankets left behind by the military. Orange juice was fresh-squeezed and pitching mounds were handmade. Baseball diamonds stretched as far as the horizon or at least as far as Eddie Rickenbacker's Eastern Airlines landing strip, formerly a night flight training base. The Dodger plane flitted in and out, bringing in hard young bodies by the hundreds. Everybody wanted to be a major-leaguer. There were seven hundred players in camp, so many they had to be assigned color-coded numbers. There were Red Dodgers, Tan Dodgers, Yellow and Purple Dodgers. If you were lucky, you didn't get assigned to Field Seven, farthest away from their minimal accommodations.

There were no televisions, no radios, no telephones. They dined off metal trays left behind by the Navy and lived in the sailors' wooden barracks. Koufax was as raw as the exposed two-by-four-inch studs in the room he shared with Charlie Templeton. The tar paper walls leaked. The rooms stayed hot when it was hot and cold when it was cold. Electric heaters and blankets were brought in; fuses blew. Guys fought over bath mats. "Amenities?" Snider said. "If we were lucky, they'd feed the spiders so they wouldn't be hungry at night and crawl all over us."

Reporters and athletes lived side by side. Sportswriters brought their families along to enjoy the weather and the pool—an inducement to cover the team. Jack Lang and his family lived across the hall from the Campanellas. They took turns baby-sitting each other's children during dinner. Poker and booze were added incentives.

The base was dry for players. The closest watering hole was a dive named Lennie's (or Lenny's, depending on which sign you believe), walking distance through swamp and bog, out there beyond the batting cages. It wasn't anywhere you wanted to get lost. There were water moccasins in residence. "Sam Jethroe went in there one night trying to get the ball," said Tim Thompson. "He came out in a hurry—without the ball."

The Bucket of Blood was a popular spot of the era, as was the Patio. Carol Decker worked the bar there. "They didn't have cars," she said. "They'd walk in and say, 'Set up seventeen beers' and we said, 'Yup.' The rookies had to be back before curfew. If they couldn't get back, we'd take 'em back. I had a big old van and they'd lie down in back and I'd pretend I was lost. A lot of times we took 'em out by the fence by the ballpark and they'd jump the fence."

Sometimes they got caught. A loose board in the bridge spanning the canal betrayed them: thump, thump, thump. "Those boys weren't the best boys," Decker said. "They were all married. Needless to say, they were all looking for a good time. Sometime down the road, the city fathers and the Dodgers got together on it. The fathers of the young girls weren't happy. The boyfriends weren't happy. My God, it was a feather in your cap if you had a Dodger."

As Johnny Podres, the veteran bon vivant, put it, "Hell, I pitched single."

Field Number One, a pristine green diamond, lies just outside the press room and cocktail lounge then off-limits to players. It was here that Koufax made his debut in a Brooklyn Dodger uniform. Lang, who covered the team for the *Long Island Press,* witnessed the event: "The first pitch he ever threw went over the screen and landed on top of the flat roof of the press room, where Harold Burr of the *Eagle* was sitting in an easy chair. It landed with a thud and woke him up."

This inauspicious beginning provided the impetus and subtext for the enduring Koufax mythology: the wild young lefty who became the greatest control power pitcher of modern times. "Nobody was ever greener," he has said of himself. He didn't know the drill or the drills. He thought having "good wheels" meant having a good head on your shoulders. It was all new to him, not just the language or the etiquette, but the punishing dailiness of throwing a ball. "The first spring I was so scared," he said. "I had never in my life thrown a baseball every day. I was so sore I couldn't throw. It took five or six years to get my body used to the fact of pitching."

When Red Smith, the preeminent sports columnist of the day, writing for the *New York Herald Tribune*, arrived at Dodgertown on March 5 looking for an angle, Joe Becker, the anonymous new pitching coach, was his subject. Koufax was a minor character in Smith's column, "a baby-pitcher" with Joe Black by his side in the string area behind Field One. In Dodger lore, this is sacred ground, where generations of phenoms and has-beens learned the art of control by throwing through a matrix of strings erected over adjoining plates. In the next day's *Tribune*, Smith noted the youngster's nervousness.

> One wild pitch sailed over the catcher's head and smacked high against the backstop. "Oh, nuts," the kid said.
>
> "That's all right," Becker said. "Just take it easy."
>
> "Everybody throws 'em there," Black said. "I know a fellow used to throw 'em over the backstop."
>
> "Sure," Becker said. "'His name was Feller, wasn't it?'"

That spring, Black was frequently by Koufax's side. Black was twenty-eight his rookie season. He remembered what it was like to stand outside the locker room trying to summon enough courage to cross the threshold into the major leagues. "Suppose I don't see Campy, what am I going to do? What do I say to these guys? I didn't even know their names. I called them by their numbers. 'Hey! Number 1.'"

He remembered his gratitude when Preacher Roe came over and introduced himself, the same Preacher Roe who was traded to make room on the roster for nineteen-year-old Koufax three years later. So when Black discovered Koufax wandering around the infield wondering what to do next, he said, "Just follow me."

Growing up, Black's baseball hero was Hank Greenberg. He copied the man's batting stance and memorized his stats, preserving them carefully in a scrapbook. He rooted for Hammerin' Hank to break Babe Ruth's home-run record in 1938 the way the Jews of Brooklyn rooted for Jackie Robinson when he broke the color barrier in 1947.

In high school, scouts started coming around. "You're good but you're colored," they told him. "Colored guys don't play baseball." He ran home and tore up all his scrapbooks. "There was pictures of Tony Lazzeri, Frankie Crosetti, Charlie Gerhringer. All white. I tore 'em all up except Greenberg."

Robinson's first season in the majors was Greenberg's last. They met on the field one day in Pittsburgh. "He got a hit and stood beside me at first base with his chin up, like a prince," Greenberg said later. "I had a feeling for him because of the way I had been treated. I remember saying to him, 'Don't let them get you down. You're doing fine. Keep it up.'"

A headline in the next day's *New York Times* returned the compliment: "Hank Greenberg a Hero to Dodgers' Negro Star."

When Koufax arrived in segregated Florida in 1955, ten years after the liberation of the concentration camps in Germany, blacks and Jews could still identify with each other as persecuted minorities. Anti-Semitism was subtle but entrenched. "Tucked away in private clubs, locker rooms, bars," the author Irving Howe wrote. Koufax didn't trumpet his background, nor did he hide it. "It wasn't as though Sandy had a Star of David on his sleeve," said Tom Villante, who traveled with the team as broadcast coordinator. "Some people thought he was French."

Drysdale, who joined the team in 1956, called him Koo-foo—the legacy of Joe Garagiola's mispronunciation—and the name stuck.

Koufax defused potential embarrassments with humor. Like the time there was a pig roast in Duke Snider's backyard and his wife worried about what Koufax would eat. "I'll have some of that turkey," he reassured her.

Carl Erskine, a stalwart of the pitching staff, remembers one particularly sweaty bus ride through Miami. "We'd played a night game. We were on the way back to the hotel on a bus. It was just a little city bus; it had been chartered. And it's hot. No air-conditioning. And Miami's got all these train tracks going all through there. So we got stopped by a train. And I mean it was *hot*. And ballplayers are edgy anyway. And they were moaning and mumbling and Billy Herman was one of our coaches, who was a Hall of Famer. And after a while, he yells out, real loud, 'You can give this damn town back to the Jews.' And Sandy's sitting right across the aisle, you know? And all of us are, 'Oh, Billy.' So after a few minutes of silence, Sandy, in a real soft voice, says, 'Now, Billy, you know we've already got it.'"

That there would be some anti-Semitism in baseball is hardly surprising. The national pastime was no bastion of enlightenment. Being a bonus baby was bad enough. Being a Jewish bonus baby was a liability. There was an unspoken calculus: Moneyed and Jewish went together like left-handed and wild. With jobs at stake and world series earnings more than just pocket change, judgments could be fierce and unforgiving. What Hank Greenberg did for Jackie Robinson, Robinson, Black, Campanella, and Newcombe did for Koufax, taking him under their sheltering wing. It was the Dodger way: Hadn't Pee Wee Reese walked across the infield in Cincinnati in 1947 to put his arm around Robinson—an act of moral courage memorialized in literature, infused in the history of the franchise, and remembered as a landmark in the American struggle for racial equality?

"We had our reasons, our one reason—it was because he was a Jew," Newcombe said. "Some of the players did not like him because he was a Jew. They vilified him because he was a bonus baby and had to stay on the roster. It wasn't his fault. He wanted to go to the minors. I couldn't understand the narrow-mindedness of these players when they would come to us and talk about Sandy as 'this kike' and 'this Jew bastard' or 'Jew sonofabitch that's gonna take my job.' And: 'I've got to go to the minor leagues because he's on the ball club and he can't throw the ball in the batting cage but he's gonna take somebody's job.' And saying it in front of us about Sandy! They hated Jews as much as they hated blacks. I don't know if Sandy ever knew that, but that's why we took care of Sandy.

"Players used to complain he threw the ball too hard. But the way they used to complain—'The wild Jew sonofabitch, I'm not gonna hit

against that'—and they'd use the f-word—'that kike as wild as he is.'
And these were star Dodger players, some of them. You think of crackers
as being from the South but a lot of those crackers they were from
California and other places. That's what made him such a strong man.
He knew some of the players did not like him because he was not pro-
ducing and he was also a Jew." (He says Lasorda was not among them.)

The perception wasn't confined to the Dodger locker room. It was
the mind-set of the era. "Sandy Koufax, being a little Jewish boy, didn't
know anything about baseball," Hank Aaron said, describing the prevailing attitude. "Everybody thought, Hey, he needs to be somewhere
off in school, counting money or doing whatever *they* do."

Around the league "there was definitely some of that: the spoiled
Jewish kid with a lot of money," said Frank Torre. "You talk to some
old-timers, I don't care what they tell you today, they used to grumble
like hell. Two things were happening. They had a good team. They felt
it could have been better without him. Then there would have been
somebody legitimate in his spot who was really going to help the team.
Down deep most of them resented the fact that he had earned more
money than them."

When, late in spring training, Koufax conveniently sprained his
ankle, the joke around Dom Fristachi's Brooklyn neighborhood was:
"He tripped over his wallet." A wallet big enough to buy a shiny new red
convertible and treat Dom and his girl to dinner at a Chinese restaurant
before the annual Dodger-Yankee exhibition game. Koufax sat in the
stands with them, a spectator, just as he was when he kept Wilpon company during try-outs. On May 9, a hairline fracture in the previously
sprained ankle was miraculously diagnosed, enabling the Dodgers to
place him on the thirty-day disabled list.

Lasorda got a temporary reprieve. Koufax kept his mouth shut. "You
wouldn't know he was there," Bavasi said. "He wasn't anything like
Tommy Lasorda, who let everyone know he was there. But Tommy had to
do it because he had no ability. I shouldn't say that. He was oh and four in
the major leagues." In four appearances with the Dodgers, he had a 13.50
ERA. Despite the grumbling of more seasoned pitchers that he wasn't

one of them, Lasorda would always be able to say he was a member of the 1955 World Championship team—a claim validated years later when Peter O'Malley had a world series ring made for him from the old mold.

On June 9, 1955, the *Times* reported: "The Dodgers released Tom Lasorda outright to their Montreal International League affiliate in order to create room on the roster for Sandy Koufax. Both are south-paw pitchers." Which is a little like saying Abraham Lincoln and James Polk were both president. "Sandy could throw better right-handed than Lasorda could throw left-handed," Black said.

Koufax made his major league debut on June 24, in the fifth inning of a game in Milwaukee with the Dodgers trailing 7–1. Johnny Logan waited at home plate, watching him walk across the grass "with his jacket over his shoulder, like a high school kid, Sandy Koufax, mop-up man."

The crowd noise, which seemed benign in the bullpen, reached up to greet him. Through the intimidating crescendo he heard the public address announcer mispronounce his name—"*Koo*-fax,"—as Logan stepped to the plate. In Koufax's recollection, Logan hit a blooper off the end of the bat. "A blooper?" Logan said. "You got to be kidding. It was a line drive over Gil Hodges's head. Hit the white line in right field for a double. *A double.* Chrissakes, I remember that just like today is—what day is it? You tell Sandy Koufax it was a double."

It was a bloop single. The next hitter was slugger Eddie Mathews, who surprised Koufax by bunting back to the mound. Koufax calmly threw the ball into center field. The third hitter was Hank Aaron, the one batter for whom he later confessed he never had a plan. He walked on four pitches. Bobby Thomson—*that* Bobby Thomson, slayer of Dodger dreams—followed Aaron to the plate. The count went to 3 and 2 before Thomson swung and missed, thus becoming the first man ever struck out by Sandy Koufax. "Hey, I'm famous," the dour Scotsman said decades later.

Koufax's first major league start came two weeks later against Pittsburgh. He walked eight batters in the 4 and ⅔ innings he pitched and didn't get another start for seven weeks. "Oh, no," coach Jake Pitler moaned when Alston announced Koufax would face the Reds on August 27.

Birdie Tebbetts, the Reds manager, who had ignored Ed Jucker's plea to sign Koufax out of college, got a scouting report from Joe Black, who had been acquired from the Dodgers in June. "He throws hard," Black said.

It was a glorious Saturday afternoon. Koufax struck out fourteen, most that season in the National League, and surrendered only two hits: a first-inning single to Ted Kluszewski and a ninth-inning double to Sam Mele. Their paths wouldn't cross again until a decade later when Mele was managing the Minnesota Twins in the 1965 World Series. Mele was heading back to the visiting clubhouse after being shut out by Koufax 7–0. "He's right in the doorway wrapped in a towel," Mele recalled. "I said, 'Nice game.' He pointed a finger at me and said, 'You hit a double off me.'"

No wonder he remembered. It was his first major league victory, a complete-game shutout. Bob Rosen, one of just 7,204 paying customers at Ebbets Field, left the game convinced the Dodgers had finally found their Jewish star. Not that he hung on to his ticket stub. Who knew it would be worth real money to latter-day Koufax "completionists"?

"Every pitch was *whomp, whomp, whomp*," Black said. "I mean, they were coming back carrying the lumber. Next day, Birdie says, 'That rookie made us look terrible. Where the hell they been keeping him?'"

On the bench. He made only twelve appearances in 1955, pitching 41.2 innings, walking almost as many men (twenty-eight) as he struck out (thirty). His only other win in 1955 was another shutout. "He was totally inconsistent but brilliant," Rosen said.

He had a fine view from the dugout in Yankee Stadium of Sandy Amoros's catch in left field that finally made the Bums world champions. Afterward, he drove across town to attend class at Columbia University, where he had enrolled in architecture school, just in case. No one in academia suspected he was a ballplayer. "I'm one of the pitchers although I don't pitch too much yet," he told the professor, who gave him permission to skip class in order to attend the victory party.

Throughout his career, Koufax was seen as an ally by black players—teammates and opponents, American and National Leaguers. Word got around, as it will, traveling from clubhouse to clubhouse: Koufax was *consistent*. He treated everyone the same. Cheesy Kawano, the clubhouse man's wife, who was at the ballpark a lot helping her husband with the players' laundry, says Koufax was the only member of the team who knew her name and addressed her by it. "If he was in a restaurant, he would never shy away from sitting with the colored fellas," Black said. "If he saw me sitting over there, he'll come sit down and say, 'How ya doin'?'"

This sentiment wasn't confined to his teammates. Earl Battey, who would face him as one of Mele's Twins in the 1965 series, paid him the ultimate compliment: "I accused him of being black. I told him he was too cool to be white."

Partly this was the legacy of a grandfather with a social conscience, partly the democratizing influence of competing under the boards in Brooklyn. But, perhaps there was something else at play. Perhaps, Dave Wallace says, Koufax identified with the black players as much as they identified with him. Fred Wilpon agrees. "Sandy had a special feeling toward the downtrodden and the oppressed, a special feeling for the black players and their plight," Wilpon said. "And I think maybe part of it was sort of a substitution for his own minority standing."

Late at night in the Dodger locker room while icing aching arms and legs, Koufax would screen Maury Wills's mail. "Funny mail," Wills called it. "I could tell when I had some hate mail. You could just look at the envelope and tell. I didn't want to read it anymore when I got to a certain point. And when he was reading it we'd have a lot of fun with it. He was—'Oh, you got to read this one.'" On occasion, Wills had the opportunity to reciprocate.

Koufax never forgot Joe Black's kindness. One day in the summer of 1965, the Dodgers were in New York to play the Mets. Black was out of baseball and working as a vice president for the Greyhound Corporation. "I'm just walking on Fifth Avenue, y'know, and all of a sudden two hands go over my eyes," he said. "I'm, like, 'What the?' Someone says, 'Guess who?'

"I turned around and it was Sandy Koufax. I said, 'Where did you come from?' He was across the street, walking in the opposite direction. He ran all the way to come my way. That's when he was a star. I was a hacker, a one-year wonder. Here's a man who says, 'You're my friend then, you're my friend now.' The same old Sandy Koufax."

Chapter 8

THE THIRD INNING

THE DODGERS WERE in the process of going three up and three down in the bottom half of the second inning when Dave Smith's father wandered past his son's bedroom in Escondido and noticed the tape recorder wasn't running. Dave wouldn't be happy about missing the first two innings of a Koufax game. Koufax was Dave's favorite player on his favorite team. The first game he ever saw, on July 18, 1958, he chose because Koufax was starting. Not too many people organized their lives around Koufax's appearances that season. (He was knocked out in the first inning after striking out two and walking four.) So, as Dave's father switched on the machine, he muttered under his breath, "This is the best I can do, David."

The machine began to record just as Scully was making a commercial pitch for Chevrolet's year-end Fall Cleanup Sale—*Hundreds off the sticker price!*—and just as Bill Buhler was turning off his movie camera. Buhler had only a hundred feet of film—enough for three minutes of live action—so he decided to conserve his resources for the top of the Cubs' order.

"Here's Chris Krug, coming up for Chicago," Jerry Doggett said, taking over the play-by-play. Krug was twenty-five, a right-handed hitter batting .219. Called up in May, he was starting against lefties by September. It was the first of what he expected would be many years in the major leagues. He was a California kid, out of Riverside. This was his first trip home as a major-leaguer. He had bought a bunch of tickets from the front office for family and friends. Gary Adams, his best friend, was sitting behind first base with his mother, a real fan, and his mother-in-law, who had never been to a major league baseball game.

Krug had heard about Koufax's fastball. *A radio ball*, the old-timers called it. *You can hear it but you can't see it.* As Casey Stengel, the Old Professor, once noted, "Umpires often can't see where Koufax pitches go, so they have to judge from the sound of them hitting the catcher's glove. He's very tough on umps who are hard of hearing."

Krug wanted to see for himself. He swung and missed at the first pitch and took another for a called strike two, turning to look at Torborg in disbelief. They knew each other some from the minors. "What the hell?" Krug said. "What was that?"

"Ball's going up," Torborg replied.

Some old catchers stuffed their mitts with falsies, protecting delicate digits with the padding women used to enhance their bust. Torborg preferred athletic tape—easier to augment. Koufax wasn't hard to catch. Not like Drysdale, who threw a heavy, sinking ball, not to mention the occasional spitter. Koufax threw a four-seam fastball, his fingers pulling back on the stitching to create backspin and lift. Drysdale threw a two-seamer, creating topspin and bite. Drysdale was a "hard hard." Koufax was an "easy hard." No matter how hard he threw, he was light. Torborg thought: He throws the ball hard so easy.

Ed Bailey, the Cubs' veteran catcher, watched from the bullpen, trying to gauge Koufax's stuff from Krug's response to it. After Krug lined out to center, he returned to the bench feeling pretty good about himself. At least he made contact. His buddy, Gary Adams, was thinking along with him: *At least you hit a good fly ball.* From the bullpen, Bailey had a more jaundiced view. *Cocky kid,* he thought. *Sandy ate 'im alive.*

Don Kessinger, the young Cubs shortstop, approached the plate not so much with trepidation as curiosity. Kessinger had been reading the papers like everyone else, stories about "this old left-hander whose elbow hurt so bad he might not be able to pitch much more." But he didn't give himself much of a chance to form an opinion, flying out on an 0-and-2 pitch.

"All right, two down," Doggett said. "Bob Hendley coming up."

Hendley took a few languid practice swings while Doggett updated the pennant race. The Giants had won. Juan Marichal was the victor, getting his twenty-first win and his tenth shutout. The Mets and Reds were all tied up in the seventh. With just twenty-one games left in the regular season, the Dodgers had to win to keep pace in the National League pennant race. "The Dodgers see the Cubs again next week in Chicago," Doggett pointed out, hopefully.

Hendley was focused not on the future, not even on his prospective at-bat, but on the mound, a handcrafted pile of dirt and clay lovingly molded into a sublime perch by Dodger groundskeepers. It was 50 percent clay, 30 percent sand, and 20 percent silt—a pitcher's butte. Major league rules mandated a fifteen-inch height limit. Everyone said the mound at Dodger Stadium was sixteen inches at least, probably higher. It gave even the least prepossessing pitcher an aura of indomitability and made the most invincible batter a supplicant. Other mounds were higher still. But none had the sheer drop-off, pitching rubber to ground level, that distinguished Dodger Stadium. With the length of Koufax's fingers, arms, and stride factored into the equation, he was no more than fifty-four or fifty-five feet away from the plate when he released the ball. *On top of you.* From the baller's box, Koufax looked like an elegant crane swooping down on its prey from the lip of the Grand Canyon.

"Bob bats right, throws left," Doggett said. "In just sixteen games, Hendley was two and two. He had a lot of trouble this year and had to go out to Salt Lake City and get straightened away. He worked just

thirty-seven innings in the majors this year and had an earned run average of 8.29."

Granted, Hendley was no longer the pitcher he had once been. But
he loved the mound at Dodger Stadium, the way the clay held your
spikes and made a pitcher secure. It leveled the playing field, giving him
a fleeting taste of the omnipotence Koufax always enjoyed. He savored
the sensation of bearing down on the batter, the way Koufax was now
bearing down on him. So even as he struck out, meekly and predictably,
to end the half inning, he was looking forward to climbing back up the
hill.

Chapter 9

TO BE YOUNG AND WILD

IN THE HALL OUTSIDE THE GYM at Lafayette High School in Brooklyn, there is a display case heralding the names of the seventeen boys who became major leaguers—among them the Aspromonte brothers, Ken and Bob, Al Ferrara, Larry Yellen, John Franco, and Sandy Koufax. His pictures are long gone from the school library, empty frames in yellowing yearbooks. "Sandy's glove was here, too," longtime baseball coach Joe Gambuzza said. "But someone broke the showcase and took it."

The school, now called "Hell High," was unable to field a team for the 2002 season. Not enough interest. Not enough passing grades. The last generation of players trained and competed on Ben Sherman Field, named for the team doctor who, according to legend, set Koufax's broken finger, thereby enabling him to fulfill his unknown destiny. Players dress in a dank, cinder-block bunker adjacent to the field where Gambuzza sat one spring afternoon, before he retired in 2001, in a three-legged chair dispensing the same paradoxical advice to two young pitchers given to Koufax fifty years ago. *Don't throw so damn hard. Let 'em hit the ball.*

One of the pitchers, Chris Dowd, had caddied for Koufax at a golf tournament in Westchester County. He cherished the advice Koufax gave him: "When you make it, be grateful."

Modern myth-making is by definition retrospective; the accretion of detail produces a portrait so outsized it seems petty to question the particulars. Take Koufax's broken finger. If Dr. Benjamin Sherman hadn't been there, hadn't been so dedicated, hadn't been so competent, then Koufax wouldn't have healed and prospered. The only problem with this bit of mythology is that it was another kid who broke his finger. Koufax only dislocated his. "A nothing," the doctor said. So much so that when doctor and patient met years later and Koufax said, "Remember me?" Sherman had to admit, "To tell you the truth, I didn't."

The essential Koufax myth is this: A fire-balling young lefty, a bonus baby whose own teammates wouldn't get in the batting cage against him, suddenly became a pitcher of such exquisite control that catcher John Roseboro said, "He wasn't throwing on the outside corner of the plate but on the *outside* of the outside." His wildness is an indispensable part of his myth. After all, if he hadn't been so wild, so unpredictable, so thoroughly unharnessed, then his reversal of form and fortune wouldn't have been so miraculous. It's a better story this way.

"The common understanding of how he emerged from someone allegedly who couldn't throw the ball near home plate to somebody who became the greatest pitcher in the history of the game for six years in a row is a misconception," says Fred Wilpon. "I actually think that six-year period where manager Alston played him one day and pitched him four weeks later was the root of his inconsistency. And had he been brought along either through the minor leagues or in the major leagues in a consistent way and handled better, in my opinion, he would have emerged as a superstar far earlier.

"There was no rationale from the beginning. He had this extraordinary talent. And it wasn't all of a sudden he discovered how to throw a curveball. He knew how to throw a curveball before. He had two devastating pitches. He suffered through that period and I thought he was poorly handled. I think he would have been pitching very successfully at an earlier age. I don't know why they didn't use him better. Why he didn't walk away was because he was a fierce competitor. He knew that given the opportunity, he could be successful."

Tall tales are an essential part of baseball's charm and they grow stilts in the retelling. Word was he had great stuff but couldn't keep it in the batting cage. Word was Joe Becker, the pitching coach, took him behind the barracks at Dodgertown to throw so he wouldn't embarrass himself or hurt anyone else. Word was he struck out seven batters in a row in a winter league game, walked the next ten, and then hit a lady in the stands. "Right here," Orlando Cepeda said, pointing to his forehead.

Duke Snider still complains about Koufax hitting him in the rear end during batting practice. Finally, Snider put a batting glove in his hip pocket to protect his hindquarters. "I gave him a target and he hit it," Duke said. "I said, 'If you've got that kind of control, you'll win a lot of games.'"

Carl Erskine tells a story about the late Sam Narron, the Dodger bullpen coach whose thumb Koufax had broken at a previous try-out in Pittsburgh. Sam wanted no part of Koufax. "Sam was a country boy from Carolina. Chewed tobacco and caught pitchers. That was his duty. So he warmed up everybody. That's all he did. So when he'd get Sandy, Sam would get hit in the chin, in the ankle, in the wrist, in the chest with balls in the dirt. And Sam, as nice a Joe as he was, he hated to warm up Sandy.

"One day at Ebbets Field, they told Sam, 'Take Sandy down to the bullpen and give him a good workout.' So Sam, knowing he was gonna have a tough time, put on all the equipment, the shin guards and the chest protector, mask. He goes down there and the bullpen was very close to the outfield fence. It was out in the open. So Sandy got really warmed up and threw a fastball over Sam's head and it hit that fence and ricocheted right back and hit him in the back of the head where he had no protection. And Sam, right there, said, 'You know, I'd rather be home workin' on the farm than warmin' up Koufax.'"

For every tale of his wildness, there is a mitigating view.

Fresco Thompson, the Dodger scout, told reporters after Koufax's try-out at Ebbets Field, "Usually, when we use a kid to pitch batting practice, the players are kind of wary. Some don't even bother to hit against the kids they're so wild. But they all hit against him. He had good control."

As for throwing behind the barracks, everyone did—that's where the string area was. Joe Pignatano caught him in the spring of 1955. "Everybody said, 'Sandy's wild, wild, wild,'" Pignatano said. "He was not that wild. A little high and low in the strike zone. Once they put that tag on you it stays with you. They never stayed with Sandy long enough to give him a chance until later when they had nobody else."

Besides, young lefties are supposed to be wild. They are valued because they're different, rare, scary. "It's good to be wild when you're young," Ernie Banks says.

But Koufax's wildness carried no such favor. It penalized him. Now it serves a mythic need and provides cover for those who chose not to use him. How wild Koufax was at a given place on a given day fifty years ago is probably not relevant or ascertainable—even by him. Friends have heard him protest, "My control wasn't that bad." Don Zimmer, a teammate from 1955 through 1959, demurs, "The thing that he don't remember, he didn't have to go up and hit off himself. The humpties like myself, we did. And we thought he was a little wild and hard."

What Koufax needed most, the Dodgers couldn't or wouldn't provide: opportunity. In 1955 and 1956, there was logic on Alston's side—he had an established pitching staff and a team fighting for a championship. Not to mention an annual one-year contract. Taking chances was not in his nature or his interest. No doubt, he resented being saddled with a twenty-four-man roster. Alston needed to win; Koufax needed to pitch. Alston was afraid of inexperience; Koufax was damned by it.

Sports columnist Jimmy Cannon once described a bonus baby as a "ballplayer who is paid a fortune to watch ballgames." That pretty much sums up Koufax's first two seasons in the big leagues. He was the first Dodger player signed under the new bonus system put in place by ownership in 1954. It acted as a deterrent to paying what passed for big money. Even then owners knew they couldn't trust themselves not to outspend each other in a bidding war. So they instituted a rule that penalized the player by inhibiting his development, the manager by saddling him with unproven talent, and themselves if they paid too much too often.

Koufax was greeted with the same skepticism that bonus babies encountered throughout the major leagues. The litany of disappointments was long. Paul Pettit, "The Wizard of Whiff," signed by the Pirates in 1950 for $100,000, the first player to receive a six-figure bonus, won exactly one game in his major league career. Ted Kazanski, signed by the Phillies for $100,000 in 1953, batted .217 in 417 games. Few expected Koufax to be any different.

The system almost guaranteed it, putting a player at odds with his teammates, his manager, and the culture. To be paid for potential was unthinkable. Nothing in life was guaranteed, much less in baseball. Entitlement was not yet endemic to the American psyche. Players signed under the system not only understood the sensibility, they shared it. They wanted to go to the minors and couldn't. The only thing worse than not playing was being paid not to play.

Koufax first met Joe Amalfitano killing time under the stands at Ebbets Field, commiserating over the awkwardness of their position. "These players were all fighting for the extra nickels—now they make thousands a day—and here we come, unproven talent," said Amalfitano, who signed with the Giants in 1954. "We're getting money up front and a signing bonus."

Frank Torre, a first baseman with the Milwaukee Braves, recalls the attitude in the clubhouse. "We almost laughed at those guys," he said. " 'Here we go again, here's another guy who's going to take one of our spots and never do anything in the big leagues.' I guess deep down most players resented it because money was so tough to come by. For somebody to earn so much without doing anything, it just wasn't the way of the times. If somebody comes along and gets twenty thousand you preferred they earned it."

Koufax's $14,000 signing bonus plus $6,000 annual salary sounded pretty good, considering that the payroll for the entire team was $500,000. Erskine remembers Koufax's discomfort. "I always felt Sandy was self-conscious about taking up a major league spot," Erskine said. "I think he showed a lot of respect for the players on the team who had made it through the minors."

He kept his mouth shut and tried not to get in the way, muttering to himself that if he didn't learn how to pitch he would be riding that subway he and Wilpon vowed to avoid. Alston used him rarely and trusted him less. Having made twelve appearances as a rookie, he saw his workload increase 33.3 percent in 1956. He pitched a total of 58.2 innings, walking twenty-nine and striking out thirty, with an ERA of 4.91. He wasn't so much unproductive, Erskine says, as unpredictable. Rarely was he allowed to work out of a jam. "The only thing that bothered Sandy was when he threw two or three balls, they got somebody up in the bullpen," said Pignatano. Often, it seemed, Alston had someone warming up in the first inning. Red Adams, who later became the Dodger pitching coach, said, "Walter didn't have a lot of scout in him."

Jackie Robinson, then in his final season, clashed with Alston on many subjects, including Koufax. Villante who was affiliated with the Dodgers throughout the fifties and sixties, said, "The one thing about Jackie was, no matter who the hell you were, Jackie appreciated talent. If you were good, he was on your side. I think he saw that in Sandy. Added to that was the fact Jackie Robinson did not like Alston.

"Jackie always thought Alston was dumb. And the very fact that Sandy would every so often show this terrific flash of brilliance and pitch a terrific game and not pitch again for thirty days would add to Jackie saying how dumb this guy was."

Eventually, reporters began to question why Koufax was "wasting his life" in idleness. Dick Young of the *Daily News* referred to him as "the young, ignored lefty."

> For some reason that escapes me, Alston manifests very little confidence in Koufax. A pitching pinch has to develop before Walt uses the kid. Then, it seems, Sandy must pitch a shutout or the bullpen is working full force and the kid will be yanked at the first long foul ball. . . . Koufax started in St. Louis the other night. He was leading, 3–1, in the fourth

when he walked the leadoff man and threw two balls to the next hitter. Carl Erskine, who had been warming up since the first inning, relieved. Erskine gave up seven hits in four innings. Koufax had given three hits in three innings. After the game, Alston said Koufax didn't have good stuff, but Erskine did.

That winter, the Dodgers sent him to Puerto Rico to play winter ball. There were cigarettes to bum and women to impress and older team-mates to shore up his confidence. He spent time with outfielder Jim Landis and his bride, who fed him egg salad, the only thing she knew how to make. Tim Thompson, his catcher, nourished his self-esteem. By then, Koufax's reputation had become a self-fulfilling prophecy. "When we first got down there, he was wild," Thompson said. "Most of his trouble, though, was that he didn't believe he could throw strikes. So many people said he couldn't do it that he believed it. We didn't change any-thing. We more or less talked to him. 'Don't believe what people tell you.'

"The reputation followed him and the umps went along. He could throw the ball close to the plate and they'd call it a ball because the umpire expected him to throw balls. I think they squeezed him."

One night, in an effort to relax him, Thompson suggested a new approach, a spitter. "He said, 'What's that?' I said, 'You put a little saliva on your finger and throw a spitter.'

"So anyway, I said to Sandy, 'When I give you the sign, you go throw the spitter.' He turned his back to me. I saw his head go down toward his glove. I thought, 'What the devil is he doing?' So he turned around and threw the ball and the saliva flew right off the ball all the way in and the umpire said, 'What's that?' I said, 'Sandy, I didn't say spit all through your hands. Just moisten your fingers.'

"He started laughing about it. We didn't throw any more spitters. Probably the only one he ever tried."

Thompson thought he'd be fine in 1957. But the season began just as the previous one ended—with perplexing inactivity. What was under-standable on Alston's part in 1955 and 1956 was inexplicable in 1957.

The Dodgers were going nowhere—except west. And he was pitching well. On May 15, the day he became eligible to be sent down to the minor leagues, Tommy Holmes of the *Herald Tribune* wrote, "There's not a chance. He has been getting his good stuff over the plate this spring."

The next day, Alston gave him a chance to justify his place on the major league roster—his second start of the season. Facing the Cubs at Wrigley Field, he struck out thirteen and won 3–2. It was his first complete game in two years. For the next two weeks, and for the first time in his career, he was a member of the starting rotation. He won two of the next four games he pitched. On June 4, he faced the Cubs again, this time in New York on Better Brooklyn Night. He had a no-hitter into the sixth inning. His twelve strikeouts gave him a total of fifty-nine in the 49⅔ innings he had pitched—most in the National League. His ERA was 2.90, twelfth in the league. He didn't get another start for forty-five days.

A small item buried in the *Sporting News* alluded to "a lame arm" and "muscle soreness," for which doctors prescribed rest. He got plenty. He was completely idle for twenty-three days. Between June 5 and July 19, he made three brief appearances in relief. When he finally made his next start, on July 19, he struck out eleven in seven innings but got no decision.

By this time, even those who had doubted him early were perplexed. Pee Wee Reese, The Captain, confronted Alston about it. "They had other pitchers who were just as wild but it didn't seem Alston wanted to pitch Sandy," he said in a letter written shortly before his death. "But I told Alston he's got to give the guy a shot with an arm like that even if he throws the ball over the damn backstop. I didn't care just as long as I didn't have to hit against him."

Danny Ozark, who had been in the Dodger system since 1942 and was a member of Alston's coaching staff from 1965 through 1972, said, "Somewhere along the line someone had to be told, 'Don't pitch this guy.' You can smell a fish here. I know he—Sandy—was upset. He's probably still upset. They could have given him a chance to pitch, especially in '57. They could have pitched him every fifth day. He should have pitched. They were going nowhere. He could have gotten twenty to twenty-five starts. He probably would have been a better pitcher in

1959 and '60. Somebody upstairs had a reason for this. It has to go back to the g.m."

These days, former general manager Buzzie Bavasi sits atop a mountain just north of San Diego in retirement. The Pacific lies outside his picture window. But the easy chair he favors faces the interior of a study lined with baseball books and photos, the accumulation of fifty years in the game. "I can't believe that," he said, when asked about Koufax's numbers. "I can't believe he went two months without pitching. In '57, who the hell did we have?"

Carl Erskine and Sal Maglie were injured. Don Newcombe and Roger Craig lost more than they won. Don Drysdale was the ace. Koufax was his forgotten foil. Later, they would come to be seen as linguistically inseparable—*KoufaxandDrysdale*. But, in the early years, their lives and careers couldn't have been more divergent. Drysdale was larger than life, the kind of guy sportswriters always referred to as "strapping." Koufax was bigger than he seemed. Drysdale, the bland California blond, was born and raised to be what he became. Tall, dark, and Semitic, Koufax became the one thing no one, including himself, expected him to be. By 1957, Drysdale was fulfilling his promise; pitching regularly, he won seventeen games. Koufax was the Great (Unfulfilled) Jewish Hope. "The Great Unwanted" is how he described himself in his autobiography.

Bavasi was especially close to Donald, as he still refers to him. Reaching now for the *Baseball Encyclopedia*, he scanned the small print of Koufax's lifetime record for the 1957 statistics. "Well, yeah, right," he said. "He pitched one hundred four innings, only gave up eighty-three hits, struck out one hundred twenty-two. That's not too bad. If I would have known that, he would have been pitching. Fifty-seven, of course, we had so many things on our mind."

Even now, former Dodger executives cannot bring themselves to use the word "betrayal" in the same sentence with "Brooklyn." In 1956, the last of the trolleys went out of service. The Dodgers played seven "home" games across the Hudson River in Jersey City. Little by little, Walter O'Malley loosened the ties that bound the Bums to Brooklyn, selling off the property on which Ebbets Field stood to a real estate magnate and then exchanging the Dodgers' Fort Worth Texas League team for Chicago's Pacific Coast League Los Angeles Angels. The handwriting was not just on the outfield wall, it was in all the papers. In the New York *Daily News*, Dick Young wrote: "Inching their way westward, the Dodgers . . ."

Koufax was the last man to pitch for the Brooklyn Dodgers, throwing an inning of relief in the final desultory loss of the 1957 season. His record after three years in Brooklyn: nine wins and ten losses.

When the Dodgers left Brooklyn it marked not just the end of an era but the end of a way of life. The day the Los Angeles City Council approved the deal to bring the Dodgers to California, the U.S. Census Bureau reported that New York City's population had decreased by 96,486. Cities were becoming inner cities. Everyone who could was getting out. In July, the Giants had announced their intention to move to San Francisco. In September, Jack Kerouac published his ode to mobility, *On the Road*. Dislocation was the new national pastime, a restlessness facilitated by technology. The country was souped-up, tail-finned, and grilled. Chrysler debuted a high-end sedan with a 16⅔ rpm hi-fi built into the dash. Ford marketed prudence, introducing a safety package on some of its '57 models (seat belts, padded dash, safety door latches). It didn't sell. America was going places and didn't want to be constrained.

The first week of October, the Soviet Union launched the first Sputnik satellite, initiating the space race. The sky was no longer the limit. On October 7, the L.A. City Council awarded the Dodgers 315 acres of land on which to build their gleaming new stadium. O'Malley wired the mayor: "Get the wheelbarrow and shovel. I'll see you at Chavez Ravine."

What Paul Zimmerman described in the *Los Angeles Times* as "a forbidding, hilly, useless piece of real estate" had once been home to many Mexican-American families. Michael Levett, then an impassioned thirteen-year-old baseball fan with liberal Jewish parents, remembers watching on television as one last family was forcibly removed by police. "It was so indelibly imprinted on my mind, I remember the name of the family, the Arechigas," he said. "My family was appalled." (Later, baseball historian Michael Gershman would discover that the family was a front for groups filing taxpayer lawsuits.) Levett was ambivalent for other reasons. He lived only four blocks from the minor league ballpark that was home to the Hollywood Stars. A kid with moxie could always talk his way into the game, free. All he had to do was get a willing adult to pass as his mother or father. That was okay with Levett's parents. They never even thought to warn him about talking to strangers.

The arrival of major league baseball inaugurated a new star system. The first game was played at the Los Angeles Coliseum on April 18 before 78,672 fans, including Gene Autry, Nat "King" Cole, John Ford, "Tennessee" Ernie Ford, Georgie Jessel, Danny Kaye, Burt Lancaster, Jack Lemmon, Gregory Peck, Buddy Rogers, Danny Thomas, and Alfred Hitchcock, who took up a seat and a half. Ray Bolger and his wife wore Army surplus helmets, his and her "Los Angeles Dodger beanball protectors." The players arrived in a caravan of shiny, new convertibles like new-age Roman conquerors. Koufax and Pignatano brought up the rear.

They shared an apartment in Los Angeles. They played cards, saw some shows, drove back and forth to the stadium together. Neither of them was a carouser but the girls chased them plenty. "The girls were crazy about anybody in uniform," Piggy said. "Sandy was one of those guys who wasn't gonna get hooked. He wanted to do the asking. I never questioned him if he was seeing anyone. That was strictly personal."

Koufax went to Erskine, a family man and paterfamilias of the pitching staff, for advice on how to meet women. "He used to talk to me kind of in a quiet way, say, 'Uh, you've got a nice family and a nice wife. How do I find girls like that?'

"And I'd say, 'Well, Sandy, what type of girl?'

"'Well, a good home girl or homemaker—you know, a domestic type. But a girl with some life.'

"I said, 'Well, you're dating, aren't you? A handsome kid like you, you've gotta be dating in L.A.' He said, 'I date.'

"I said, 'Well, who do you date?' 'Oh, these young starlets, these beautiful girls that come out here who have stars in their eyes to meet movie stars.'

"And I said, 'Well, where do you meet these girls?' 'Cocktail parties and the bar, you know.'

"I said, 'Sandy, you go to synagogue, don't you? How about the symphony and cultural things in L.A.? Why don't you start spending more time in those places?'"

Over the next three years, Koufax was in and out of the starting rotation, up and down in the strike zone, on and off the disabled list. He told reporters he wasn't sure whether he was a *shlemiel* or a *shlemazel*. "In Yiddish," he explained, "a *schlemiel* is someone who spills soup on people. A *schlemazel* is someone who has soup spilled on him." Either way it was messy. In July 1958, he had a record of 7 and 3 and four consecutive wins when he sprained his ankle in a collision at first base. He finished the year 11 and 11 and led the majors only in wild pitches.

There were intimations as well as lamentations. One June evening in 1959, he struck out sixteen Phillies, a record for a night game. Two months later, he broke that record in Los Angeles, against the Giants, tying Bob Feller's major league record of eighteen strikeouts. There were 82,794 people in the reconfigured ballpark that night to see the most heated confrontation of the pennant race. Koufax struck out the side three times and allowed Willie McCovey the only home run he ever hit off him. Naysayers noted the Coliseum's poor lighting.

The win reduced the Giants lead in the National League to one game. The *Los Angeles Times* pronounced it "one of the most momentous victories in the Dodgers' glorious history." Columnist Mal Florence wrote that the former bonus baby was a "bargain baby at any price." Even so, Koufax was close to coming out of the game; a pinch hitter sent up to bat for him in the seventh inning was called back from the on-deck circle.

Though he struck out forty-one men in his last three appearances of the season, he remained an afterthought, a spot starter and reliever for the 1959 National League champions. The Dodgers traveled to Chicago to meet the "Go Go Sox," where Koufax made his first world series appearance, pitching two perfect innings in relief in an 11–0 rout.

Alston gave him the start in game five—after determining that Larry Sherry was unavailable to pitch. The game was played at the Coliseum in front of more than 92,000 fans. Joe DiMaggio was in town but refused to attend on the grounds it was no place to see a ballgame. Koufax lost

1–0 when Nellie Fox scored on a double play. It is tempting to wonder how different the trajectory of his career might have been had the Dodgers elected to throw home. They won the series in six games without any further assistance from him. He was a world champion without portfolio.

The 1960 season began in sorrow and ended in disgust. On February 2, Ebbets Field was demolished. That morning one last ballgame, a charity event, took place at the old ballpark on Bedford Avenue. A jaunty iron wrecking ball painted with baseball stitching hovered over home plate, the message as subtle as the intent. To Robert Pinsky, the emerging poet, it said: "Not only are we going to screw you but we're going to grin while we're doing it."

Koufax's career had progressed hardly at all since the Dodgers left Brooklyn. He was despondent. His relationship with Alston was at best uneasy. Alston was solid and stolid, conservative by nature, a "company man" in Erskine's opinion. Koufax was "a young hard thrower and a hardhead," his friend, Dick Tracewski, later said.

"He doesn't know what it means to pitch and win in the majors," Bavasi was quoted as saying in the newspapers. "He's got one of those silent tempers. He gets mad at himself and decides to overpower the hitter."

In early May, Koufax confronted Bavasi in the tunnel behind the batting cage at the Coliseum. It was the classic player's lament: Play me or trade me! Dodger pitcher Ed Palmquist overheard the conversation, as did Giants Sam Jones and Willie Mays. Mel Durslag reported what Mays told him in the next day's *Los Angeles Herald Examiner*. "Trade him to us. He's got a fastball you can't see."

A sanitized version of the conversation appeared in Koufax's autobiography:

> "Buzzie," I said, "why don't you trade me? I want to pitch, and I'm not going to get a chance here."
>
> "How can we pitch you," Buzzie said, "when you can't get anyone out?"

"How can I get anyone out when I'm sitting around in the dugout?"

Bavasi remembers the conversation differently. "Sandy stopped me one day and he said, 'Buzzie, I think I'll quit. I think I'll go home.' Now as I'm walking, I'm saying to myself if I beg him to stay, it's not going to do him any good. If I agree with him and tell him that he should go, maybe he'll have some of his mother in him and tell me, 'You no-good sonofabitch, I'm better than you think I am.'

"So I said, 'Sandy, when do you want to leave? I'll get a ticket for you.'

"He said, 'Grrrrr, I'll let you know.'

"So I'll be darned, three days later he went out and pitched a hell of a ball game, a one-hitter. So help me, that was the toughest decision I ever made in my life."

A third version casts events in a different light. "I'm behind you," Bavasi said. "Every spring I bet Walt you'll end up with more wins than Don." To which Koufax reportedly replied, "Either you're a liar or a moron. He gets forty starts, I get fifteen." And in the background high-pitched Willie Mays was chortling, "We'll take him. We'll take him."

Bavasi swears he never contemplated trading Koufax, never doubted the pitcher he would become. "Everyone in our organization knew that he was gonna be one of a kind. But all of us were afraid that he would go out there and not do the job and get disgusted. I think Sandy thought we were all nuts. And he might have been right."

By 1957, there were only twenty-one bonus babies left in the majors; Koufax was perhaps the most prominently disadvantaged. He became an object lesson to others. Jim Kaat's father cited Koufax's experience in turning down a $25,000 bonus deal with the Chicago White Sox. Kaat accepted a lowly offer from the Washington Senators instead. "That probably represented about six years' salary for my dad," Kaat said. "Washington offered me four thousand dollars and said, 'You go to the rookie league.' My dad had the foresight to see that the success and the money is on the other end, not up front."

The bonus rule was replaced by the amateur draft in 1965. The animus toward bonus players remained as long as the system survived. When Joe Moeller received an $80,000 bonus from the Dodgers in 1962, he was excluded from team meetings and parties, voted the same share of postseason money as the batboys. He was one of the first major leaguers to have his own room on the road. "Because no one wanted to room with me," he said.

By the end of 1960, Koufax was ready to quit. His belated passion had become an unrequited love. His record for the year was 8 and 13. He was a career losing pitcher. Maybe he should have stayed in school. There were other things in the world. He had a part ownership in an electronics business. He always loved fixing things, carried around a suitcase he had rigged up with a reel-to-reel tape deck, a prototype boom box. "He had a year of college," said teammate Ed Roebuck. "He wasn't as hopeless as the rest of us. He was either going to become a real good pitcher or quit. He couldn't cope with mediocrity. He wouldn't stand for it."

Wills, who was perhaps his closest friend on the team, said: "There's no telling—he may have quit a lot of times and changed his mind before he got to the ballpark. Something was in his craw all the time. It ate at him, the way they treated him early. He had a resentment going. Part of his greatness might have come from that *I'll show you.*"

After the Dodgers' final game in 1960, he tossed his gloves, his spikes, and his dreams into the trash bin, keeping one mitt in case he wanted to play softball in the park on a Sunday afternoon. Nobe Kawano, the clubhouse man, watched as he threw his career away. "If you want to quit, go ahead," Kawano said. "But I wish you'd leave your arm."

When the clubhouse emptied and only the season's dirty laundry remained, Kawano retrieved Koufax's gear from the trash, packing it away to be shipped to Florida for spring training. The impulse was both sensible and empathic. "In those days, they had to buy their own gloves and shoes," Kawano said. "They're not cheap. If he didn't show up, somebody might be able to use them. You can't just get those shoes. He had pretty big feet, you know."

Chapter 10

THE FOURTH INNING

IN THE FOURTH INNING, the authorities caught up with Bill Buhler. He was standing by the screen behind home plate, near the gate where the umpires came out, his camera ready for the top of the inning. He always shot from the same place, the same angle, and always the same usher raised hell. He was vigilant—and adamant. It didn't matter that Buhler was a Dodger employee, using Dodger equipment. *No photographers behind the screen by order of the fire marshal.* "Quit jamming up the aisles," the usher said, "or I'm going over your head."

Over the years, Buhler had filmed loads of footage of Koufax, maybe a third of a mile. His eye was practiced if not professional. There was no art to it, nothing fancy. His job was instructional, not historical. With only a hundred feet of film he had to skip around, leaving out the pauses between pitches, the idiosyncrasies that give a game its feel. No hitching up the pants, dusting off the plate, rubbing up the ball. The film, consequently, had an edgy, jumpy feel, at variance with the rhythm of Koufax's delivery. But his view was unimpeded and undiluted. After Koufax quickly retired the first two batters in the top of the fourth, Buhler thought, He looks great.

Scully thought so too. "Koufax, of course, among other things is trying to rewrite the strikeout record, and he's getting very close to Bob Feller's mark. Koufax, at the start of the night, needed thirty-one strikeouts to break Bob Feller's record and he's picked up four so far tonight. The major league record is three forty-eight. Koufax right now has three twenty-two."

One of which was his first-inning strikeout of Billy Williams, the Cubs' hottest hitter, who was at the plate for his second at-bat. "Billy is trying to become only the third player in Chicago Cub history to hit .300, score a hundred runs, have two hundred hits, thirty home runs and drive in a hundred," Scully said. "It's never been done by Mantle, Mays, or Mathews."

In the first inning, Williams was fooled by a hanging curve. This time, the curve made him look foolish. "Sandy broke off a dandy," Scully said as Williams admired it for strike three.

"There just hasn't been a visitor to first base," Scully was saying, when the officious usher returned with an unnamed club vice president who gave Buhler hell for blocking the fire exit. "Pack up and get out," he said. Buhler had shot two minutes and fifty-six seconds of scratchy, jumpy, black-and-white footage, no runs, no hits, no errors. But he had captured the turning point of the game, Koufax becoming Koufax, getting stronger with each pitch, the sweet, self-replicating motion that lulled and mesmerized; the perfect synchronization of muscle and thought. Afterward, he would turn the film over to the club. As always, it would be developed and screened for Koufax's use. Sometimes the film would prove helpful. Other times, it broke and ended up in the garbage.

Buhler made his way back to the dugout. The bench remained sanguine even as the Dodgers went three up and three down again. Koufax was pitching. And so was Hendley. The Dodgers knew they were going to win. "At the end of four innings, perfect," Scully said. "Nobody has gotten nowhere with nobody."

Buhler promised himself he'd find a way back to his spot behind the screen if Koufax still had it going in the ninth inning.

Chapter 11

1961

JOHN ROSEBORO SAID TO MEET HIM in section 123 of Dodger Stadium. It's tucked beneath the overhang behind third base, far removed from the action and the limelight, offering an oblique angle on home plate, which has always been Roseboro's outlook if not his view. Section 123 was empty except for an oversized man in faded jeans and a denim shirt trying to get comfortable in a space far too confining for his bulk. His knees knocked against the row in front of him. Roseboro was too big, too outsized to be a spectator. He belonged behind the plate on the other end of what poet Gail Mazur calls "the delicate filament" of concentration that connects pitcher and catcher.

Roseboro looked sturdy enough. In fact, he had been ill. Prostate cancer and a bad heart were taking their toll. He had come to Dodger Stadium on this May evening in an official capacity, surveying National League umpires for the league office. It was his preference to sit apart, away from the scouts and the know-it-alls, the has-beens and the wanna-bes.

In his playing days, opponents called him Rosie, which he never was. Teammates, who knew him better, called him Gabby, which he wasn't either. But time has made him effusive. Roseboro says he doesn't like to talk baseball, never took the game home. But the corrosive memories of what it was to be a black man in baseball in the early 1960s have made him voluble.

Branch Rickey created Dodgertown, the original spring training oasis, as a safe haven where black players could live and train with their teammates away from the discrimination of old Florida. Not everyone in town was happy to have them. In the early 1950s, the mayor of Vero Beach went to general manager Buzzie Bavasi to complain about the racial makeup of the team. "He was concerned because we were getting so many black boys in camp," Bavasi recalled. "He said, 'We're worried about our young women.' I sent Lee Scott down to Gulfstream racetrack, gave him a check for forty thousand dollars, and told him to come back with twenty thousand two-dollar bills. We stayed up all night stamping Brooklyn Dodgers on each of 'em. We had seven hundred fifty people in camp. I gave them all about fifty dollars. I said, 'Go downtown, have haircuts, go to the movies, eat dinner. If you come back with one dime, you're going to get fined.'

"When you take forty thousand dollars and spend it in a town of three thousand, they're going to notice. The mayor came back the next day and said, 'Buzzie, I get your point.'"

Over time, Dodgertown became burnished in memory as a place where everyone was family and everyone had everything they needed. "Movies! Mass!" exclaimed Chickie Anderson, granddaughter of Steve McKeever, one of Charles Ebbets's eventual partners. "Oh, it was wonderful."

For white players, it was an era that generated boys-will-be-boys anecdotes, stories that always begin . . . Remember when Duke and Zim and Podres got stuck on the railroad tracks racing to get back from the dog track before curfew? Zim, who already had been famously beaned, smashed his head against the dashboard. Duke, who was driving, jammed his bad knee against the steering column. Podres's head practically went through the roof of the car. "God, was he bleeding," Zimmer said. "But there's a train forty, fifty, sixty yards away. And it's got its light on and it's at night." They didn't wait to find out if it was in locomotion. Jumping out of the car, a Volvo Duke received in an endorsement deal, they lifted it off the tracks and beat it back to Dodgertown.

It wasn't as carefree a time for black players in Florida. "We were captives," Maury Wills said. There was nowhere in town to get a haircut; no Laundromats that would accept their laundry. For a good time, they had to go to Gifford, the black quarter, where Junior Gilliam got his nickname, the Devil, playing pool.

"We couldn't go to the movies," Roseboro said. "I couldn't rent a goddamn motel room when my wife and son came down. I had planned to hurt somebody and run into the swamp and stay there a couple of weeks until they found out I wasn't around."

When spring training opened in 1961, the stands at Holman Stadium were still segregated; bathroom facilities and water fountains were decidedly separate and unequal. But that spring was redolent with change. There was a young man in the White House, stirring passions with virility and wit, asking impertinent questions of Americans. A sense of imminence pervaded the air, a sub-rosa conviction that the future was now. Tommy Davis, of Brooklyn, New York, was then a lean, scholarly-looking man in wire-frame glasses. He is rounder now. Hunched over a plate of Buffalo wings, he searched for an explanation of the insurgent feelings that overtook him that spring: "It was just there," he said. "Nobody was really complaining. We didn't even think about it until one day we looked and said, 'Let's change the seating arrangement in the bleachers.'"

He led a contingent of players—he remembers Roseboro, Gilliam, and Willie Davis being with him—to see Peter O'Malley, who was running Dodgertown for his father. "We went to Peter and said, 'We gotta change this.' We walked in and said, 'This what we want to do.'"

O'Malley immediately ordered the bathroom facilities desegregated. He kept a photograph of the groundskeeper taking down the "White Women" and "White Men" signs and "putting just 'Men' and 'Women' up instead." Integrating the grandstand took a while longer. When the players went back to the field the next day, the black folks were still sitting deep in the right-field corner on the concrete stands that had always been set aside for them. Davis and his teammates walked across the lush green grass to speak with them. "We said, 'We want you to go behind home plate. You can sit anywhere you want. You don't have to sit here anymore.' They said, 'No, no, no.'"

So the players took them by the hand and led them out of the stands. "Directing traffic until they got used it," Davis said.

Tommy Davis would go on to become the National League batting champion in 1962 and 1963. But it's the walk across the grass that he recalls when he remembers when.

Perhaps, the mood of rebellion was inspired by the giddy optimism that annually accompanied the opening of spring training. The day pitchers and catchers reported was still an occasion observed by tomboys who wore their Mary Janes to school in celebration. On the day Dodger camp officially opened in 1961, cameras from the *News of the Day* swept the manicured playing fields and found Koufax tossing the ball around with his mates. "Baseball's bustin' out all over!" a cheerful newsreel voice intoned. "The popular Sandy Koufax, still a potentially great moundsman, pitches one to shortstop Maury Wills." The announcer sounded surprised to see him.

Koufax returned to baseball with new priorities. He had spent the winter reacquainting himself with the real world through his electronics business. He hated selling. He ended up telling customers, "You don't want this shit. Let's go have lunch." He also began to look inward. Maybe he hadn't done all he could. He began to take responsibility for his fitful career. "Growing up, it's called," he would tell friends and reporters. "Baseball didn't even become important to me until two or three years after I started to play. I didn't work hard enough. I didn't do what I should have done."

Decades later, he elaborated on the theme, telling his friend Kevin Kennedy, "That winter was when I really started working out. I started running more. I decided I was really going to find out how good I can be."

When he arrived at Dodgertown, the equipment he had tossed into the garbage at the end of the 1960 season was waiting for him at his locker. "I thought you might want these," Kawano said.

Deliverance was at hand. People had been telling him the same thing in different ways for years. *Quit throwing so hard. You gotta sacrifice speed for accuracy.* Don Newcombe used a military analogy. "See, when you throw a baseball, it's like firing a pistol. If you go, 'bang, bang, bang, bang,' just fire shots off, you're not gonna hit a thing. But if you squeeze the shots off you might hit what you're aiming at."

One night, over beers at Lennie's, Kenny Myers, the old scout, was talking with Norm Sherry and Ed Roebuck. Myers was a baseball man, as invaluable as he was invisible. "I remember Kenny was smoking one of those cigars," Roebuck said. "That bar was the pits but it was right by the batting cage so you didn't have to go too far. He took out his cigar and marked a spot on the wall. He said, 'Sandy, take an imaginary baseball and try to hit that spot.' So when Sandy got up to take his windup, Kenny said, 'Wait, Sandy, you can't even see that spot. You're taking your whole body back and your head is going way above the spot. Why not try taking your hands back and keep your head level and naturally correct the trajectory. Your release point will become lower.' "

In Sherry's recollection, the conversation continued for another half an hour in the men's room. He was scheduled to catch Koufax the next day in a B game against the Minnesota Twins in Orlando. None of the coaches or the team brass was making the trip. Only three pitchers were going. One of them, Ed Palmquist, known as Wally Weird, was sitting on the steps of the barracks the next morning nursing a hangover when the plane took off. "Oh my God," he said. "There goes the Dodger plane."

The Dodgers fined him twenty-five dollars. They should have given him a lifetime annuity. In his absence, Gil Hodges, the designated manager, told Koufax he would have to pitch at least seven innings. Then Hodges got beaned in batting practice and had to go to the hospital for X rays, taking trainer Bill Buhler with him. There was no one to give Koufax his customary pregame rubdown. The ever-accommodating Kawano gave him a special Oriental massage with Joy Oil.

Norm Sherry is a mild man, diminutive by today's bulked-up athletic standards. He looks more like your uncle in the rag trade than the man Drysdale called "Catcher Face." "You have a face like a catcher," Drysdale always said. And hands too. His features are sun-worn and freckled, his fingers as gnarled as the roots of a eucalyptus tree.

On the plane ride to Orlando, Koufax told him he wanted to experiment with his change-up. Sherry had a more modest proposal: Get the ball over the plate. "I started out by calling a curveball on the first pitch. It was a ball. Then I came back with another curveball: a ball. I called for a change-up and it was a ball. I called for a fastball on three and oh. It was high, ball four."

Next batter. "Now we start out with a change-up, then a curve. Sandy's frustrated—he hasn't thrown a strike. So we go fastball, fastball, and he walks the guy. We start the next guy out with a curveball and then another curveball. Koufax is mad. He's shaking me off. He's throwing fastballs, higher and higher. The last two got up there good. He walks the guy. Now the bases are loaded. Nobody out. I went to the mound. I said, 'Sandy, we only got nine guys. You've got to throw the ball over the plate or we'll be here all day.'"

In his autobiography, Koufax remembers Sherry telling him to "take the grunt out of the fastball." In truth, there was less poetry and more vehemence to it. "What I actually said was 'Take something off the ball and let 'em hit it. Nobody's going to swing the way you're throwing now.' I went back behind the plate. He wound up like, 'Here, hit it' and strikes out the side. It was like, 'I'll show you, you smart-ass.'

"We went back to the dugout, I said, 'Sandy, I got to tell you something. I'm not blowing smoke up your rear end. But you just now threw harder trying not to than you did when you were trying to.'"

At the end of the requisite seven innings, Koufax had struck out eight and walked five without allowing a hit. The change in him was immediate and apparent to Kawano. "I could tell when he came in," Kawano said. "It was the first time he really enjoyed himself playing. We joked about it later—it was the Oriental rubdown that did it. You could see how elated he was. My God, a no-hitter!"

That night, Koufax broke curfew, returning late from a pizza run to

Port St. Lucie with Norm's brother, Larry. Stan Williams, Koufax's roommate, also was late getting in. Unfortunately, their room was directly across the hall from manager Walter Alston's. "You could not put your foot on one part of the barracks without it creaking two hundred yards away," Williams said. "Now Walter kept his wife there with him when she was in town. She had left that particular day and so I guess Walter decided he was going to keep an ear open that night for any creaks. I came in, not inebriated but a little tipsy. I learned to walk on the very edge of the floor by the wall because it didn't creak quite as much there.

"I walked in, two o'clockish, and the sitting room light was on. I said, 'Oh, dear old Sandy, he left the light on for me so I'd know that he left the door unlocked.' So I took the door and went to open it and it was locked. And there was a thump and the minute I made the thump, I heard a rustling and it's Walter getting out of bed across the hall. So I immediately tore into my pocket, got my key out, let myself in, and locked the door so he couldn't follow me. Of course, I had my shoes off already. I went into the bedroom, put my shoes under the bed, and just as I sat down on the bed there was banging on the bedroom door.

"Well, I had a reputation of being a real sleeper. So I let him pound on the door for a while. But as he's pounding, I'm undressing and throwing my clothes under the bed. And finally I said, 'God, who is this?' He said, 'It's Walter, open the door.'

"I says, 'Who?'

"He says, 'Alston. Open the damn door.'

"And I said, 'Oh, just a minute, skip.' I tore the blankets back like I'd been sleeping and then I went and opened the door. I covered my face like I was very sleepy so Walter couldn't smell the beer on my breath. And I said, 'Yeah, Walt, what is it?'

"He said, 'Who just came in?'

"I said, 'I don't know, Walter, I've been sleeping. I've got a ballgame I got to pitch at eight A.M. over at Field Seven.'

"He says, 'Who's your roomie?'

"I said, 'Sandy.' And I pointed to Sandy's bed, and he wasn't in it.

"And he says, 'Where is he?'

"I said, 'I guess he's in the sitting room. The light's on.'

"So he pushed me out of the way and walked back in there and said, 'He's not in there. You tell him when he comes in to go over to my room and knock on the door.'

"I said, 'Well, Walt, I probably won't hear him. I sleep awfully sound.'

"And he says, 'Then you tell him I want to see him in the morning.'

"So my heart was pounding a mile a minute but I figured I must have pulled it over on him because he went across the hall and pounded on Roseboro and Gilliam's door asking, 'Who just came in?'

"Anyway, I lay back down in the bed and finally went to sleep. Just about the time I went to sleep, all hell breaks loose. Boy, there was all kinds of noise. What had happened is that Sandy came creeping up the stairs with his shoes in his hand just the same as I did. He got to the sitting room and said, 'Good old Stan, he left the light on for me.'

"So he thought the door was open. Well, he grabbed the door and started to push on it and it was locked because I locked it so Walter wouldn't follow me in. So Sandy hits the thing and the minute he hit it, Alston's out of his room like a shot. Now Sandy's plastered up against the door not knowing what to do and Alston starts after him. But just as he starts after him, he looks down to the other end of the corridor and here's Larry Sherry walking around the corner in his shorts, carrying his clothes, and teetering all over the place. So Alston forgets all about Sandy and tears after Larry. Larry sees him coming and he runs into his room and locks the door. Alston's yelling, 'Come out of there and fight me. I'll whip your so-and-so butt.' And Larry's afraid to open the door because Alston's so mad."

Alston pounded on the door so long and so hard, he broke his world series ring. The characteristic monotony of the next morning's bus trip was interrupted by Koufax's cheerful inquiry: "Hey, Larry, had your door appraised for diamonds yet?"

Throwing a baseball sixty feet six inches with exactitude and intent is a kinetic event with intangible dimensions. Try too hard and you overthrow. Tighten your grip and you lose control, infusing tension in the ball's trajectory. Now, it's easy to tell young pitchers he sees tossing the ball, "Just pitch like that." But it's hard to relax when you're hanging on to each opportunity for dear life. The changes Koufax made in his delivery were as subtle as they were overpowering. As his friend Dave Wallace, the pitching guru, puts it: "The mechanics of the delivery is such a precision thing, it's almost Zen-like. When you have it, you know it."

In the privacy of the Dodger clubhouse, Norm Sherry, aka "Catcher Face," was also known as "the Jolly Jew." His brother, Larry, was "the Rude Jew." Koufax was on his way to becoming "Super Jew." Why was he able to listen to Norm when so many others had failed to get through? "Catcher Face" grinned, his features crinkling like old leather. "*Landsman*, eh?"

Now when they went to the string area to work, Sherry would cover home plate with dirt. "Take my finger and make a line so there's a line of white, right?" Sherry said. "The rest is nothing, dark. Just the width of a finger and he'd put it right on the money! He realized how good he could be. I don't know what he did the rest of the year, but by '62, you couldn't hit him."

Finally, he was pitching regularly, a member of the starting rotation. He knew what to expect and exceeded every expectation. He began to avail himself of Allan Roth, the team statistician, the first employed by a major league club. Over the years, Roth charted 26,450 Koufax pitches and 313 of his 397 games. Roth tracked each at-bat and the count on which the decisive pitch was made. His numbers demonstrated the obvious: It's better to get ahead on the batter. But he quantified how much an advantage it was, showing Koufax the difference in the batting average against him when he was ahead in the count (.146) and behind (.286). From then on, whenever anyone asked what his best pitch was, Koufax would answer, "Strike one." In the last five years of his career, he allowed only 2.1 walks per game, compared to the 4.8 he averaged his first seven seasons. In 1962, more than half the hitters he faced (55.6 per cent) found themselves in the unenviable position of hitting with two strikes against them.

As Robert Pinsky, the poet, would later write: "People were amazed by him"—among them Pee Wee Reese. They weren't close as teammates. But, Pee Wee's son says, in The Captain's final years, Koufax called more often than any other Dodger. Though Reese was too ill to be interviewed, he wrote shortly before his death: "To be honest about it, I thought the guy would never be a great pitcher. But he sure proved me wrong. When I retired and I was announcing the CBS *Game of the Week*, I came up to him while he was warming up. And he was really making the catcher's mitt pop. So I went up and asked him, teasing him, 'Where in the hell did you learn how to pitch like that? You can't be that damn good.'

"He said, 'Grab a bat and get your ass up there at the plate.' So I did. Here I am standing with a bat in my hand in my street clothes and I never saw anybody throw that hard in my life, and I've faced some of the greatest in the game. He had pinpoint control. I said, 'How is your control on the outside part of the plate?' I was amazed. He then said, 'Do you want me to show you how good my control is inside?'

"I said, 'Hell, no.'"

Chapter 12

THE FIFTH INNING

Sanitary hose were the only socks Lou Johnson ever wore. He wore them high and he wore them the way he did everything else, ebulliently. Out of uniform, he went sockless. Socks were confining. He disliked anything that cramped his style. He had waited too long to get where he was going to keep his feelings to himself. It was one of the first things his teammates noticed about him when he was called up to replace Tommy Davis in May. The socks, or lack thereof.

Louis Brown Johnson was a thirty-one-year-old bush-leaguer, a Southerner whose only previous claim to fame was being named outstanding rookie in the Cubs' 1962 spring training camp. Davis was a two-time National League batting champion from Brooklyn. He wore socks. When Davis broke his ankle sliding into second base in May, the players expected a big name to fill his shoes. Instead, Bavasi summoned sockless Lou Johnson from the Dodgers Triple A team in Spokane,

Washington. Johnson was the father of two young children, one a new-born. He liked to say he earned so little he cashed his check at the concession stand. His was a "not-quite" career: not quite a major-leaguer, not quite the Pacific Coast batting champion (he lost the 1964 title by a single point). A talent so marginal no big league club bothered to invite him to spring training in 1965. Others might have considered quitting. Johnson told his mother, "I can't retire. I haven't succeeded yet."

Peter O'Malley, the heir apparent who was running the Spokane club for his father, called Johnson into his office to tell him he was going to Cincinnati. Johnson was disconsolate, wondering how he would ever break into an outfield that boasted Frank Robinson and Vada Pinson. He figured if he was consigned to another year in Triple A, he might as well stay in Spokane. He told O'Malley he wouldn't report. O'Malley replied that he wasn't going to play *for* Cincinnati, he was joining the Dodgers *in* Cincinnati. "Phew!" Johnson replied, hugging his most proper boss.

When Johnson arrived at Crosley Field, Koufax was the first to greet him, walking across the diamond to shake his hand. "He made me feel like a star amongst stars," Johnson said.

Every day Koufax greeted him the same way, ambling over to his locker, pulling up his pants leg, saying, "You've got the same socks on." One day, Johnson came to the ballpark and found six boxes of new socks in his locker. "I get tired of seeing you wear the same color," Koufax told him.

That's awful nice, Johnson thought. He was halfway across the clubhouse before he got the joke.

In clubhouses and other salons where races mingled, people were learning to be careful about what they said. The new idiom, Black Power, was becoming part of the American vocabulary. But Koufax was a man so comfortable in his own skin he could tease a black teammate about his and thus make him feel welcome. Soon Johnson was fully integrated into the fabric of the team. He patrolled left field with the joie de vivre of a junkyard dog. Fans renamed the bleachers the "LBJ Ranch" in his honor.

As the summer progressed and the pennant race heated up, Johnson rallied his teammates with the appropriated slogan "All the Way with LBJ."

He was in the middle of every rally and every conversation, carrying the Dodgers with his exuberance. "Tell 'em about the ear," teammates would say. And "Sweet Lou" (as he quickly became known) would launch into the story about how he lost his ear in a bus accident and the doctor sewed it into his midriff, intending to reattach it later. Then Johnson would lift his shirt—and Dodger spirits—revealing an odd fleshy nub where the skin had shriveled up and died. "Doesn't it bother you to have an ear down there?" visitors would ask. "Naw, it don't eat much," Johnson would reply.

His allegiance to Koufax was intense. "Sandy and Lou, that's all you need," he liked so say. So as he settled into the batter's box in the bottom of the fifth inning, he was thinking, How am I going to get a run for Sandy?

Koufax started every game assuming he would get nothing. "Pitching fine," Johnson called it. The Dodgers scored fewer than four runs a game for him, one less than they did for Drysdale, who could help his own cause. First in the league in earned run average, the Dodgers were seventh in batting. They didn't just manufacture runs, they cobbled them together like piecework. They rarely got shut out. "Speed doesn't have a slump," Koufax always said. But laughers were as common as stand-up comedy in the collected works of Sophocles. When Koufax was on the mound, Alston often played for one run.

"This year, Bob Hendley has worked thirty-seven innings and he has allowed ten home runs," Scully said, hopefully, as Johnson came to the plate. "That's averaging three home runs a game."

The Dodgers had only sixty-nine home runs, fewest in the league, and Drysdale had six of them. He was the team's best pinch hitter, their only .300 batter, possessor of the highest slugging average on the club. But he wasn't in the lineup. He was in the clubhouse getting a rubdown, listening to Scully apologize to area schoolchildren for his use of double negatives in the previous inning. "We were just having fun," he said.

Upstairs in the press box, beat reporters were beginning to speculate about the last time two pitchers threw nine innings of no-hit ball. Hendley was matching Koufax pitch for pitch. Inspired by the memory of that Oklahoma crop duster, he was pitching the game of his life, holding the Dodgers hostage to an assortment of unapologetic junk. For four innings, Hendley had seen nothing except Chris Krug's target. It was as if his field of vision had been reduced to sixty feet six inches. Then, inexplicably, with the count 1 and 2 on Johnson, his concentration wavered. By the time he regained his composure the count was full.

It could happen to anyone. Koufax had fallen behind three balls and two strikes on consecutive batters, Banks and Browne, in the top of the inning. Banks even had a good cut at a fastball, fouling it straight back through the gate behind home plate, where Buhler had been standing an inning before. Koufax got both outs. Hendley was not as fortunate.

The payoff pitch to Johnson could have been called either way. "The three-two pitch . . ." Scully hesitated, not wanting to presume on such a close call. "Taken high, ball four, there it is, the first base runner of the night. Some of the Cubs are howling at Ed Vargo and Vargo motions with his right hand to indicate the pitch was high, above the shoulder."

The notation BB was made on a thousand scorecards. In a season of limited means, a bunt was inevitable. Hendley fielded the ball tentatively and threw to first. "Hendley had a play at second if he had fielded the ball cleanly," Scully said, "but in his haste, he dropped it and had to go to first."

As Johnson slid safely into second base, Krug thought: We had him by ten feet! Johnson thought: I'm going to steal third.

Hendley looked over at second base. Scully noted Johnson's liberal lead. There's only one out, Johnson reminded himself, as Hendley went into the windup. Somebody's gonna hit a high chopper or something, get me home.

On the first pitch, he went to third. He could tell the fielders were shocked by their belated response. It was an enlivening play, the kind Johnson had been making ever since joining the team. The languid tension that had been building for five innings erupted as he slid into the bag.

The rookie catcher hurried his tardy throw to third. The left fielder, playing in his first major league game, ended up with the ball, wondering, Why did he throw it to me?

Krug knew he shouldn't have thrown it. Johnson had gotten too good a jump on Hendley. Still, Krug thought, It wasn't a bad throw. High. Maybe a little higher than a little high but catchable.

The way he saw it, Santo was late covering third. Johnson knocked him down making his slide, making the ball uncatchable. Santo saw it differently. He saw the ball sail over his head. He thought, When you rush that throw, you throw it wild.

Hendley agreed with both of them. But it wasn't their fault. He had allowed the walk to Johnson and allowed him too big a lead off second. He thought, It wasn't a terrible, terrible throw. But it wasn't playable, either.

Johnson had the clearest view of all—safe at home plate. "The ball got there first, Lou got there second, and Santo got there third."

The verdict flashed on the scoreboard: E-2. Richard Hume marked his program with baseball's terse shorthand: no hits, a walk, a sacrifice, a stolen base, and an error. The Dodgers had scored a run without an official at-bat.

Chapter 13

WHEN WE WERE YOUNG

IT WAS THE HOMELY ENVELOPE that caught Robert Pinsky's poetic imagination. Cobbled together with precision, Scotch tape, and a razor blade, this ad hoc parcel was the handiwork of a person, not his people, the singular vision of the man whose name appeared in block print in the upper left-hand corner: KOUFAX.

Pinsky, poet laureate of the United States, was staying with friends in Cambridge, Massachusetts, for the summer. No one knew he was at that address. So the fact of the envelope's finding him the way it did, in pristine, almost divinely sanctioned condition, was magical. Then he opened it and it was another time.

October 1963. The pregame world series handshake is ritual theater, part of autumn's emotional calendar. Pitchers embrace. Shutterbugs snap. Scribes mill. They've seen this act before. On October 2, 1963, the requisite photograph was taken at Yankee Stadium. Sandy Koufax and Whitey Ford clasping hands at home plate: two New York kids who made good.

This image, an eight-and-a-half-by-eleven-inch missive from another time, was what Pinsky found inside the improvised package. It was autographed by both, Koufax citing the page number of the poem Pinsky had written about them. Though it arrived without fanfare or padding, no protection at all except God's, the photo was unblemished and unlined, like the two young lefties. Koufax had heard a family member was ailing. He thought a surprise might cheer him up. Pinsky thought: It doesn't get any better than this.

The photograph is not so much a portrait of their youth as Youth, adolescent America exploring New Frontiers. Cynicism and assassination were not yet cultural imperatives. John Glenn was a hero. *Camelot* was a Broadway hit. Khrushchev had backed down. That October, that month before November 1963, was an apotheosis. So much was imminent. So much hadn't happened.

But things were "blowing in the wind." In June, the University of Alabama was desegregated and John Kennedy went to Berlin. In August, Martin Luther King Jr. proclaimed his dream on the steps of the Lincoln Memorial and McDonald's sold its one billionth hamburger. In September, four little girls were murdered in the Sixteenth Street Baptist Church in Birmingham, Alabama. "A terrible day, a day that never ended," the minister called it. (That day finally ended on May 22, 2002, when a former Ku Klux Klansman named Bobby Frank Cherry was convicted of the crime.)

A housewife named Betty Friedan published *The Feminine Mystique*, a revolutionary treatise dedicated to "All the New Women and the New Men." Annette Funicello and Frankie Avalon, stars of *Beach Party*, presumably were not among them. Trolls and elephant jokes were big. "Sugar Shack" was number one—with a bullet!—when Koufax and Ford posed together before game one of the world series.

In the photograph, the reporters recede into the background the way they did then: balding white guys in white shirts and black ties who'd still look black and white even if the picture had been taken in color. They wore thick, black horn-rims and fedoras over thinning brush cuts. The story was still the story, not the telling of it.

Over their shoulders, the scoreboard loomed, blank and expectant.

And in the distance the Bronx County Courthouse, not yet the symbol of urban decay Tom Wolfe would make it in his 1980s novel *Bonfire of the Vanities*. Unseen children played hopscotch on the steps of the Beaux Arts mansions of the Grand Concourse—fashioned after the Champs Élysées—the tenants as white as Whitey's home uniform. Co-Op City, the vast, misguided urban renewal project, which would displace the white population and turn the neighborhood into a slum, wouldn't be a fact for another two years. The Concourse Plaza Hotel at the corner of 161st Street, where the Babe once stashed his babes, was still a swank joint.

The foreground belongs to Sandy and Whitey. The stubble on their cheeks reveals when the picture was taken: Starting pitchers never shave. They are looking in opposite directions, their eyes diverging even as their fates intertwined. Whitey's pitching arm is draped casually over Sandy's shoulder in a kind of embrace, their caps perched lightly on their heads. The stitched white satin lettering signified and summarized like hieroglyphs: L.A vs. N.Y. Brooklyn vs. The Bronx. The Pacific Rim Upstarts vs. the East Coast Establishment. The Dodgers vs. the Yankees. Koufax vs. Ford.

It was this set of opposites that Pinsky invoked in his poem "The Night Game," describing Whitey's pink skin "shining like a burn" and the "white unpigmented halo of his hair/So ordinary and distinct." He spoke for generations of ethnic Americans when he wrote, "To be white and called/Something like *Ed Ford*/Seemed aristocratic,/A rare distinction." And: "Possibly I believed only gentiles/And blondes could be left-handed."

There beside Whitey stood Koufax with his decidedly Semitic visage. He was still a pitcher, not yet a symbol, a man who welcomed his fate. Perhaps that accounts for the dimpled, sideways grin, the lightness of bearing, the openness of his face.

He had his coming-out party in 1961 along with JFK. Vigor and speed would be served. Kennedy wanted twenty-five Thunderbirds for his inaugural parade but they were all sold out. As Todd Gitlin observed in his cultural history *The Sixties*, there was implicit bravado in all that chrome: We had the goods and we could afford the goodies.

Going into the 1961 season, Koufax was a career 36-and-40 pitcher, a study in mediocrity. He announced himself in May with a 1–0 victory over Bob Gibson in St. Louis, a taut three-hitter decided by Tommy Davis's seventh-inning home run. In the next day's *L.A. Times* Gibson was described "as the former Harlem Globetrotters' melon manipulator." Koufax's name was misspelled. That wouldn't happen again.

By July, he was an All-Star. By season's end, he had broken Christy Mathewson's fifty-eight-year-old single-season strikeout record, needing only 256 innings to fan 269 batters. The achievement was overshadowed by more ominous events. The East Germans began building their wall. The Bay of Pigs proved a quagmire. Duck and cover drills were practiced. Freedom riders were attacked. The Domino Effect was invoked. The first two military companies were dispatched to a place called Vietnam. Roger Maris's hair fell out as he pursued Babe Ruth's record sixty home runs. Koufax's record received scant attention. Stan Hochman wrote in the Philadelphia *Daily News*: "Nobody called from Cooperstown to ask for the baseball that blurred past Pancho Herrera. . . . A guy breaks a record that has stood for fifty-eight seasons and he gets treated as if he has German measles."

Sixty-two should have been his year. Walter O'Malley unveiled his new state-of-the-art stadium tucked in the Elysian Hills, a pitchers' paradise with generous foul territory and a terrible hitting background configured to enhance Dodger pitching. And it did. In his first season at Chavez Ravine, Koufax lowered his home earned run average from 4.29 to 1.75; Drysdale lowered his from 2.83 to 2.11.

It should have been the Dodgers' year too. They hit better than the 1961 Yankees. Tommy Davis led the league in batting. Maury Wills revolutionized the game by stealing 104 bases. "Before Maury it was just a bunch of slow white guys playing," Koufax liked to say.

The year began promisingly. One night during spring training, Norm Sherry prevailed upon Koufax to join him at the Flame, a joint popular with stewardesses and ballplayers. Koufax wasn't a boozer; he generally preferred a good book, a good bottle of wine, and a smoke. "There were three stewardesses sitting at a bar," Sherry said. "One of them grabs Sandy's arm and says, 'You're coming with me.' He said, 'See ya, Norm.'"

The memory stuck with Sherry because it was so out of character.

Maybe, finally, it was Koufax's turn to get lucky. It was a sexy year. Liz and Dick fell in love, Henry Miller's licentious fiction finally gained admission to the New World, and Helen Gurley Brown topped the best-seller list with *Sex and the Single Girl.* The Pill celebrated its second birthday, making sex safe in a way it had never been before. Phil Collier began referring to Koufax in the *San Diego Union* as "the playboy bachelor." He was as telegenic as JFK but without the hubris and a whole lot more discreet.

There were tremors of cultural upheaval but they did not register on the collective Richter Scale. The Port Huron Statement, the manifesto of the nascent student movement, was issued by the Students for a Democratic Society and ignored. Marilyn Monroe committed suicide in August and no one thought it had anything to do with the Kennedys. So what if The Twist was banned in Tampa? The Russians backed down in Cuba, didn't they? And we weren't going to have Dick Nixon to kick around anymore. Americans were having too good a time to intuit what lay just ahead.

In his first start of the season, the second game played at Chavez Ravine, Koufax gave up four hits, at least one of which was lost in the new untested lights. It could have been a no-hitter. In his fourth start, he struck out 18, equaling the record he shared with Bob Feller. Four days later, he beat the Pirates, 2–1. More significant than the victory was Alston's decision to allow him to bat with the score tied in the bottom of the eighth, an uncharacteristic act of trust duly noted in the morning papers.

In late May and early June, he pitched four consecutive complete games, striking out forty-nine men. On June 13, he beat Warren Spahn, 2–1. His golfing buddy, Ken Still, flew in to see the game. Koufax was altering itineraries. It was a cold night in Milwaukee and Still huddled in a blanket giggling as Koufax drove in the winning run with his first major league home run. Spahn slammed his glove to the ground, yelling at Koufax as he giddy-yapped around second base.

Five days later, Koufax teamed up with Tommy Davis to beat "the old melon manipulator" again. Another 1–0 loss for Gibson, another game-winning home run for Davis. For the first time in his career, Koufax pitched a complete game and walked no one. They celebrated by dancing around the clubhouse crowing: "Us Brooklyn boys got to stick together."

Later, Davis and his wife had the misfortune to run into Gibson at an L.A. nightspot. "I walked over to him and he said, 'Hi, how you doing, Tom?'" Davis remembered. "My wife says, 'Oh, is this the guy you hit the home run off?' I'm thinking, 'I'm dead. I'm dead. I'm dead.' He looked at her and said, 'Yes, I'm the guy that he hit the home run off.' With that mean look in his eyes. I said, 'Honey, we have to go.'

"I told him, 'I'm not saying no more about it because I know you're gonna get me in the hereafter.' He says, 'You're right. I'm gonna get you up there, boy.'"

Gibson's still growling about it. "They are not fond memories. People come and ask how it was to pitch against Sandy Koufax. Sandy Koufax was a pain in the ass. You pitched against him and you knew the score was going to be two to one, one to zero. Normally, two to one, one to zero, *I* won."

In eight games between June 13 and July 12, Koufax was 6 and 2, allowing only five earned runs in 67 ⅓ innings. His ERA was 0.67. He struck out seventy-seven batters and walked twenty. On June 30, Koufax pitched his first no-hitter, a 5–0 triumph over the Mets. You could see it coming—particularly if you had Ron Perranoski's seat in the bullpen. Dodger relievers always enjoyed the day Koufax pitched—and the evening before too. Their exploits became the stuff of team legend. "This one time, Pete Richert did go out and have a good time and wasn't feeling well the next day and, lo and behold, Koufax was struggling on the mound," Ron Fairly said. "And Alston walked out to the mound and asked, 'Sandy, how do you feel?' And Sandy said, 'A lot better than the guy you have warming up.'"

Another time in Philadelphia, Larry Sherry and Stan Williams hatched a plan in the bullpen to rob a bank while Koufax was pitching. "What do you think you got to do down in the bullpen for two and a half hours?" Sherry said.

The bank was just across the street from Connie Mack Stadium and there was a door in the bullpen to a maintenance room with an exit directly across the street from the bank. Williams cased the joint and planned their escape route. "We'd wear street clothes underneath our uniforms, take our uniforms off, go over there about maybe the seventh or eighth inning, rob the bank, come back, and put the money in our base-ball bags," Sherry said. "It was getaway day. The stuff goes right to the plane. We had our own private plane. Put the money in the big bag with all the catching equipment. Stanley says, 'It'll work, it'll work.' He started figuring up a time line. You know, he got serious about it, Stanley."

Perranoski put his seat in the Dodger Stadium bullpen to better use. From his vantage point—feet up on the wire, chair tilted back—he could gauge the quality of Koufax's stuff. On June 30, 1962, he knew right away the Mets were in trouble. "From my angle back there, sitting in the bullpen, his curveball used to break from the first deck, it looked like," he said. "And all of a sudden it's breaking from the second deck and I said to the guys, 'They're in for a tough day.'"

Solly Hemus, coaching third base, was first among the Mets to real-ize just how tough it would be. After Koufax struck out the first three men on nine pitches, they crossed paths along the third base line. Hemus murmured, "It's not that easy, is it?" At the end of the third, Hemus murmured to him again, "Still got a no-hitter going." Hemus kept murmuring, inning after inning, hoping that agitation would accom-plish what the Mets' bats could not.

Felix Mantilla was the last batter. They had been teammates in win-ter ball in Puerto Rico back in the mid-fifties, a time Mantilla remem-bered well: "He pitched a no-hitter but we lost, two to nothing, because he walked a few guys. Like eight or nine. Or ten." When Koufax retired him for the twenty-seventh out of his first major league no-hitter, a message flashed on the scoreboard in left center field: "Koufax, report to Buzzie Bavasi and have your contract torn up."

He was engulfed by teammates and a downpour of cerulean seat cushions. Hemus intercepted him by third base one more time. "He didn't acknowledge me," Hemus said. "He didn't look at me. I wouldn't let anybody in the ballpark know, so I congratulated him under my breath. Casey would have killed me. Ah, hell, Casey probably would have done the same thing."

Stengel, the Mets' inimitable manager, said: "You put the whommy on him but when he's pitchin', the whommy tends to go on vacation."

Koufax acquired a patina of omnipotence. Even his clothes matched. Larry Sherry used to worry whether Koufax would criticize his tie when they went out to dinner. It got annoying, his perfection. Larry was determined to beat him at something. One night in San Francisco, he challenged Koufax to a drinking contest. The bartender set up twenty drinks on the bar, ten shots of vodka for Sherry, ten shots of gin for Koufax, which Larry concedes "was not real smart, but in those days, you know."

Koufax started at one end of the bar and Larry started at the other, while his brother Norm looked on. "Anyway, I still have the seventh one in my hand and he'd already finished the tenth," Larry said.

"And he didn't get drunk!" Normie said. "If he set his mind to it, he'd do anything to beat you."

Koufax pitched in San Francisco on July 8, his last start before the All-Star Game in Washington. The index finger on his pitching hand had been bothering him since that April game against Pittsburgh, when in a futile and misguided attempt to improve his hitting he had batted left-handed, and Earl Francis had jammed him with a pitch. The heel of the bat dug into the palm of his hand. A week later, numbness and dread set in. He told no one. Newspapers reported only his triumphs. By May, his index finger had turned white and lifeless. By July, the tissue was close to gangrene. By the time he went to the mound in Candlestick Park, the seams of the ball felt like a serrated edge. Still, he held the Giants hitless into the seventh inning. He left the game in the ninth when his hand went numb.

In Los Angeles, he consulted a vascular specialist. The National League refused the Dodgers' request to excuse him from the All-Star Game. Who would believe he was hurting?

Four days later in New York, he had another three-hitter going when his hand went numb again. "I touched it," Stan Williams said. "It was ice cold." (It remains susceptible to cold even today.) Still, he insisted upon taking his next turn in Cincinnati. Duke Snider, the team captain, took one look at the dessicated finger and said, "Don't even try it. Do you think anybody around here is going to thank you?"

After years of bitching about not pitching, he wasn't about to ask out. Before the first inning was over, the finger had split wide open. Newspapers reported he had a mysterious circulatory ailment called Reynaud's disease, which Williams heard was caused by the diet of a Jewish male, none of which was true. In fact, he had a crushed artery in the palm of his hand. Ten days of experimental intravenous medication successfully reopened the artery. Amputation was the only alternative. He did not pitch again until the end of September. The Giants won the pennant.

In the off-season, "That Index Finger" was the subject of cover stories and anxiety attacks. It was a sight gag in a Vegas lounge act headlined by Milton Berle. Uncle Miltie and several Dodgers—Wills, Snider, Drysdale, Willie Davis, and Koufax—played the Vegas strip for eleven days before taking their act to spring training for a two-week engagement at the Fontainebleau. "How's the finger?" Berle demanded, nightly.

And Koufax would reply on cue: "I've been to the doctor and he says it shouldn't bother me at all. But now I've got a little problem with my thumb." And he would hold up an outsized thumb, swaddled in bandages.

The concern was misplaced. For the last five years of his career, Koufax was unassailable. He led the majors in every pitching category: most wins (111), lowest ERA (1.95), winning percentage (.766), strikeouts (1,444), shutouts (33), and no-hitters (4). He won the Cy Young Award three times (when only one trophy was awarded for both leagues), the world series MVP award twice, and was named Player of the Decade.

"As far as I'm concerned, no other pitcher in the history of baseball ever put together five years like Koufax did from 1962 to '66," Gibson wrote in his 1994 autobiography, *Stranger to the Game*. "But in light of the fact that Koufax put together nothing more to speak of, I'm unwilling to take a backseat to him as a pitcher. . . . For that reason, it bothers me somewhat, just as I'm sure it bothers [Juan] Marichal, to hear and read so often that Koufax was the leading pitcher of our generation. A generation lasts more than five years."

You can say that. Or you can look at it the way Willie Mays does, his voice rising in incredulity at Gibson's logic: "For him to do all those things in five years, what guys take twenty years to do, *that's* remarkable."

The 1963 season opened without any intimation of what the fall would bring for the Dodgers or the nation. The pennant race was taut and bracing. Koufax was impeccable. He was, no doubt, aided by the newly redefined National League strike zone and by a full season in pitcher-friendly Chavez Ravine. Twenty of his twenty-five victories were complete games. He finished the year with the most wins, most strike-outs (306), most shutouts (11), and lowest ERA (1.88) in the major leagues. For the first time in his career, he was not called upon to pitch in relief.

In May, there was another no-hitter, against the Giants of Mays and McCovey, no schlubs. The San Francisco broadcasters, mindful of Koufax's eighteen-strikeout performance in 1959, asked that the game be preserved on videotape, an unusual request. Videotape came in two-inch rolls then. Nobody had room to store them. The game was played on a Saturday night before 55,000, the largest crowd in Chavez Ravine's short history, the largest crowd in the major leagues. Koufax's parents, recently relocated to the West Coast, were not among them. He had for-gotten to leave them tickets.

The night before, general manager Buzzie Bavasi called Tommy Lasorda and asked if he still had a left-handed catcher's mitt. Koufax wanted to throw. Throw, he did. "It's boom, boom, boom," Lasorda said. "I said, 'With stuff like that tomorrow you gotta throw a no-hitter.'"

Chuck Connors, the onetime ballplayer turned TV star, had invited Lasorda to Saturday-night dinner. "I said, 'I can't,'" Lasorda remem-bered. "'I've got to go watch Koufax pitch a no-hitter.' He said, 'If you don't come, I'm going to kill you.' So I went and listened on the radio. I'll be goddamned if he didn't pitch a no-hitter."

Playing behind Koufax, it was easy to be seduced by passivity. Tommy Davis would not soon forget the look on Koufax's face when one day he allowed a line drive to sail over his head, having forgotten that Koufax was capable of surrendering one. Nobody in uniform is a spectator during a no-hitter. Davis had just moved from third base to left field when Felipe Alou, the league's leading hitter, came up in the seventh. "Don't hit it to me," Davis was saying to himself when Alou did. Oh, God, it's a home run, Koufax thought, as Davis retreated for a backhanded "there but for the grace of God go I" catch against the left-field fence. "Did I catch it?" he asked decades later, smiling only when assured he had. "I'm *good*," Davis said, relieved.

It was a perfect game until Koufax walked Ed Bailey on a 3-and-2 pitch in the eighth inning. ("Finally, he threw one I couldn't reach and he walked me.") In the ninth, Joey Amalfitano, the leadoff batter, popped out. Jose Pagan flied out. McCovey walked on four straight pitches and Harvey Kuenn came to the plate. The score was 8–0. Only the no-hitter was in doubt. Kuenn took one strike before tepidly bouncing back to the mound. Fairly, the first baseman, took a deep breath. He knew from painful past experience that Koufax was constitutionally incapable of tossing a ball softly. Years earlier, in Fairly's initial game at first base, Koufax had fired a ball at him at point-blank range. "Threw it between my legs and chipped my cup," Fairly would remember. "It almost killed me."

Koufax remembered too. He thought to run the ball to first and then changed his mind, scooping it underhanded instead. Fairly caught the ball and exhaled.

By August 25, his record was 19 and 5. He was one out away from his first-ever twenty-win season when Alston removed him from the game. As Alston walked to the mound, Koufax stalked away from it, leaving the manager to wait alone for the unwelcome reliever. Heading back to the dugout, Koufax hurled his glove against the bench; Alston was inundated with home-grown boos. For Dave Smith, a young fan sitting high above home plate, the display of temper was as stunning as Alston's decision. It was such a departure from Koufax's usual elegant self-containment. He wouldn't lose again until 1964.

In his next start, Koufax got his twentieth win, beating the Giants 11–1, to give the Dodgers a seven-game lead over San Francisco. On September 6, he beat the Giants again, his twenty-second win, and returned to Los Angeles to be with his father, who had suffered a minor heart attack. Beat reporters respected his request and did not write about Irving Koufax's illness. When his father was out of danger, Koufax rejoined the team in Pittsburgh. The three-way pennant race had grown so tight, St. Louis TV stations were showing Dodger and Giant games—this in an era when few home games were broadcast.

By the time the Dodgers arrived in St. Louis on September 16 for a decisive three-game series, their National League lead was down to a single game. The Redbirds had won ten straight. The number one hit in town was the Spike Jones standard "Pass the Biscuits, Mirandy," the anthem of the 1942 Cardinals. "The series has already been banned by the American Heart Association," Jim Murray wrote in the *Los Angeles Times*.

There were twelve games left in the season and in Stan Musial's career. One hundred sportswriters wrote one hundred thousand words about game one. Musial, a new grandfather, defied time, pulling a fast ball over the right-field wall. The Dodgers went on to win the game, a thriller, in the ninth. But it was Musial's at-bat that Koufax would remember when he pitched the next day.

He spent the morning before the game reading *Nation of Sheep*, William Shirer's definitive essay on the passivity of the German people during World War II. That evening, he delivered a doctoral dissertation in pacifying hitters. As Pee Wee Reese liked to say of him, "He doesn't think like a left-hander—he's smarter than that."

Koufax believed in the outside corner of the plate the way some people believe in reincarnation. It was a tenet of his faith that anyone who can put a fastball on the outside corner of the plate 85 percent of the time can win fifteen games in the major leagues. He never believed in just getting a pitch over; every one had a purpose. Throwing strikes? Overrated dogma. Challenging a power hitter inside? Macho posturing. His job was to train the home plate umpire to define the strike zone as he saw it, expanding it inch by inch, inning by inning, cajoling him into giving a little more, and then a little more. When, finally, he had a batter where he wanted him, leaning out over the plate, he'd come inside—and then go outside again. "You pitch outside, you throw inside," he liked to say.

Roseboro was catching that night. His solemn, masked face was the one Koufax envisioned on the receiving end of every successful pitch. Theirs was a telepathic battery. They always tried to exploit a hitter's vanity. "The littlest SOB wants to be a star," Roseboro said. "He doesn't want to hit a blooper to right. He wants to hit a ball out of that dang ballpark. And we're saying: 'Here, hit this goddamn fastball on the out-side corner, I *defy* you to hit it.' Hit that sucker four hundred and fifty feet to right field.' God can't hit it to right field."

Mike Shannon, the Cardinals' outfielder, prepared for Koufax with an imaginary cigar box. All night before the game, he'd visualize this cigar box hovering over the outside corner of the plate. He saw it when he went to bed and he saw it when he got up in the morning and when he finally got up to the plate, carrying the image with him like a baby's blankie. If a pitch happened to land in the box, he swung. Occasionally, he got lucky. Cardinals manager Johnny Keane had grown so tired of watching his players trying to pull those outside pitches, he threatened to fine anyone who attempted it five hundred dollars. "Ten minutes before the game he called us all in and said, 'You know, we haven't hit Koufax very well,'" catcher Tim McCarver recalled. "This was sup-posed to be like a vision that John had. He said, 'And I've decided that we all ought to try to go the other way against him.'"

Musial didn't need to be told. The score was 1–0 when he led off in the bottom of the seventh, determined to do what he had done the night before. Koufax was equally determined not to allow it. Musial lined the second pitch, a low outside fastball, to left center for the first of the Cardinals' four hits. It wasn't a mistake; it was just where Koufax wanted it to be. He lost the no-hitter but won the contest and the game, 4–0. It was Koufax's eleventh shutout of the season, a major league record for left-handers. He had thrown eighty-six pitches, only twenty of them balls. After the game, Drysdale told reporters: "He's the only pitcher I've ever seen if he pitched a no-hitter every time I wouldn't be a bit surprised." Las Vegas bookmakers took the pennant race off the board.

The next evening, a Dodger rookie named Dick Nen officially put the Cardinals out of their misery. Nen had been called up from Spokane that morning. After he pinch-hit for Fairly in the eighth, coach Lee Walls told him to ask Alston if the manager wanted him to stay in the game and play first. Nen couldn't decide which was worse: talking to Alston or disobeying the coach. He approached the manager with trepidation.

"Skip says, 'Oh, that's right, you're a first baseman, you go play first.' That's how I got to stay in the game."

When he came to bat again in the ninth, the Cardinals were ahead by a run. Nen's father, Sam, and his sister, Donna, were at home watching on TV. His mother was at church praying for the Dodgers. "Back in those days, there weren't a whole lot of sporting events on TV," Nen said. "But that game was on TV. It seems like everyone in Southern California watched it. No matter where I go, what I do, people recognize the name. People say, 'You're not . . .' And I say, 'Yeah, I am.'"

When Nen tied the game with a home run into the right-field stands, his mother rushed back from church to make his favorite spaghetti sauce. By the time the Dodgers won it in thirteen innings, the pot was boiling on the stove. When the Dodger plane touched down in Los Angeles at 4:08 A.M., a spaghetti breakfast was waiting for him.

Koufax didn't know anything about Nen's home run until he read about it in the paper the next day. He had flown home to Los Angeles to be with his parents for the Jewish New Year.

By the fall of 1963, television had insinuated itself into the fabric of American life. Newton Minow, chairman of the Federal Communications Commission, had already declared it a vast wasteland. Live TV took on a new meaning for those who saw Lee Harvey Oswald shot to death in Dallas. Four days later, at the annual Army-Navy game, instant replay was used for the first time. Writing his world series preview for the *San Diego Union*, Phil Collier confidently predicted the largest nationwide television audience ever to witness a sporting event. Phil Silvers, the TV comedian and guest columnist for the *Los Angeles Times*, bragged about *not* going to the games. Silvers wrote that he was staying home to watch on color TV: "This is a strange way to cover a world series but I suppose I and all my sportswriting colleagues might as well face it. This is the trend of the future." NBC estimates that 22 million American homes tuned in to the 1963 World Series. Games three and four remain on baseball's top-ten list of the most-watched broadcasts in history.

Among the viewers was Bob Costas, a sixth-grader in Burlington,

Connecticut. "Mr. Tomasi and Mr. Landy, who were our teachers, they had a black-and-white television set," Costas recalled. "And they brought the TV set in and suspended class and let us watch the world series on a black-and-white TV set with rabbit ears. Whitey Ford against Sandy Koufax—I mean, how great is that?"

Mel Allen and Vin Scully, voices of the Yankees and Dodgers, respectively, called the series for NBC. Scully, who was hired by the Dodgers as a radio announcer in 1950, watched as television usurped the prerogatives of reporters. "In those days, it was strictly between the lines," he said. "I mean that's about all we did. You know the classic change in the media. In the old days, even in the early fifties, you had two kinds of newspapermen following a club: a morning man and an afternoon man. The morning man answered all the great questions of journalism: who, what, where, when, and how. And then television came along. Television gave you the who, what, where, when, why, and how. So the morning man's job had to change. So the morning man started looking for an angle. So now you had a morning man looking for an angle and an afternoon man looking for an angle."

As television appropriated the old questions, reporters began to ask new ones. The sports pages had come a long way since Red Smith filed his first dispatch for the *St. Louis Star* in 1927, writing an account of an evening event from the point of view of a glowworm outshone by newly installed floodlights. The old bald guys with inky fingers were being nudged aside by a new species of sportswriter. Chipmunks, Jimmy Cannon called them, after noticing Phil Pepe, a toothy *Daily News* reporter, and a horde of other sportswriters surrounding Jim Bouton's locker in Yankee Stadium.

The chipmunk revolution is often traced back to the 1962 World Series when a reporter named Stan Isaacs, interviewing a pitcher named Ralph Terry, inquired about the eating habits of said pitcher's new baby. "Breast or bottle?" Isaacs asked.

He saw the lighthearted inquiry as an example of a new, less reverential view of athletes. To Isaac's dismay it became interpreted as an example of how sportswriters intruded on private lives. The protective bubble around them was imploding. "It was the ultimate chipmunk question," said former sports columnist Larry Merchant. "It would be the chipmunk letterhead or T-shirt. Now we can be reporters, not just fans, which was revolutionary in those days—sportswriters as reporters. No one was getting into social issues or the heads of athletes. I felt the personal was the professional. We wanted to know who these people were."

Chipmunks found their voices in irreverence. Distance and irony were the tools of their trade. Old-school reporters like Collier perceived themselves as being in the same business as the players. They knew more and wrote less about the people they covered than their journalistic heirs, whose mandate to *understand* their subjects has grown while their access has diminished. "None of them ever feared me," Collier said before his death in February 2001. "I wasn't going to squeal. I rode in the back of the plane and the bus with the guys. I went out and drank with them every night. I always said I was going to write a book and call it, *The Bases Are Loaded and So Was I.*"

In time, the excess of one era was replaced by another. Purple prose, underwritten by free food and free booze, gave way to sports page psychoanalysis. Sportswriters became interested as much in how players felt as in what they did. "Measuring the ego and id of ballplayers," Red Smith called it with distaste.

For athletes of Koufax's generation, the rules changed mid-game. Everything became fair game: adoption, divorce, marriage; remarriage, wife-swapping, wife-beating. Suddenly, ballgames were not just events but media events; and, thanks to the *Game of the Week* and postseason play, ballplayers were TV stars, especially telegenic ones like Koufax.

The return of the Bensonhurst kid, coming home to fulfill the thwarted dreams of all those cuckolded Brooklyn fans, was an obvious and compelling angle. The tabloids made him their own. Even his head cold made headlines. Speculation about his health was fueled when he failed to show up at Dodger Stadium for the last weekend of the regular season. It was Yom Kippur, he explained later.

New York reclaimed him. And so did his biological family. Maury Allen was a young reporter for the *New York Post*. Shortly before the series began, Allen said, the *Post* received a tip saying that Koufax was adopted. People didn't talk about divorce in 1963, much less adoption. "All of sudden we get a call: 'I'm related to so-and-so Braun, that's Koufax's natural father. He's adopted.' The big scoop is that he's not a Koufax—not *born* a Koufax. Ike Gellis is the sports editor. Gellis says, 'What kind of bullshit is this?'"

Gellis gave the information to Milton Gross, a *Post* columnist, who was close to Koufax. "Gross talks to the guy," Allen said. "He spells out the background."

The background was this: Koufax's biological father, Jack Braun, had left the family when his son was three years old. They had not spoken since before he signed with the Dodgers. The paper made arrangements to bring Braun to Yankee Stadium in the hope of meeting his estranged, biological son. "I wrote a story about him," Allen said. "Sandy was very hurt. He never said, 'I'm never going to talk to you.' You could read in his face such anger, such disappointment. We were Jewish. We were also the Jewish paper. It was a very, very strained thing through that series."

Ed Linn, the writer who later collaborated on Koufax's autobiography, also recalled the story. "I said, 'Maury, 'how could you?' He said, 'You think I didn't fight this?'"

Merchant recalled it, too: "It was considered by a lot of people at that time a sort of breach of some kind of journalistic etiquette. It made a lot of people uncomfortable. It didn't have anything to do with his being a player.

"Part of the deal here is Sandy Koufax, a Jewish kid from New York, coming to New York to pitch in the world series, a superstar, somebody who seemed almost perfect—handsome, beautiful to watch, except when he hit, and brilliant at what he was doing. Here was this perfect guy, and this was seen as some bump in the road, some slight imperfection. We're talking about the time just before the sexual revolution, before divorce became a norm. I guess it was something of a shock. It was public. It was during a world series."

Koufax did not see Braun. Nor was he aware that *Post* reporters were responsible for bringing him to the Stadium. His concern was for his father, Irving Koufax, who was still recuperating in a Los Angeles hospital.

The Koufax clip file in the *Post* morgue no longer exists. What was actually published in 1963, if anything, is lost to history. Three years later, the *Post* did publish an exclusive interview with Braun the day after Koufax's last major league start in the 1966 World Series. Braun appeared on the front page of the paper in a photograph showing him at home on Long Island watching his biological son on television.

The headline blared: "Sandy's Dad: The Ordeal." The caption read, "Where Sandy's Loss Hurt." Arthur Greenspan, the rewrite man who got the byline, quoted Braun as saying: "Please say in your story that you came looking for me, not that I sought you out. Tell people that I didn't really want to talk because I don't want to do anything which could even remotely harm Sandy. Say that I don't want to seem to be trying to profit from my son's fame. And say I am very proud of my son."

The *Post* printed snapshots Braun had taken of his eight-year-old son, a boy in short pants and high socks trying to hit a baseball, and revealed that he attended every game at Shea Stadium that Koufax pitched, sitting as close to the visiting dugout as possible.

The wire services reprinted the story, and the pictures, noting the coincidence that both world series starting pitchers had been adopted. Jim Palmer, of the Orioles, was born Jim Wiesen, the Associated Press reported. As the story gained circulation, the zone of privacy—a new concept for a new media age—began to shrink. Dodger general manager Buzzie Bavasi remembers Koufax showing him "a telegram he got one day from somebody saying his grandmother was dying and 'Goddamn you, you sonofabitch, why don't you take care of her?' And I said, 'Well, Sandy, you had nothing to do with that. Whoever sent you the letter should take care of your grandmother.'"

Nobe Kawano, the protective clubhouse man, began to screen his mail. "I remember one letter from Brooklyn. It said, 'I went to the Hall of Records. There is no Sandy Koufax.' I didn't want to tell him about it. I just threw that letter out."

The adoption story became not only public record, but also a de facto part of his public persona—a perception perpetuated even today. Writing in the *Los Angeles Times* in 1999, Roger Kahn, the celebrated author, suggested that the *Post* piece drove Koufax into a shell, a refrain that drives Koufax nuts. "What shell?" Koufax asks friends, plaintively.

"The shell," Kahn responds, "that Pee Wee Reese encountered when he asked Koufax to work with his son, Mark, on a 1997 television series about the Dodgers in the Hall of Fame. Despite his warm feelings for Reese, Koufax declined, whereas Snider and Rachel Robinson and even Roy Campanella, who was very ill, cooperated wholeheartedly."

It was during a cross-country flight that Reese broached the subject. "We're up there in first class, going to North Carolina. Sandy had just bought a place in North Carolina. He started talking about how lucky he was to play baseball in Brooklyn. He'd see all those people riding the train, doing nine to five. He said, 'Man, I am the luckiest man on the earth.' I said, 'Sandy, that's great stuff. I'd like to use that in the documentary.' He reamed me. He said, 'No, that's just for me, that's not for everybody to know.' Later, he said, 'Okay, call me.' But I never pursued it. I respected that. He was a lot like my dad about things like that. Whenever he was approached about scripts and things, he always said no. I can't say anthing bad about Sandy Koufax. Every single week when my father couldn't distinguish a clock from a coffee cup, when the cancer was going to his brain, he was still talking to Sandy. Sandy called regularly, every week."

Sometimes, near the end, when Pee Wee wasn't entirely lucid, Mark got to wondering what they could possibly be talking about. "One time, he was on the phone talking to Sandy, I picked up the phone to listen. There was no one on the other end of the line." Deep in the twilight of terminal illness, Pee Wee took solace in an imaginary conversation with Koufax.

"I wouldn't say Sandy denied me," Mark Reese said. "A lot of people think Sandy is an uptight, reluctant, elusive guy, which he is, but not around teammates. When he got around my dad, they were like two little kids."

After Pee Wee's funeral in 1999, Koufax told reporters, "He was a teammate for four years, a friend for forty. What else is there to say?"

Privately, he told friends, so many former teammates were dying, he needed to pack a dark suit on all his travels.

It is one thing to be publicity shy. It is another to be just plain shy. Koufax doesn't view himself that way. "People have been writing it for forty years," he told a press conference in 1999, "because someone said it forty years ago." Friends consider it a "reserve" (evident only among those he doesn't know) and trace it not to the publication of the *Post* story but, as Charley Steiner suggests, to the fact of Jack Braun's absence from his son's life, a formative event in any childhood.

Allen, who did the legwork for the story, believes it served as a cautionary tale. "It allowed him to accept that he was a public figure and that everything in his life was going to come out," he said. "It was a hurtful thing. In journalism, you have one, two, three stories in your life— that's the line that's drawn. Sometimes you cross it. We crossed it. I regret it from the standpoint of hurting a beautiful human being."

Koufax did not see Braun until decades after the *Post* published its account, shortly before his death. Braun gave him some old snapshots, the same sort he had supplied to the tabloid.

Yankee Stadium was strictly S.R.O. for the first game of the 1963 World Series. For once the announced attendance—69,000—wasn't inflated. It was the eighth time the Yankees faced the Dodgers, but the first time New York faced L.A. Teachers suspended class. New York dailies printed page one pleas to readers not to call for information. A special city-wide telephone number had been set up. Five hundred and forty radio stations carried the radio broadcast with Joe Garagiola and Ernie Harwell. Everyone else watched on TV.

The Vegas boys made the Yankees 8-to-5 favorites to win the series—6 to 5 to win the opener—and posted 10-to-1 odds against the Dodgers' being swept. The odds against the Yankees' being swept: 25 to 1. No wonder. The Dodgers had finished seventh in the National League in home runs, and sixth in runs scored. Bill Skowron, "The Moose," who had come over from the Yankees in an off-season trade for Stan Williams, entered the Dodger clubhouse one day and found a baseball dangling from the ceiling—the handiwork of Koufax and Drysdale. "This is a baseball," they said. "You're supposed to hit it."

The Yankees were the Bombers. They had won the American League pennant by ten and a half games. "It was the last great Yankee team," said Dodger infielder Dick Tracewski. "We had our meeting and we said, 'Holy Christ, how are we ever going to compete against them? I hope we don't get embarrassed.' They were so potent."

Whitey Ford, "The Chairman of the Board," was the winningest pitcher in world series history. Koufax had never pitched in Yankee Stadium except in the bullpen in 1955. On the way to the ballpark, he entertained his teammates with impersonations of Bill Dana, a comic of the era who made the entire country laugh by pretending to be Hispanic. ("Hello, my name is Jose Jimenez.") Koufax wasn't nervous until he stepped onto the mound. Being on the mound in Yankee Stadium, he decided, was like being at the bottom of the Grand Canyon.

"I was scared crapless," Roseboro said. He was at his locker worrying about the winds that swirl around home plate when his father showed up with a flask of peach brandy. "I was going to take my little sip to cool myself down," Roseboro said. "Somebody tapped me on the shoulder. I had my head up in the locker. It was Alston. He said, 'Have a good day, boy.'"

It was seventy-six degrees at game time. Ladies wore lampshade-size hats. Men wore white shirts. Guy Lombardo and the Royal Canadians played "The Star-Spangled Banner." Stan Musial threw out the first pitch.

"The world series had a tremendous mystique then because the leagues didn't meet," Costas recalled. "And teams had more of an identity then. The Dodgers had a certain continuity in their roster. In fact, one of the things that was almost jarring was Moose Skowron playing for the Dodgers.

"And I knew all about the lore of Yankee Stadium and the world series with the hitting background coming down behind the monuments. And everyone then wore white shirts. And so, I fully understood, even watching on this black-and-white TV, that here's Koufax coming out of the white shirts, out of the sunlight, into the shadows. And I could tell that not only was he throwing incredibly hard but this curveball . . . I don't know that his curveball was ever more effective than it was on this day.

"And I was a Yankee fan, too. As a Yankee fan, you had a certain belief, a certain haughty belief in your team. And you know he didn't just *beat* the Yankees. I think the first five guys struck out, didn't they?"

The first three Yankee batters—Tony Kubek, Bobby Richardson, and Tom Tresh—struck out on twelve pitches. NBC's cameras panned the crowd: Stogie-shaped men with fat cigars jammed between their teeth were speechless. Umpire Shag Crawford was grateful. Taking a drag on a last cigarette before the game, he ruptured a blood vessel in his throat and began spitting up blood. He wasn't about to bail on Koufax and Ford. He waited to go to the hospital until after the game and never smoked again.

Koufax's confrontation with Richardson, the Yankees' diminutive second baseman, was the touchstone of the game and perhaps the series. Born the same year, retired the same season, they had little in common other than manners and civility. Richardson, a born-again Christian, who returned home to Sumter, South Carolina, when his playing days were over, answers the phone with courtliness: "I will be happy to receive your call."

They weren't happy memories but he was glad to share them. "There was an air of expectancy. We had won in '61 and '62. We were confident, overconfident. That was set straight right away. I was just overpowered."

Richardson had struck out only twenty-two times in more than 600 at-bats. Koufax didn't just strike him out, he did it three times, and he did it the way everyone said you couldn't—throwing to his power. Koufax and Roseboro were in complete agreement about what they wanted to do with the fastball-hitting Yankees. "After a while you're on the same wavelength," Roseboro said. "It becomes so easy that if Sandy didn't want what I put down he wouldn't do anything but look at me for a couple of seconds and I said, 'Oh, shit, he's going to the next one.'"

Like most of his teammates, Richardson ignored the scouting reports. "The report comes in and says, 'His fastball really takes off.' You think, 'I've seen lots of fastballs.' When you see it for the first time, I couldn't believe it. I had not seen stuff like that before. By the third time up, I was honestly just trying to hit the first pitch because I didn't want to strike out again. Mantle was in the on-deck circle and when I walked past him, he said, 'No use even going up there.'"

After Koufax struck out the side in the first inning, writers and other observers reported that he looked into the Yankee dugout as if to say: There, take that. Others, who know him better, swear it never happened. "That's not him," Ford said. "He might have been thinking it but he sure as heck didn't say that or give that impression."

Frank Howard, the slugger whom Jimmy Cannon once described as a "one-faced totem pole," came to bat in the second inning. John Gregory Dunne, the novelist, then a *Time* magazine reporter and aspiring TV writer, watched from the left-field grandstand as Howard hit the ball to center field, a drive as clear and straight as a narrative line. Kubek, the shortstop, had the fleeting impression he might catch it. Ford ducked instinctively and needlessly. "Mantle took one step and the ball was over his head," Dunne said. "It was like a projectile. Of course, it *was* a projectile."

It hit the black protective screen around the public address amplifier on the fly, landing by the monuments in the deepest part of Yankee Stadium. Howard, as huge as he is modest, claims to have hit balls harder. "You're running, not looking," he said. "But it came right back to Mantle. With most normal individuals, it would have been a three-base hit. With me it was a double. I had to slide headfirst to get a double. They almost threw me out."

Mantle, who had a unique appreciation for a hard-hit ball, hid his admiration in the webbing of his glove. Clete Boyer, the Yankee third baseman, caught him laughing into his leather.

Skowron stepped to the plate with a .203 batting average and some ambivalence. On the field he was known for his fierce demeanor and his closely cropped hair. Neighborhood kids nicknamed him "Moose" after his grandfather shaved his head. They thought he looked like the Italian dictator Benito Mussolini, who, Skowron notes, "was big at the time."

Skowron had played badly all season, in a funk about having been traded by his beloved Yanks. Alston started him at first base in place of Fairly and Moose vindicated Alston's hunch with the first of two run-scoring singles. "I felt bad playing against guys I played with all my life," Skowron said. "I knew Mickey since 1950. I was surprised I was in the lineup. I saw my name and choked a little bit. Fans in the stands were calling me Benedict Arnold. I'm no traitor. I had nothing to do with the trade."

Tracewski, another unlikely starter, was up next. He was in the line-up because of an injury to Ken McMullen. Trixie singled in his first world series at-bat. Fortified by his father's schnapps, Roseboro stepped to the plate. "I went out there and hit a three-run home run," he said. "It changed everything. Sandy was throwing bee-bees. He was hitting his spots. We won the first game. After that it was a real relaxing series."

Pitching with an ease facilitated by an unaccustomed 4–0 margin, Koufax struck out the first two men in the bottom of the second: two guys named Mantle and Maris. With those five consecutive strikeouts, he tied a world series record.

The first mention of Carl Erskine's world series strikeout record came in the fifth. Erskine had struck out fourteen Yankees on an October afternoon ten years before. Inning by inning, the strikeouts mounted. *Six. Seven. Eight.* Everyone in the Stadium—everyone in Erskine's box— was keeping count. In the seventh, Elston Howard went down swinging. *Twelve.* And then pinch-hitter Phil Linz in the eighth. *Thirteen.* And the hometown folks who accompanied Erskine to Yankee Stadium were saying, "Carl, he's got eleven, twelve, thirteen—wow, you gettin' nervous?"

"And," Erskine remembered, "the crowd kind of picked up on that after a while and so every time he'd rack up another strikeout, the whole section of people would be looking at me to see what I was doing."

Briefly, Koufax wavered, his delivery "elbowish," in Roger Angell's apt description. He lost his rhythm and his shutout in the eighth on a two-run home run by Tom Tresh. But that moment of vulnerability only served to heighten the drama of the denouement. The Yankees kept going down swinging, and the shadows crept across the outfield grass. Cannon wrote: "Koufax seemed alone, a man engaged in a game of manual solitaire. Only occasionally are you aware of the other eight men on the field."

When, in the bottom of the eighth, Richardson struck out for the third time, the big scoreboard in center field flashed the number four-teen. Koufax had tied Erskine's record. "I can't say I felt a sense of loss because here's a teammate who's doing this," Erskine said, "and I was just kind of in no-man's-land watching to see what happened."

Koufax led off for the Dodgers in the top of the ninth. The crowd voiced its appreciation. The Brooklyn kid had done the impossible. He had made the Dodgers at home in the Bronx. They gave him a standing ovation and never bothered to sit down. The Dodgers went out in order quickly. As Koufax walked to the mound for the bottom of the ninth, Bob Shepard's voice reverberated through the stadium, asking fans not to walk on the grass. Horns blared and fans roared, a crescendo with every pitch.

Elston Howard, the first batter, lined out on the first pitch. Sixty-nine thousand new Dodger fans groaned when Joe Pepitone lifted a foul behind home plate, imploring Roseboro to "Let it go!"—and exhaled when the ball landed safely in the screen behind the plate.

Pepitone silenced them momentarily, singling to right. Boyer, the only Yankee who hadn't struck out (though not the only one to claim the distinction), came to the plate. Harry Bright stepped into the on-deck circle behind him. They had ridden to the park together that morning and would ride home again together that night. "I could have been the record, all right?" Boyer said. "But I happen to hit the ball to short or something. So we rode home and he told me, 'Why didn't you strike out? I was pulling for you to strike out.'

"I said, 'Well, if I had struck out, that's only two outs, and you would have *extended* the record.' We knew we weren't going to hit it."

Bright, a career journeyman, known to his teammates as "Not Too," gamely approached the plate for his first world series at-bat. He was well aware he represented the potential record-breaking fifteenth strikeout. "I couldn't miss it," he said. "It was up there on the Fan-o-tron."

He told himself, I'm going to hit the ball out of the ballpark.

Koufax offered nothing but fastballs. As Scully put it on national TV, "Bright is swinging at thin air." Each pitch was accompanied by a roar which barely abated before Koufax delivered again. On the radio, Garagiola tried to affect a professional, understated calm.

> *Oh and one, fastball swung on and missed.*
> *High; one and one. Just watching Koufax pitch, you gotta believe he knows he's one away from breaking it. He's rearing back. Humming it.*
> *High; two and one. That's ball two.*
> *And the tension builds.*
> *Swung on and missed! He struck him out!*

Having called Bright out prematurely, Garagiola did not acknowledge either his own excitement or the error it induced.

> *Two balls, two strikes. Sandy Koufax within one pitch of breaking it.*

There was no mistake about the next pitch. It wasn't the shadows creeping across the diamond—they had long since moved out—or the white shirts in deep center field that stymied Bright. It was pure speed. Koufax was quickly engulfed by his teammates, the beak of his cap knocked sideways. He never looked younger. The Yankees never looked older. In the clubhouse, Bright told reporters: "I wait seventeen years to get into a world series and I strike out. That isn't bad enough: Sixty-nine thousand people were rooting against me."

As with Sisyphus, Bright's fate was inescapable. But Sisyphus didn't have to see the replays. "I see it every year," Bright said. "Seems like they always show that segment. People—especially my family—call up and say, 'Did you see yourself on TV?'"

He isn't any happier about it now than he was then. "It was more or less a joke," he said. "It was true, I was waiting a long time to get in the world series. And here was this nice Jewish boy from Brooklyn and all the fans were rooting for him."

Yogi Berra would have been the next hitter—a prospect which, he allowed, made Yogi leery. Instead, Yogi remained on the sidelines, asking the question on everyone's lips: "How the hell did he lose five?"

No one, including Sandy Koufax himself, ever thought he would grow up to be a baseball player. Jack Braun, his biological father, provided this snapshot to the *New York Post* long after his famous son had taken his stepfather's name. "When I speak of my father, I speak of Irving Koufax, for he has been to me everything a father could be," Sandy wrote in 1966. (*New York Post*)

Sandlot manager Milt Laurie (*left*) was the first to recognize the potential in Koufax's left arm. His parents (*right*) didn't even know he played baseball.
(*Richard Auletta*)

Sandy Koufax, as a college freshman, at Cincinnati's Coney Island with his catcher, Danny Gilbert. Both made the team as walk-ons.
(*Danny Gilbert*)

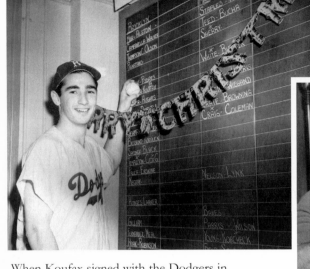

When Koufax signed with the Dodgers in December 1954, the *Brooklyn Eagle* dubbed him a "boro star," though he had pitched only four intercollegiate games.
(*Bettmann/Corbis*)

The children and grandchildren of his late sister, Edie, are the only surviving members of his immediate family. He was leading the National League in strikeouts on June 13, 1957, when he was photographed with his nephew Martin.
(*Bettmann/Corbis*)

If you want to understand how he did what he did, you must see the ball in his hand. "When Sandy Koufax holds a baseball, there's no question who's in control," says former Dodger Rick Monday.
(*AP/Wide World Photos*)

Sandy Koufax's back leg was his anchor. Every other part of him was flying. The sweet, self-replicating motion lulled and mesmerized—the perfect synchronization of muscle and thought. In 1961, Koufax broke Christy Mathewson's National League strikeout record. In 1962, he was unhittable.

(*AP/Wide World Photos*)

Everybody watched or listened. (*National Baseball Hall of Fame Library, Cooperstown, N.Y.*)

Pitching off the mound at Yankee Stadium for the first time was like looking up from the bottom of the Grand Canyon. (*Bettmann/Corbis*)

World Series starting pitchers Sandy Koufax and Whitey Ford at Yankee Stadium on October 2, 1963: two New York kids who made good. (*Bettmann/Corbis*)

After breaking Carl Erskine's world series strikeout record, Koufax told his former teammate, "You know, Carl, in the eighth inning I just thought to myself how great it would be to share that record with you." (*Bettmann/Corbis*)

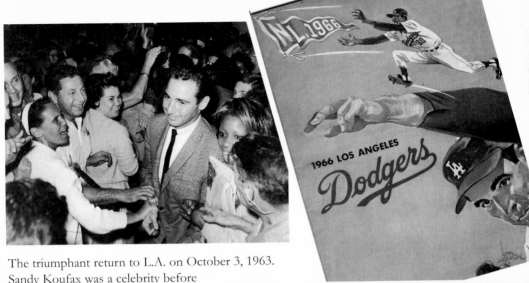

The triumphant return to L.A. on October 3, 1963. Sandy Koufax was a celebrity before celebrity became an entitlement—hound's-tooth and Glen plaid, a crisp white shirt, and a skinny black tie held in place by a discreet gold tie tack. (*AP/Wide World Photos*)

The more unassailable he appeared, the more vulnerable he became. Heat was his salve, ice his salvation. Trainers fashioned a rubber sleeve from an inner tube, the height of medical technology. (*Bettmann/Corbis*)

When Juan Marichal of the Giants smashed his bat over John Roseboro's head, on August 22, 1965, it was the culmination of a savage summer and the end of a kind of innocence. Roseboro had a two-inch gash in his skull. For Koufax, the pain was heartfelt. (*AP/Wide World Photos*)

Perfect form during the perfect game, September 9, 1965. (*Bettmann/Corbis*)

In the last inning, he threw so hard his hat wouldn't stay on his head. (*National Baseball Hall of Fame Library, Cooperstown, N.Y.*)

Once before, when he was with the Milwaukee Braves, losing pitcher Bob Hendley came this close to a no-hitter. (*AP/Wide World Photos*)

Koufax and Drysdale on the set of *Warning Shot* during spring training on March 28, 1966. Their joint holdout was a revolutionary act, received as heresy. (*Bettmann/Corbis*)

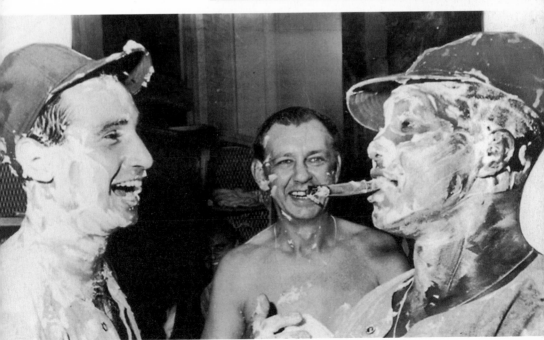

Celebrating the 1966 pennant-clinching game with teammate Wes Covington in Philadelphia. It was the ninth time in his career that Koufax pitched on two days' rest. Seven times he won, six times he threw complete games. Umpire Doug Harvey called this 6–3 win "the greatest exhibition of baseball I've ever seen in my life." (*AP/Wide World Photos*)

The retirement press conference on November 18, 1966, was funereal. No one from Dodger management attended. (*AP/Wide World Photos*)

Prior to Sandy's 1969 marriage to Anne Heath Widmark, sportswriters referred to him as baseball's most eligible bachelor. Both that marriage and a subsequent one ended in divorce. (*AP/Wide World Photos*)

Working with Dodger pitcher Terry Mulholland at spring training, 2002, in Dodgertown. Friends say he has never been happier. (*Los Angeles Dodgers*)

("He didn't," Maury Wills would say later. "We lost them for him.")

Erskine was first to greet Koufax at his locker. Four years earlier, when Koufax got his first world series start, Erskine had told him, "I hope you break my record." Now he'd done it. "And," Erskine said, "against the same team on the same date, ten years almost to the clock, the hour. An afternoon game on October second against the Yankees. Some of the same lineup—Mantle, at least.

"Well, I go to his locker and he looked at me and said, 'You know, Carl, in the eighth inning I just thought to myself how great it would be just to share that record with you.'"

That evening, Richardson went home to New Jersey and turned on the television, hoping for diversion. But every channel carried the same image. "All they showed was Yankee bats whiffing," he said. "All those empty swings."

Koufax was the "Man in the News" in the next day's *New York Times*. It was an understated encomium, headlined "Man with Golden Charm," and began: "To a gushy Hollywood columnist he is Clark Gable, Gregory Peck and William Holden rolled into one." The paper of record also noted his fondness for alpaca sweaters and "Hollywood cupcakes." And his refusal to do liquor or cigarette commercials.

Johnny Podres, winner of the seventh game of the 1955 World Series, beat the Yankees in game two. On the team bus en route to the airport, Boyer wondered out loud: "Aren't there any more Jewish holidays?"

"You mean like *Yom* Koufax," Mantle replied.

Later, the Dodgers would concede the series was a lot closer than it appeared. "One little break could have turned it around," Tracewski said. But after game one, there was an operatic quality of predestination.

Some would argue that in the course of those four games, you could sense a seismic shift; the reorganization of the plates beneath the crusty surface of American society. The Bombers were the incarnation of moneyed, East Coast WASPdom: the old-boy network in flannel pinstripes. The Dodgers were the future: the coming of cool. And Koufax was "The Mostest"—as *Life* magazine described him on its August 2 cover. They were Jews and blacks, speed and daring. Dem Bums had become a symbol of the ascendancy of style.

Jim Bouton, future author and starter of game three, rejects the cultural imperative analysis. "The seismic shift in power from East to West, the redefining of power from clout to ingenuity, the remaking of the economy from postindustrial to service? No, we're baseball players. We were not sociologists. None of us knew any sociologists or anthropologists and none of us cared to. After the fact, we didn't care to talk to any anthropologists either. We wanted another crack at Koufax. We were all convinced we would get to him."

The night before game three in Los Angeles, Bouton, the optimist, and Phil Linz, the utility infielder, went to Hollywood Boulevard "hoping people would recognize us and buy us dinner." Unrecognized and undeterred, they headed for a honky-tonk joint and had a fake headline made up: "Bouton Pitches No-Hitter and Linz Hits Home Run as Yankees Beat Dodgers, 2–0." They unveiled it on the team bus the next morning.

None of the 700,000 words filed that day with Western Union resembled theirs. Drysdale pitched what may have been the best game of the series and his career, beating Bouton, 1–0. The Dodgers were one game away from sweeping the mighty Yankees. And they had Sandy Koufax going against Whitey Ford. The Yankees' bags were packed before game four began.

On Sunday, October 6, Los Angeles awoke to what Cannon called a "Warner Brothers sky." It was another star-studded, California day: Danny Kaye, Yul Brynner, Doris Day, Fred MacMurray, Sammy Cahn, Stanley Kramer, and George Stevens were there, as was Eddie Fisher, who sang "The Star-Spangled Banner." Women wore sunglasses as big as fantails, their hair stiff as egg whites. Men wore white straw boaters provided by the home team. Irving Koufax and Dick Nen did not attend. Irving was just home from the hospital. In defiance of doctors' orders, he sneaked an occasional peek at the television. Nen was not on the world series roster and had given away the seats Dodger management had sold him in the upper reaches of Blue Heaven.

Ford was superb. He gave up only two hits, both to Frank Howard, including a fifth-inning home run he hit one-handed. Koufax was numb, his foot anyway, which had been injected with novocaine for a bothersome corn. He allowed only one run, a Mantle home run so prodigious it made Tracewski's ears ring. Mel Allen lost his voice on national TV.

The game was tied 1–1 in the bottom of the seventh inning when Junior Gilliam sent a high bouncer Boyer's way at third. The morning papers would feature photographs showing Boyer leaping high, cradling the ball, and making the seemingly routine throw to first, where Pepitone, Skowron's successor, waited. Arrows superimposed upon newsprint traced the trajectory of the ball as it hit Pepitone in the midsection and careened away, trickling down the right-field line. Gilliam raced all the way to third and scored the winning run on a sacrifice fly by Willie Davis.

Pepitone said he lost the ball in all those white shirts behind third base. Boyer saw it differently. "Joe got there late is what happened," Boyer said. "It didn't get lost in the shirts like he said. But the funniest part of the whole thing was in the clubhouse before the first game Whitey had told him, 'Joe, you're going to screw up one of these games.' And now Joe's sitting talking to the press, feeling bad. And Whitey interrupts him and says, 'See, Joe, I told you you'd fuck up one of these games.'"

In the top of the ninth, Koufax faced the heart of the Yankee order, minus Maris, who was injured. Richardson led off with a single. Tresh struck out and Mantle strode to the plate with the opportunity to put the Yankees back in the game and the series. "The press box is throbbing with action," Scully reported, as cameras panned rows of immobile reporters pecking diligently in anticipation of East Coast deadlines.

Koufax got ahead in the count: no balls and two strikes. Fans rose, their voices broke; Roseboro got down in his crouch. He never wanted to be a catcher. The Dodgers made him one, he says, because he was big and black and mean and could block the plate. Smart, too, though nobody mentioned that. He and Koufax were more comrades than friends. Rosie liked to say they met at eight o'clock and said, "Let's kick some ass." His memories of their times together are not particular: games, counts, at-bats, the asses they kicked. What he remembers is a symbiosis so finely tuned that he could change his mind about the pitch he wanted to call even as Koufax went into his windup and it wouldn't matter. Because Sandy would have thought of it already.

As Mantle waited for the 0-and-2 pitch, Roseboro belatedly wiggled two fingers, telling Koufax: Take something off the curve. The book on Mantle said: Never give him anything off-speed to hit, especially when he is batting right-handed. Koufax looked in to Roseboro for the sign, thinking, I'd like to take something off the ball. Then he saw the fingers wiggle.

It was a huge curve that broke like a cheap folding chair. Mantle took the pitch for a called strike three with arrested equanimity. Then he looked at Roseboro and said, "How in the fuck are you supposed to hit that shit?" The Yankees were down to their final out.

It figures that the last man up would be Elston Howard, the catcher for whom Bavasi once considered trading Koufax. Howard hit a meek grounder to short. Umpire Tom Gorman called Richardson out on the anticipated force at second. Blue seat cushions drifted down like snowflakes, Koufax leaped high, and Richardson screamed, "Tracewski dropped the ball!" "Calm down," Tracewski said, admitting he was right. "Sandy didn't see what happened. He's jumping. He had to compose himself and pitch to Hector Lopez."

Watching at home, Irving Koufax felt a flutter in his chest and turned off the television. Later, his son would tell him, "Dad, at that point I felt a little flutter too."

The Yankees had a reprieve but no chance. One out later, Koufax leaped again, though not quite as high. "I had two great thrills that inning," Koufax said later. "One when I thought it was over. Two when I *knew* it was over."

In the Dodger locker room, there were lox and bagels, beer and champagne—giggly-water, the papers called it then. Koufax and his teammates serenaded Skowron, the Yankee killer, who finished the series with a .385 batting average. "M-I-C-K-E-Y M-O-O-S-E!" But Moose was glum. In his heart, he was a Yankee. "I'm no Dodger," he told Mantle years later. "I was only there one year." (In fact, he was no longer a Dodger even then: Bavasi had already agreed to trade him to the Senators for the 1964 season.) "What's the winner's share?" Moose wanted to know. The answer momentarily assuaged the lump in his throat. It was a record: $12,794.

After the interviews were done and the champagne sprayed, Koufax went to the Yankee hotel to visit Roger Maris. They'd gotten to know each other a little and Koufax wanted to spend some time with him before Maris left for his home in Missouri. Then he joined his teammates, late for the victory party, just like 1955. But this time he didn't ask permission. Phil Silvers, the moonlighting comic, reported that the Yankees all signed a petition asking that Yom Kippur be moved permanently to the first week in October.

The morning paper declared: "The North American continent, said the late Frank Lloyd Wright, tilts to the west and everything loose slides into Southern California. Sunday afternoon the continent tilted once more."

Koufax was its axis. Suddenly the game revolved around him. He was the guy who made heads swivel, who made colleagues into fans, so that decades later they would ask to have their picture taken with him and hang it in the front parlor as Richardson did. His guests may not recognize the other guys in the photograph, Stan Musial or Ted Williams. "But they all know Sandy Koufax," he said.

Two days after the series ended, Koufax returned to New York to receive the gold '63 Corvette presented to the Most Valuable Player. He also got a fifteen-dollar ticket from New York's Finest for parking on the sidewalk outside of Cavanaugh's Restaurant. Ford provided the ultimate testimonial. "Koufax had only two apparent weaknesses," Ford said. "He can't park and he can't hit."

Chapter 14

THE SIXTH INNING

CLAUDE OSTEEN WAS LYING in his shorts on a training table in the club-house listening to Jerry Doggett tout the virtues of Royal "76" Premium gasoline. It was getting late in the game and late in the season when arms tire and bodies need assuaging. Drysdale, who was scheduled to start against Houston the next evening, lay on the table beside him. It was Osteen's first year with the Dodgers, having escaped last place in the American League in an off-season trade with the ignominious Washington Senators. At twenty-six, Osteen was no rookie but he felt like one in Drysdale's presence. Everyone felt small in Drysdale's presence. He was the team enforcer; whether standing on the dugout steps, bat ominously in hand, the day-game sun glinting off his California-white teeth, or getting treatment in the training room. His entire being commanded authority. "Get up," Drysdale said suddenly. "Get your uniform on. You gotta watch this."

When Drysdale said "Get up," you got up—even if you were lying on the training table half naked and it was the sixth inning and a violation of baseball etiquette to do so. No one in the dugout or the press box could say how many times before Koufax had carried a no-hitter into the sixth inning. His teammates generally accepted the fact that he'd have one through four or five because it seemed like he always did. Later, they would count them up and be astonished all over again: nine times, not including the no-hitters, he had held the other team hitless through six innings.

The sixth inning of a no-hitter will either be remembered as the necessary pause before a classic denouement or it won't be remembered at all. The dramatic tension derives from not knowing which. The line between the mundane and the heroic is drawn with every pitch, every potential passed ball, every errant bounce. In this instance, the tension was compounded by the improbable symmetry of the line score. On the field, in the stands, on the respective benches there was a coming to consciousness of what lay ahead. Hendley was hanging on. Koufax was getting stronger. "You could smell that something big was about to happen," Osteen said.

It figures that Drysdale would smell it before anyone else. Their lives and fates were inextricably linked. After all, they virtually grew up together. They had been teammates for eleven years. The Dodgers were nothing without them. And without each other, neither would have been what each became. Righty, lefty, gentile, Jew. Everything about them was opposite except their purpose. Drysdale came sidearm; Koufax came over the top. Drysdale's ball beat you up, Koufax's rose to greet you. "Drysdale was like going to the dentist without Novocain," Joey A. liked to say. "Sandy had the Novocain." Facing him was painful only in retrospect.

If Koufax was a shooting star, Drysdale was a full moon. Both were essential but one was sublime. The closest Drysdale had ever come to throwing a no-hitter was a one-hitter against the Cardinals in May. A first-inning single removed all the anxiety from the effort. Big D knew better than anyone the infinitesimal difference between excellence and dominance; he inhabited that place. So there he was, all six feet six inches of him, climbing off the training table in his undershorts, going to his locker, and putting on the uniform, that big 53. That's what stunned Osteen most: "Drysdale's acceptance of what this guy could do that no one else, including himself, could do."

Drysdale's arrival in the dugout compounded the hush and the sense of occasion. Everyone knew what was going on. The Cubs were no longer just facing Koufax. They were facing an inchoate realization: *Uh-oh, he found it.* The curveball was breaking. The fastball was gathering force. "Each pitch," Osteen said, "harder than the last."

The Cubs were restive, jiggling with nervous energy, everyone desperate to change something, anything. For five innings, they had been telling themselves all the right things: We still got a chance. *We're only down one. One swing of the bat, you never know.* But due up in the sixth was the bottom of the order: Krug, Kessinger, and Hendley.

It would be human to weaken in the face of such tepid opposition. Koufax was unrelenting. "Two-hundred hitters hit two hundred for a reason," he liked to say. Drysdale knew if he got past the seventh, eighth, and ninth men in the batting order, the seventh, eighth, and ninth innings would be something to see.

The Dodger dugout exuded a studied nonchalance that soon gave way to superstition. The impulse was conservative. If you change nothing, then perhaps nothing will change. So you sit in the same seat, cross your legs the same way, tilt your cap in the same direction. If you're Maury Wills and you've been sitting beside Koufax on a stool in the runway between innings where you can have a smoke without being noticed, you make sure to sit there again. The one thing you don't do is mention the obvious.

We got a double no-hitter going here, Krug thought, swinging a bat in the on-deck circle. His errant throw was all that stood between what was and what could have been. It is baseball's way to juxtapose failure and redemption with comic regularity. Thus, Krug would remember this at-bat with uncommon specificity. How the pedestrian grounder he hit to short was gobbled up by Wills who threw it in the dirt to first baseman Wes Parker. And how Wills hollered thank you across the diamond after Parker dug it out. In truth, Parker had never been so scared in his life. God, he thought, I don't want to blow this guy's chance at immortality.

Kessinger, the shortstop, was next. After fouling back a fastball for strike one, Kessinger stepped out of the batter's box and exchanged a meaningful look with the home plate umpire. Vargo had seen that look before. Scully too: "Mitts are popping," he said. "The Cubs have a couple of fellas loosening up down there. But Hendley's out on deck."

Kessinger hit a hopeful dribbler down the third base line. It was a nothing ball—the kind on which so much can turn. Its weakness was its potential strength. In its timid trajectory Kessinger found cause for optimism. But Gilliam was playing in at third to guard against a bunt. "I thought I had a chance to beat it out," Kessinger said. "I got thrown out by half a step."

As he headed back to the bench, Kessinger couldn't help thinking about the Hollywood crowd: late to arrive, early to leave, slow to grasp what they were seeing. Arriving just as *we're* leaving, he thought, with a small smile.

The dugout lacked the usual baseball chatter, a form of surrender. Byron Browne kept waiting for someone to say something, break the spell: "This fool is trying to throw a no-hitter at us!" But he was a rookie. It wasn't his place.

With two down, Klein allowed Hendley to hit for himself. The man was still pitching a no-hitter. Besides, Klein was saving Amalfitano for later. As Hendley meekly and predictably struck out again, Richard Hume recorded the totals: no runs, no hits, no errors. Nothing had happened but everything had changed.

"In case you are speculating, down through the years, there's been one gem, one double no-hitter," Scully noted. "We'll tell you more about it if and when we get to that stage. There's never been a perfect game on one side and a one-hitter on the other side . . . yet."

Musing aloud, Scully gave everyone within the sound of his voice permission to consider the possibilities. What had been murmured (or muttered) was now articulated. Adams, Davis, DeLury, Buhler, Hume, and God knows how many others were thinking the same thing. *I think he has a chance.* When Koufax returned to the dugout, Drysdale vacated the stool in the runway. In abdicating the seat, Drysdale was yielding not just to superstition but to reality.

In the Cubs dugout, Joey A. got up from his seat too and sought out Ron Santo: "Hey, Ronnie, somebody must have pissed him off." Santo nodded. Jogging back onto the field, he told Beckert, "Yeah, you're right. He doesn't have shit."

Chapter 15

PULLING TEETH

Two months after arthroscopic knee surgery, Koufax stepped to the first tee at the Shadow Ridge Country Club in Omaha, Nebraska. No one, including him, thought much about it. Walking eighteen holes eight weeks after knee surgery was in no way extraordinary for a sixty-three-year-old man in the last year of the twentieth century. What may have been just another round of charity golf was also evidence of the revolution in the treatment of movable human parts.

Koufax looked good, especially compared to the other notables Bob Gibson had corralled for the annual event. Jim McMahon, onetime prime-time quarterback for the Chicago Bears, showed up in Ray-Bans and flip-flops, cradling a six-pack. Orlando "Cha Cha" Cepeda, newly inducted into the Hall of Fame, was resplendent in a three-piece, burnt-orange zoot suit. "Sweet Lou" Johnson packed his effusive self into a snugly fitting "Bob Gibson All-Star Classic" golf shirt. Koufax wore his own shirt—an impressionistic tableau of palm trees and blue skies.

The course, carved out of a former cornfield, was named Shadow Ridge but there weren't any shadows except for the ones cast by the celebrities, none bigger than Koufax. At the first tee, a gallery of two hundred eager midwesterners awaited him, old guys wearing replica Jackie Robinson jerseys, young kids in Yankee caps, and a few enterprising autograph merchants lugging duffel bags full of memorabilia and disguises to change into once Koufax caught on to their act. The pros are always easy to spot—they come equipped with accoutrements and attitude, affecting the easy pose of townies on every main drag of America, eagle eyes searching the horizon for prey. They mobilized at the sight of him, pushing less mercenary souls out of the way. Al Meyers, a twenty-eight-year-old man in a Celtics jacket, stuffed his one ball back in his pocket. "I came for my dad," he said.

His father, a Koufax devotee ever since seeing him play basketball in high school, had a Legion ball game to coach. His stand-in, Al, hung back, too shy to venture forward as Johnson wrapped Koufax in a bear hug; but close enough to hear Koufax whisper, "My neck's killing me."

Johnson cackled when Koufax's first shot soared straight and long off the tee. By the thirteenth hole, however, Koufax was surveying the crowd for a chiropractor. Dr. Mark Cobleigh stepped forward and wrenched Koufax's neck into alignment. "If I get a hole in one you had nothing to do with it," he told Cobleigh, smiling.

Sometimes his neck is so bad he can't get out of bed; sometimes it's his back. He's had surgery on his rotator cuff and arthroscopic surgery on both knees and he still can't straighten his left arm. Vin Scully, the Dodger broadcaster, was with him one day on a golf course when a well-meaning pro suggested Koufax would shoot better if he straightened his arm on his follow-through. "If I could straighten my arm, I'd still be pitching," he replied.

People ask all the time how it is. "Does it bother you?" an Omaha reporter inquired, trailing him down the fairway. "Only when I throw," Koufax said. He doesn't.

When Koufax was a rookie, there was no such thing as sports medicine. You didn't rehab injuries. You lived with them, grew old with them. You ached, you got a rubdown. You hurt, you put on some heat. Ice was for martinis, not elbows. "Milking your arm" was considered high-tech medicine. Rubbing the fluid out of engorged fingers enabled married guys to put their wedding rings back on—when they chose to. In the spring of 1955, Karl Spooner was the pitching phenom that Koufax eventually became. When his arm went bad, the Dodgers were understandably reluctant to give up on him. They tried everything, including pulling his teeth—they thought maybe poison was leaking into his shoulder joint.

Every pitching arm is doomed. Soft tissue and bone can only give so much. Koufax, like so many other pitchers before him, was doomed by the time in which he lived. He pitched on the cusp of a revolution. He was born a decade too soon. "He came from an era of sacrificial lambs," said Dr. Marilyn Pink, former director of the UCLA biomechanics lab. "You wore people out until they anatomically could not proceed."

As regard for him grew, so did an inchoate sense that he was living on borrowed time. He and the Dodger trainers understood the paradox of his build. That which made him special also made him vulnerable. "Doc" Anderson, who worked on him for an hour and a half before every start, told reporters Koufax had "extreme" muscles, "the largest I ever worked on, and that includes Ted Kluszewski and Frank Howard. Muscles like that aren't ideal for a pitcher, but then I've always said that Sandy Koufax wasn't built to be a pitcher."

It was an anatomical pact with the devil. "Since I have accepted all the advantages of the way I am built," Koufax said, "I don't see how I can complain about the disadvantages."

Spring training 1964 arrived with high expectations and cautionary notes. He had won the 1963 Cy Young Award (unanimously), the National League MVP Award, and the Hickok Belt as Professional Athlete of the Year—not to mention the B'nai B'rith Sports Lodge Award and the Barrett Belt, a rhinestone-encrusted jockstrap from a steak house in Vero Beach. He was voted the Associated Press Male Athlete of the Year, United Press International Player of the Year, the *Sporting News* Player of the Year, Fraternal Order of Eagle Man of the

Year, Southern California Athlete of the Year, and Comeback Player of the Year. He was feted while JFK was mourned.

It was also during that cruel off-season that the Beatles debuted on the *Ed Sullivan Show* and Cassius Clay shocked the world, first by defeating Sonny Liston and then by changing his name to Muhammad Ali. Koufax was busy eating rubber chicken at dinners in Toronto, Columbus, Rochester, Boston, Philadelphia, Houston, and Chicago, where Jerry Holtzman, the baseball writer, took him to his daughter's twelfth birthday party and all the girls squealed like he was John, Paul, George, *and* Ringo. In New York, he was serenaded by the Baseball Writers Association of America. "You're a Jewish Walter Johnson, Sandy boy, Sandy boy."

Casey Stengel opined: "Forget the other fellow, Walter Johnson. The Jewish kid is probably the best of them."

Camp opened and the great expectations of winter soon gave way to a desultory spring. Koufax threw an unusual number of slow curves and change-ups. He confided in Phil Collier: his arm was hurting and he hadn't signed his contract yet. In an exhibition game on April 6, Koufax went nine innings and beat the Yankees—again. Johnny Werhas was his roommate that spring—young, impressionable. "The next morning his arm had almost doubled in size," Werhas said. "I guess water, fluid, had gotten on his elbow. It scared me to death for him. I yelled, 'Sandy, your arm!' He says, 'Oh, man, that happens.'"

On April 22, in St. Louis, Koufax made his third start of the season. Top of the first, one ball and two strikes on Bill White, he felt something let go in his arm. White went to first on the strikeout wild pitch. "Only way I got to first on him," White would say later. Koufax left the game at the end of the inning. Allan Roth, the Dodger statistician, noted on his scorecard that Koufax's elbow was "stiff from the start."

The injury would be variously described in the morning papers as a torn muscle or torn adhesions that had built up in his pitching arm. The examination by the Cardinals' doctor, I. C. Middleman, revealed "exquisite tenderness." "Sandy told me his arm had been hurting on and off since spring training," Middleman said. "He hadn't bothered to report it, feeling he could work it out. He is extremely tender and has a swelling on the inside of his left forearm. It is rigid and just like a hot dog."

Ominously, Middleman added, "He also has an inflammation on his left elbow."

Koufax flew back to Los Angeles to be examined by Dr. Robert Kerlan, the Dodgers' team physician. He had three cortisone shots and skipped three starts before returning to the rotation in May. In a time of national cataclysm, baseball injuries were an afterthought. President Lyndon Johnson signed the Civil Rights Act in July. In August, Congress passed the Tonkin Gulf resolution, legalizing the escalation of the war in Vietnam. Two days later, the bodies of three civil rights workers, Michael Schwerner, James Chaney, and Andrew Goodman, were found on a farm outside Philadelphia, Mississippi. The Republicans nominated *über*-conservative Barry Goldwater for president. The Democrats countered with the notorious and short-lived political ad showing a little girl picking daisies in the shadow of a mushroom cloud.

Koufax was struggling with a 5-and-4 record when the Dodgers arrived in Philadelphia in early June. In the modern era, a staff of team videographers would have provided him constant visual feedback on his mechanics and delivery. Today, at Dodger Stadium, hitters immediately review their at-bats in a screening room adjacent to the clubhouse. On the road, they carry camcorders. But, the world was a more random place in 1964. By chance, Koufax came across a dog-eared issue of *Sport* magazine in the Philadelphia locker room and a photo taken during his 1963 no-hitter over the Giants. The picture was shot from an angle he hadn't seen before and it revealed an undetected flaw in his stride. Three innings into his start against the Phillies, he was himself again.

In the bottom of the fourth, with the count full on Richie Allen, catcher Doug Camilli called for a curve. Koufax shook him off. Allen, he knew, was one of the few truly great curveball hitters in the game. "Then while I was winding up I thought to myself, Doug's right, a curveball would be better," he told reporters later. "But I didn't think fast enough and instead of stepping off the rubber I went through with the fastball and it was low, no doubt about that."

The difference between a ball and a strike is the width of a pencil in an umpire's eye. He has a third, maybe a fourth of a second to make the call. "It was close," Camilli said.

"They're *all* close," home plate umpire Ed Vargo said.

No one complained. And, a few pitches later, Camilli threw Allen out trying to steal second. Who knew he would be the first and last Phillie to reach base all night?

By the bottom of the ninth, Philadelphia manager Gene Mauch was desperate. Koufax had a 3–0 lead, thanks to Frank Howard's preemptive home run, and a chance to become only the second man in the modern era (after Bob Feller) to pitch three no-hitters. Werhas watched Mauch's managerial maneuvering from the Dodger bench: "He sent a couple of players to the bullpen, which was way out in right field. They had to go across the field to get to the bullpen. Then he brought them in one by one to try and throw Sandy's timing off, try and break up the no-hitter."

To no avail. Tony Taylor struck out. Ruben Amaro popped out. With two down, Mauch summoned Bobby Wine, one of the guys he had sent to the bullpen, to pinch-hit for pitcher Ray Culp. "Sandy's just staring at Mauch, knowing exactly what Mauch was doing," Werhas said. "I remember thinking, There's no way they're going to get a hit off him. To me that was tugging on the cape. You don't do that."

Wine had a .203 batting average and an unenviable task. "We had thirty thousand people in Connie Mack Stadium," Wine said. "They always sold out when the Dodgers were in town. I go up and I know none of these people are rooting for me. Let's face it, there were not a lot of people outside my family rooting for me. Guys in the on-deck circle were saying, 'God, I hope he makes an out so I don't have to hit.'"

The first pitch was high; the second was fouled off Vargo's mask. The Phillies' trainer came quickly with smelling salts—too quickly in Wine's opinion. "He's half chokin', half coughin', and says, 'C'mon, c'mon, I don't want him to get cold.' I said, 'Eddie, take your time.' Two pitches later, he was in the clubhouse and healthy again."

Vargo celebrated his first no-hitter by drinking a beer with a straw; Koufax celebrated his third with three beers and a date with a tub of ice.

As always on nights when he pitched, he was last to board the team bus. Nobody minded. The Dodgers weren't going anywhere without him. Drysdale, the other vital cog in their pennant hopes, wasn't with the team. He was in Washington on business when he heard about the no-hitter over the radio. The announcer neglected to mention the score. "Yeah," Drysdale said, impatiently, "but did he win?" With the Dodger offense, you never knew.

The bus idled. The team was headed for New York. Joe Moeller, the $80,000 bonus-baby pitcher, was sitting by himself contemplating his scheduled start the next evening. As usual, the seat beside him was empty. What if he sits down? Moeller thought. What am I going to say to this guy?

"Guys cheered when he got on. He was shy, making some joke about it, like, 'Let's get to a real city.' He sat down, turned to me, and said, 'You know, I got away with a pitch. I hung a curve to Wine.'"

One pitch shy of perfection and all he can talk about is a pitch that could have been hit but wasn't. Mauch was so impressed, he resolved not to allow Koufax to face his team again. The Dodgers were due back in town at the beginning of August and again in early September over the Jewish New Year. He knew Koufax wouldn't pitch then. So August was his only problem. For seven weeks, Mauch plotted. On the morning of August 3, the day Koufax was to face the Phillies again, Mauch called the stadium manager: "If one drop, *one drop!* of rain falls, I want this game called." In fact, he threatened to go up on the roof of Connie Mack Stadium with a hose.

That afternoon, Alston called a meeting at the team hotel. The world champions were a .500 ball club, languishing in seventh place, nine games behind the Phillies. The year before, on another East Coast road trip, Alston had challenged his players to fisticuffs. The Dodgers were traveling in an un-air-conditioned bus at the time. When they saw the Pittsburgh Pirates sail down the highway in a state-of-the-art Greyhound, there had been a near mutiny. But, Alston was loosening up, becoming more modern, "more smiley," as Tracewski put it. During the meeting at the Warwick Hotel, he made the mistake of asking if anyone had anything to say. "Everybody was airing their grievances,"

Tracewski said. "Sandy said something about him being no fun to play for and being too subservient to Buzzie. He said he should be more assertive with running the ball club. He said, 'This is your ball club.'"

When, finally, the meeting was interrupted by a telephone call informing Alston that the game had been called on account of rain, the sun was shining brightly over the team hotel. And over Connie Mack Stadium, too. When Wine got there, the clubhouse man said, "The game's been called. They *think* it's going to rain."

Mauch's triumph was short-lived. The Phillies managed to fold without facing Koufax again. His season was over by the second week of August, his career in jeopardy. August 8 found the Dodgers in Milwaukee and in sixth place. That night, Koufax won his seventeenth game, becoming the first National League pitcher in the modern era to strike out 200 hitters four consecutive seasons. He also singled and scored to begin the winning rally. Reaching base proved a costly mistake. Diving back into second to beat a pick-off throw, he jammed his pitching arm into the bag. He was safe; his elbow wasn't.

The morning paper made no mention of it. The big news was that he was experimenting with a new pitch, a forkball. He won his next two starts and was leading the league with a record of 19 and 5. But the morning after his nineteenth win, a shutout in which he fanned thirteen, he couldn't straighten his arm. The joint squished. Pockets of fluid protruded from beneath the skin like hard-boiled eggs. His elbow was as big as his knee. The only difference was his knee bent. He had to drag his arm out of bed like a log. A waterlogged log.

Tests were run; X rays were ordered. Kerlan took one look at the films and gave him the bad news: traumatic arthritis. A diagnosis without a cure. Arthritis is an acute inflammation of a joint usually associated with old age. Koufax's arm was old even if he wasn't. Pitch by pitch, season by season, the cartilage in his elbow was breaking down.

Kerlan knew the long-term prospects weren't good and the options weren't much better. His diagnosis was not made public. "Sore arm," the Dodgers said. Headlines grew progressively dire as he missed first one, then two, then three starts. "Koufax Injures Elbow"; "Koufax Out

Indefinitely"; "Koufax Arm Test Proves Washout." And finally on
August 31: "Koufax Probably Through for Year."

Pitching *is* trauma. The human elbow may be God's greatest invention but He didn't anticipate a major league fastball during those first
seven days. The moment of maximum stress, the subject of so many
grim-great photographs, occurs just as a pitcher finishes cocking his arm
and it begins to accelerate forward. The elbow is flexed 85 to 95 out of
a possible 150 degrees, the anatomical arc just shy of a semicircle. The
change of direction, as the arm propels itself forward, is an insult to
flesh and bone. It lasts, scientists now know, no more than 3/100s of a
second. But in that wisp of time, the arm is moving at a speed of 7,000
degrees per second. At that rate, the second hand of a clock would complete nineteen and a half revolutions in a tick of a clock. The elbow is
subjected to what doctors call "maximum load" as two contrary forces,
momentum and inertia, converge on the joint. The medical name for
this violation is a "valgus torque." It causes ligaments to stretch like salt
water taffy on a hot summer day.

Kerlan's diagnosis was circumscribed by technology. It wasn't until
the invention of the arthroscope that doctors gained a real understanding of the interior landscape of the joint. The first rudimentary arthroscope, a diagnostic tool fashioned out of urological instruments and a
flashlight, was invented in the 1930s. Modern arthroscopy did not
become available until the early 1970s. Initially, it was solely a diagnostic
tool, literally giving surgeons the ability to "scope out" the inside of a
joint. Surgical procedures using the arthroscope did not become available until the mid-1980s, first on shoulders and knees. Elbows were too
small to explore.

"Repetitive impulsive loading"—the clinician's way of describing the
act of throwing—isn't good for human cartilage. Cartilage doesn't swell
and it doesn't heal. It only breaks down, causing a plethora of outraged
responses in surrounding tissues. The medial collateral ligament, the
major stabilizing force in the joint, bears the brunt of the assault. The
collagen fibers which compose it stretch and tear. The synovial lining
fills the joint with liquid in an attempt to protect ligament and bone.

(Water on the knee or elbow, it used to be called.) Bone spurs form as the body attempts to replace weakened tissue with something stronger.

Today, "scoping" elbows and knees—to use the locker room vernacular—allows professional athletes and middle-age golfers like Koufax to return to competition in a fraction of the previous time. Dr. Frank Jobe, Kerlan's partner and successor, performed the first elbow reconstruction less than a decade after Koufax retired. Tommy John, the surgical pioneer, returned to baseball and pitched for another twelve years. Koufax never had the surgery; it was unnecessary for civilian life. "Today," Jobe said, "we'd take off the spurs, but not any extra bone. We'd replace the medial collateral ligament using a tendon out of his forearm, then give him a year of rehab and he'd come back to pitch.

"If you had said to Dr. Kerlan, 'Why does his arm hurt?' he'd say, 'Because he throws so hard.' That's true. What he didn't know was that he threw hard enough to stretch a ligament. It wasn't torn but it was stretched enough to allow two bony surfaces to rub together. Now we understand that if you have loose ligaments, then you have impingement into the arm bone whenever you throw. I can understand now a lot better than I could when he retired. It must have just killed him."

Koufax always scoffs at such reports. "My heroism is greatly overstated," he'll say, as he did to the floating gallery following him through the former Nebraska cornfield. On occasion, he's been known to admit, "Maybe I just didn't want to think about how bad it was."

At the time, draining, icing, and waiting were his only options. A recurrence was inevitable.

March is the cruelest month for pitchers: when rested arms renew the annual struggle for controlled velocity. Today pitch counts and early outings are meticulously monitored. Pitching a complete game in spring training is unthinkable, even without an arthritic arm. On March 30, 1965, Koufax did just that. The next morning, his roommate, Tracewski, was at the sink shaving when Koufax walked in. "He says, 'Look at this.' And he had this elbow. The elbow was black. And it was swollen. There was muscles that were pulled and there was hemorrhaging. From the elbow to the armpit, it looked like a bruise. It was a black, angry hemorrhage. It was an angry arm, an angry elbow. And all he says is, 'Roomie, look at this.'"

Quickly and quietly, Koufax returned to Los Angeles to see Kerlan. "All of a sudden, toward the end of the day, I'm looking around, thinking, Jeez, where's Koufax at?" teammate John Kennedy said. "And somebody says, 'Yeah, where is he?' And everybody starts asking around. And then one of the trainers said, 'We had to send him back to L.A. Something's wrong with his arm.' His arm was so swollen that it looked like if you poked it with your finger that the skin would burst. And everybody was saying, 'Oh my God.'"

Kerlan told Koufax he'd be lucky to pitch once a week. Eventually, and irrevocably, he would lose full use of his arm. Koufax made Kerlan promise to tell him when that time was near. He told the doctor, "I'm trusting you to keep me going. I'm also going to trust you to say when you think I should quit."

They mapped out a tentative schedule for 1965 that called for him to pitch every five days, which would have meant starting only thirty-four games instead of the expected forty-one. Pitching every fifth day wasn't the norm. Nor was six innings of work considered a quality start. Quantity was quality. Koufax said the hell with it. He promised Kerlan he'd quit throwing between starts, no small concession for a man who routinely dragged Tracewski out of bed in the middle of the night in order to go throw. And Tracewski would get in his car at one end of Los Angeles and drive all the way across town so that Koufax could throw.

On April 2, Phil Collier broke the news in the *San Diego Union*: "Sore Arm May Signal End of Koufax Career." Privately, Koufax told him, "I'm really worried—this might be the end."

Palliatives and temporizing were all medicine had to offer: cortisone shots in the joint, Empirin with codeine for the pain (which he took every night and sometimes during the fifth inning), and Butazolidin (phenylbutazone alka), an anti-inflammatory drug prescribed for broken down thoroughbreds, so poisonous to living things that it was taken off the market in the mid-1970s. It had only one major side effect. "It killed a few people," Jobe said.

Koufax didn't think twice. Kerlan, who suffered from degenerative rheumatoid arthritis, was taking it. Their blood was tested weekly to determine the toxicity level. Doctors and patients alike were in the thrall of modern medicine, seduced by the notion of a magic little pill for every woe. Housewives dropped Valium, football players downed greenies, and baseball players ate Darvon between innings. The drug culture and its pharmacological cowboy mentality would eventually engender a holistic reformation. But Americans weren't there yet. Koufax would recall years later: "I think the next two years, I never missed a start. I started a lot of games with two days' rest and couldn't believe it but the medical staff, the trainers, the doctors, they got me through it. They drained it. I lived on medication. Dr. Kerlan had arthritis at that time and he'd test them. He'd say, 'Boy, this is working great but it's killing my stomach.' I said, 'That's okay. If my arm's all right, I'll take it.'"

Koufax rejoined the Dodgers in Washington, D.C., where they were scheduled to play an exhibition game against the Senators. Tossing a ball on the sidelines, he made headlines. "Sandy Plays Catch!" an ardent headline writer declared the next day. He was wondered at and wondered about. No one knew what to expect, least of all him. Improbably, he pitched three innings in his first outing, striking out five of the ten men he faced. Doug Camilli, his old catcher, was the last of them. He popped up. "Sore arm my eye," Camilli yelled, as he trotted back to the Senators dugout. It was the prevailing opinion.

Koufax used an old pitcher's salve called Capsolin, derived from red hot chili peppers grown in China. The active ingredient, capsaicin, works by depleting substance P, the brain's pain messenger. It is the medical equivalent of hitting your head against a brick wall. Players called it the "atomic balm": thick, gooey, relentless stuff which is no longer marketed in the United States. (Health food books provide homemade recipes.) Most pitchers diluted it with cold cream or Vaseline. Koufax used it straight, gobs of it. Nobe Kawano always made sure to wash his laundry separately. When Dodger trainers donated a used jersey to a local Little League team, the lucky kid who got Number 32 ran off the field screaming, "I'm on fire." He wasn't the only one.

Lou Johnson wore one of Koufax's sweatshirts one cold night in Pittsburgh thinking it would keep him warm in left field. First he began to sweat. Then his skin blistered. Then he threw up.

If heat was Koufax's salve, ice was his salvation. They didn't have ice-packs then. They just plunged your arm in a bucket of ice and waited for frostbite to set in. Koufax hated it. Trainers fashioned a rubber sleeve out of an inner tube, the height of medical technology, later donated to the Hall of Fame. Buhler and Anderson tracked his treatment with an egg timer.

Who could have predicted that by season's end he would pitch 335 ⅔ innings, and set a major league record by striking out 382 men (an average of 10.25 per game)? Not only did he never miss a turn, he pitched both the pennant-clinching game and the seventh game of the world series on two days' rest.

Today stat geeks compile averages and percentages Babe Ruth never dreamed of. Delving into the numerological past, they seek wisdom buried in data, missionaries of what historian Jacques Barzun calls "the stat life." Rany Jazayerli and the authors of *Baseball Prospectus* have created a sliding scale of Pitcher Abuse Points (PAP) that proves beyond a reasonable doubt that Koufax abused his arm. That's what pitchers did. And they took pride in it. In a 1961 game, Koufax threw 205 pitches. That's nothing. Joe Hatten threw 211 pitches in a 1948 game. It was the ethos of the time. Playing hurt wasn't a cliché. It was an economic necessity.

Baseball has always been a numbers game. Owners routinely depreciated the value of their players as their bodies deteriorated. When clubs were no longer able to write them off as tax losses, they simply wrote them off. There was safety in the sheer number of people who wanted to play baseball. Players were fungible. "Just send 'em back to the farm or wherever they came from and bring up a new one," Jobe said.

"If a hundred guys went down with bad arms, you signed another one hundred," Koufax says. "It was basically survival of the fittest. The guys who could do that kept going. We didn't know any better and had some pride in running out there as often as you could."

So when fans clustered around Koufax at the fifteenth hole of

Gibson's tournament wanted to know his definition of a competitor, he didn't hesitate. "It's the guy who keeps coming back. It's the difference between the grass and an oak tree. The oak tree, you cut it down, that's it, it dies. You cut the grass, it just keeps coming back."

The Dodgers opened the 1965 season with worry. Doubt was compounded by panic when Tommy Davis, the former National League batting champion, fractured his ankle in May. Maury Wills's invaluable legs began to hemorrhage a month later. Drysdale developed shingles. Koufax kept throwing. He was an improbable constant in a tremulous world.

There was a sense that summer, in the clubhouse and the country, that events were careening out of control. America was on the precipice of something but no one was sure exactly what. Andy Warhol turned Brillo Pads into art. Martin Luther King won the Nobel Peace Prize. Malcolm X was assassinated. The Astrodome opened in Houston, making the world (but not players) safe for pretend grass. (Asked his opinion, Tug McGraw, of the Mets, replied: "I don't know. I never smoked the stuff.") Casey Stengel bade farewell to Shea Stadium. Branch Rickey died the day *A Charlie Brown Christmas* debuted. And Barry McGuire, a one-hit wonder, topped the pop charts with "Eve of Destruction."

There was civil war in the Dominican Republic and something close to it in Watts, the black neighborhood of L.A. known as South Central. On August 6, Congress passed the Voting Rights Act. Five days later, at 7:05 P.M., a young black man named Marquette Frye was arrested for drunk driving by a white L.A.P.D. policeman and a riot began. By the time it ended six days later, thirty-four people were dead. The National Guard arrived on Friday, the thirteenth, and King five days after that. He was shouted down and sent packing by rioters weary of his message of passive resistance.

On August 14, the night a citywide curfew was imposed, Koufax won his twenty-first game—his twenty-ninth start of the season. The Dodgers were in first place, two and a half games ahead of the Braves. Los Angeles was in flames. Residents of Beverly Hills began arming themselves. Rioting spread south to San Diego and north to San Francisco. "It was the first time I began to pick up a paper and skip the sports section altogether," Roseboro said. "Much of the time I was on the field I had to keep reminding myself that baseball was important. I'd wake up in the morning and say to myself, 'Why are they playing games? Why can't we do something about Watts and the people who live there?'"

In consideration of the riots, Dodger management offered season ticket holders an opportunity to exchange their seats for the September 9 game against the Chicago Cubs. Koufax wouldn't win again until then.

It was a mean, raw time, punctuated by an ugly brawl on the field in San Francisco on August 22, when Juan Marichal hit Roseboro over the head with a bat. The Dodgers, who were in first place with a half-game lead over the Braves and the Giants, went into a collective swoon; the Giants won fourteen straight. On September 16, there were sixteen games left in the season and the Dodgers were struggling to stay in third place, four and a half games behind the Giants. When the players arrived at Wrigley Field that morning, there was a sign-up sheet for any-one wanting to purchase world series tickets as guests of the host American and National League cities. Wally Moon, the player represen-tative, tore it up, saying, "We won't need these."

Armed with that vote of confidence, Claude Osteen held the Cubs to five hits. It was a dour day in a very Windy City and when Osteen tired in the ninth, walking Billy Williams, only 550 paying customers saw Koufax come out of the bullpen to save the game. It was his second relief appearance of the season. "We were all upset at Walter Alston for using him," Tracewski said.

The Dodgers won fifteen of their last sixteen games—three of them Koufax shutouts. On September 18, he beat the Cardinals, 1–0. A week later, he beat them again, 2–0, breaking Bob Feller's 1946 record for most strikeouts in a season. Feller was a last-minute no-show and missed the moment when Mike Shannon proudly became Koufax's 349th victim.

"Uecker was hitting in front of me," Shannon said. "And he had two strikes on him and he's trying to do anything but strike out. He's taking half swings and stuff. So finally he strikes out. So as he walks by me, he says, 'Okay, it's your turn, big boy.' And I said, 'Well, I'm going down fighting. I'm not going down like you did.' So I went up there and I took my strikeout and I got a standing ovation from thirty thousand people at Chavez Ravine and I tipped my cap."

Collier reported the next day: "Koufax and Feller have met two or three times socially. A person present at one of the meetings says Feller, a man never noted for tact or diplomacy, embarrassed Koufax by contending that the hitters were better in his day than they are now. . . . When Feller set his record in 1946, many of the established major league hitters had not yet returned from the war and those who had were below form as a result of their diamond layoffs."

Slightly mellowed forty years later, Feller commented: "I'll say only this. He is the best pitcher I ever saw in my lifetime."

The second-to-last game of the regular season was broadcast nationally from Dodger Stadium. Four hundred and twenty miles north in San Francisco, the Giants were facing the Reds. If the Giants won and the Dodgers lost, a play-off would decide the pennant. Again, Koufax pitched on two days' rest. Alston was hesitant to start him. Doc Anderson prevailed upon him in a closed-door meeting prior to the game to allow Koufax to pitch.

The Dodgers, the weakest-hitting championship team in the modern era, scored three runs—two on bases-loaded walks and another on a wild pitch. Koufax allowed one run on four hits, striking out thirteen, and the Dodgers won their most improbable pennant. "I've never seen him that tired before," Roseboro said. "He pitched the last four innings on nothing but guts."

Sometime in August, Collier wasn't sure exactly when, Koufax asked him to hang around the locker room after the other reporters had gone. "We went into the clubhouse lunchroom at the front end of the Dodger clubhouse," Collier said. "He says, 'I made a very important decision tonight. Next year is going to be my last.' I said, 'Oh, my God, that's going to be a helluva story.' He said, 'If you won't tell anybody, I won't.'"

Collier kept Koufax's confidence, sitting on the biggest story of his career for more than a year. He wrote a draft of the piece and locked it away in his desk. But he saw what the medicine was doing to Koufax.

"Because of the Bute," Collier said, "he had to eat four or five meals a day just to keep his stomach from rotting out. He took codeine before he pitched. Because of the codeine, it affected his reaction time. He was afraid sooner or later someone was going to hit him in the head with a line drive."

In years to come, many young pitchers would try to emulate Koufax's grand overhand motion, how his arm looked like the cathedral at Chartres rising out of the mist. They quickly understood why it hurt as it did. Among them was thirteen-year-old Al Meyers, who took Koufax's autobiography out of the library in hopes of mastering the curve, and never returned it. He never threw the curve, either. It hurt too much.

By the seventeenth hole at Shadow Ridge, the gallery following Koufax had thinned to a hardy scrum, Meyers and two oily-looking guys lugging equipment bags full of athletic memorabilia not yet signed. His surgically repaired knee was beginning to bother him and he was looking forward to refreshments at the nineteenth hole. On the last tee, Meyers finally summoned the courage to ask Koufax for an autograph for his dad.

Having signed every ball and magazine cover proffered, Koufax was about to sign his scorecard when he noticed one of the autograph merchants arming local boys with cases of balls, promising they could keep one for every three they got signed. "You're a professional," Koufax said to the bleach-blond stalker. "You changed your clothes. You didn't have a cane before."

"You smartin' off at me?" the stalker replied, shaking his cane for effect. "You want to see my medical records?"

Koufax limped off down the fairway rather than lose his temper. Meyers was glad he had never returned the book to the library.

Chapter 16

THE SEVENTH INNING

In their respective dugouts, benchwarmers John Kennedy and Joey Amalfitano contemplated the immediate future. "JK," as he was known by his teammates, was a late-inning defensive replacement for Junior Gilliam at third base. Kennedy's sole reason for being on the roster was to provide a defensive edge, to help maintain an invariably slim lead. *Oh, my God, I've gotta go in there and he's got a perfect game going,* he thought. *Am I gonna screw this thing up for him?*

Across the field, Joey A. was hoping for the chance. He was described in Chicago's newspapers as the Cubs' "best emergency swinger." Twice before he'd come to bat in the ninth inning of a no-hit game. Twice he had done nothing to spoil the occasion. Twice before this season, he had successfully pinch-hit against Koufax. He knew he would hit in the ninth.

Koufax always wanted to pitch a perfect game. But perfection is relative. If he was working on a ten-hitter, perfection meant not giving up the eleventh hit. If he surrendered two first-inning home runs as he had earlier in the year in Pittsburgh, perfection meant no more scoring. Torborg was catching that night, too. Alston blamed him for the two home runs. He was convinced that the tendons in Torborg's arm wiggled when he called for a curve and ordered the young catcher to change into one of Koufax's atomic-balmed sweatshirts. It felt like he was being electrocuted. Torborg told himself he'd better learn to do things right or be burnt alive.

Now, Koufax needed only nine more outs for a perfect perfect game. The stadium was amped; Torborg was gunned up. As Don Young came to bat in the top of the seventh inning, Torborg promised himself nothing was going to happen around the plate to cost Koufax his chance.

The game was only one hour and eleven minutes old. Quick, Danny Ozark thought, as he returned to the first base coaching box. Everybody's swinging. Nobody's walking nobody.

Koufax threw one nervous pitch that sailed past Young and went all the way to the backstop, betraying his anxiety; when the next batter, Beckert, hit a timid fly ball to right, fans gasped, betraying theirs.

"Two down, Billy Williams coming up," Doggett said calmly. "He has struck out twice."

Torborg called for a curve and then another one. Both were low, the first bouncing in the dirt. When a 2-and-0 fastball sailed high, Doggett said, "Koufax is really in the hole now." The next two pitches were fastballs right down the middle of the plate; cripples, pitchers call them. Williams allowed one to go by and fouled off another. The count was full.

You don't get to Cooperstown by just standing there. Williams swung late at a third calling-card fastball, flying tepidly to left for the final out. Well, now, maybe there's a chance, Koufax thought as he left the field.

It was the first time he had gone this deep into a no-hitter without being reminded of it. Sometimes, an opposing coach will mention it, as Solly Hemus did (every chance he got) during the 1962 game against the Mets. Sometimes, a guy will make a rookie mistake, as Dick Calmus had when he stood up in the dugout to applaud in 1963 and Leo Durocher told him to sit down and shuddup. Sometimes, a pitcher will break the silence himself. *Okay, let's knock this off, I know what's going on.* Koufax didn't do that. And no one said a word to him about it. No one talked to him at all.

No one said anything to Hendley either. It wasn't a matter of superstition. What was there to say? He was pitching a no-hitter and losing 1–0. He was vying not just with Koufax but with the memory of his former self. In 1961, he was a fireballing young lefty, "a big old country boy who could just turn it loose." The previous season in Triple A, he won sixteen games, including the final game of the Little World Series. He was sure his time had come. He spent the off-season in the Army at Fort Knox and reported late to the Braves' spring training camp. His first day on the mound, he felt something pop in his elbow. "Like a string snapped," he would recall. "I just went too quick. I was not ready. We did a lot of strength things in the Army, pull-up types of things. Probably had something to do with it. The next day was the real problem because my elbow was like a balloon. They sent me to the team doctor in Milwaukee. He said it was a strain and with time it would heal."

By the time he was called up to the majors in June 1961, he was a completely different pitcher. He tried not to think about the fastball he once had, the curve he once threw. He came up with a compensating repertoire: a slider, a slip pitch, a knuckle curve. He knew all too well what it meant to stay within himself. He had adjusted.

As he took his warm-up pitches, Helen Dell, the Dodger Stadium organist, tried to interest Dodger fans in the Mexican Hat Dance. But they were thinking about only one thing: the first potential double no-hitter since 1917, when "Hippo" Vaughn of the Cubs and Fred Toney of the Reds each pitched nine innings of no-hit ball. "Bob, who had to go out to Salt Lake City in midseason to try to regain his pitching form, apparently found it out there," Doggett said. "Hendley's pitching one of the finest games we've ever seen him pitch against the Dodgers, and he's pitched some good ones, especially when he was with Milwaukee."

Once before, when he was with the Braves, Hendley had taken a no-hitter this far into the night. In the ninth inning, someone hit a slow roller to Frank Bolling at second, who threw the ball away. Then Curt Flood hit a triple. Hendley gave up one earned run and won 9–3. Everyone in Dodger Stadium was rooting for him to get this no-hitter—including Walter O'Malley. Now that his boys had a run, it was okay to cheer for baseball.

There were two outs in the bottom of the seventh when Lou Johnson came to the plate, not sure what to look for. It wasn't this. Hendley threw him a letup of an off-speed slip pitch. Johnson reached out and poked the ball toward right field, a ball so poorly hit it seemed in slow motion. Hendley watched aghast as it landed just beyond the second baseman, Beckert, and just out of reach of Banks at first. The ball barely carried to the outfield grass, hit in fair territory, and trickled across the foul line. By the time Banks retrieved it, Johnson was at second.

It was variously described as a bloop, a flare, a humpbacked liner, just one of those things. "A duck fart," Krug's friend Gary Adams called it. In the scorecard, it was a double. Hendley allowed himself a moment of disappointment, backing off the mound, pausing a few extra seconds between pitches, trying to put the what-if behind him. The no-hitter's gone, he told himself. I can't bring it back. I can only face what's in front of me.

Which was: Johnson on second with Fairly at the plate, the Cubs down by a run. What was required was a kind of tunnel vision that admitted neither the past nor the future. He had to ignore the voice inside telling him it was Koufax's night. But it was hard and he fell behind in the count, three balls and one strike. He reminded himself to do his job, stay in the present, prevent the run from scoring.

He got Fairly to bounce out to short—a routine play that was for him anything but routine. History and Sweet Lou were left stranded at second base.

Chapter 17

KING OF THE JEWS

ZABAR'S, THE FOOD EMPORIUM ON MANHATTAN'S WEST SIDE, isn't just a delicatessen. It is a Jewish institution, a locus of ethnic tastes and smells, aspirations and celebrations that can be traced back to King David. Smoked salmon (fifteen varieties, not including seasonal designer salmons) and creamed herring! Bagels and bialys! And on Friday nights fresh-baked challah.

The aisles at Zabar's are always crowded before sundown on Friday like a Reform synagogue on the High Holidays. Observant Jews hurrying home for Sabbath vie for the counterman's attention. One such Friday evening, George Blumenthal, a New Yorker who made his fortune early in the cellular phone revolution, edged his way through the crowd, a cardboard box from Air Express under his arm. Inside was Sandy Koufax's 1955 rookie jersey: road gray, "Hall of Fame Flannel," size 44, with the name Koufax stitched in red script. Just below the tail of the "s" on Dodgers was an inky inscription: "My first uniform, 1955, Sandy Koufax, 11/22/89."

Blumenthal, chairman of NTL Inc., purchased it at auction for $25,000. He is a fan, certainly, the son of Holocaust survivors. He grew up in Cleveland playing bad baseball. He owns Hank Greenberg's rookie jersey and Shawn Green's, too. For him, Koufax's uniform was no mere totem. It was an investment in the preservation of his faith. He would use it as a fund-raising tool in a campaign to build the Center for Jewish History.

"So, I'm in Zabar's," Blumenthal said. "I give this woman a Sandy Koufax ball. Big deal, these things go for seventy-five dollars. I've got tons of them. I give 'em away. A fella standing next to me says, 'Sandy Koufax? Sandy Koufax!' He starts talking about Koufax. I said, 'Wait a second, I have Sandy Koufax's uniform right here. Let me take a picture of you.' These people are levitating. This man is so symbolic.

"This is what I do. I go around with the shirt and people write me checks. Sometimes I get a hundred thousand dollars, sometimes a hundred. What I do is I go around and ask these people, 'What is the importance of Sandy Koufax?' Then I take out this rumpled shirt from an Air Express box and say, 'Here, put it on.' And they give me money. I've sold it twenty to thirty times over. I told Mel Brooks, 'I've sold this thing five thousand percent.'"

He's got the snapshots to prove it: a stack of glossy three-by-fives featuring captains of industry with Koufax's rookie jersey draped over their shoulders like a prayer shawl. "This guy—a hundred thousand dollars," Blumenthal said, flipping through a stack pictures. "This guy, a hundred thousand." He's raised over $2 million this way.

It isn't the money that's impressive. It's the faces: aging, wealthy, accomplished men—industrialists and bankers, investors and mergers-and-acquisitions specialists, capitalists all. These balding, concave-chested bar-mitzvah boys put on Sandy Koufax's uniform and *kvell*. They are transformed.

Yom Kippur is the holiest day of the Jewish calendar, the Day of Atonement. Those who repent their sins are inscribed in the Book of Life. On October 6, 1965, Koufax was inscribed forever in the Book of Life as the Jew who refused to pitch on Yom Kippur. Bruce Lustig, who would grow up to be the senior rabbi at the Washington Hebrew Congregation in Washington, D.C., was seven years old and attending services in Tennessee with his parents that day. He took a transistor radio with him, the wire running up the inside of his starched white shirt. When the rabbi called upon the congregants to stand and pray, the earpiece came loose and the voice of Vin Scully crackled through the sanctuary. His mother walloped him with her purse and banished him to the synagogue library, where the television was tuned to NBC's coverage of the game. Live and in color when live and in color was something to brag about.

The Dodgers lost but Koufax won. In that moment, he became known as much for what he refused to do as for what he did on the mound. By refusing to pitch, Koufax defined himself as a man of principle who placed faith above craft. He became inextricably linked with the American Jewish experience. As John Goodman put it in the movie *The Big Lebowski*: "Three thousand years of beautiful tradition: from Moses to Sandy Koufax."

In Jewish households, he was the New Patriarch: Abraham, Isaac, Jacob, and Sand*ee*. A moral exemplar, and single too! (Such a catch!) He was every Jewish mother's dream, and some with eligible daughters didn't hesitate to say so. During the 1966 World Series in Baltimore, one very determined matron got his roommate, Norm Sherry, on the phone. "I vant to talk to Sandy. I got a lovely daughter I vant him to meet."

Jewish mothers with sons were equally enthralled. Kenny Holtzman faced Koufax at Wrigley Field in September 1966, the day after Yom Kippur. They had moved their scheduled starts back a day so they could attend services. There had even been some discussion, Holtzman recalls, about going to synagogue together. A TV producer at WGN took Holtzman's family to his temple, where Kenny prayed he would beat the sonofabitch the next day. His mother prayed for guidance about whom to root for. "He was every Jewish mother's idol and now he's pitching against her son," Holtzman said. "Clearly, she didn't want anyone to lose. I said, 'But, Mother, one of us has to lose.' She said, 'Maybe you can get a no-decision.'"

Dr. Jonas Salk volunteered to procure tickets for Koufax, making the offer through coach Danny Ozark. Salk—whom Ozark refers to as "the polio guy"—presented the Catholic coach with a religious medal in honor of the occasion. It had Saint Christopher on one side and the Star of David on the other. "When you go to see the Jews, turn it over," Salk told him.

The next day, Holtzman's mother and his girlfriend, and her best friend, president of the Sandy Koufax Fan Club at the University of Illinois–Champaign, were in the stands watching as Kenny held the Dodgers hitless for eight innings. Mrs. Holtzman's son won; her hero lost. She told Kenny she had decided to root for him to be just like Koufax.

A bumper sticker from the era proclaimed: "You don't have to be Jewish to love Sandy." His predominantly Christian colleagues admired his chutzpah. For them, the decision not to pitch was a political act, one that would not have been tolerated from a .500 pitcher, one that sent a message to baseball's hierarchy. As Jim Bunning put it, "We have our rights and my choice is not to play on Yom Kippur." The political subtext did not go unnoticed among the generation of Baby Boomers who would grow old still thinking of themselves as sixties kids. To Charley Steiner, a sixteen-year-old growing up on Long Island, it was "a quintessential sixties move. And it predated Ali and the draft. For Jewish teenagers, it was like, 'Wow.' "

He was an object lesson to bar mitzvah boys (reform, conservative, and orthodox), a standard to which Jewish parents held their children, as well as a measuring stick of their assimilation into American culture. In the Brooklyn yeshiva where Alan Dershowitz studied as a boy, they discussed his parentage with Talmudic fervor. They heard he was adopted but (thank God!) Jewish by birth. "That's all we ever cared about. We wanted to make sure we can claim our rights."

The Jewish community laid claim to him, ascribing to him a religiosity he never acknowledged or displayed. "Did you know the day he blossomed was the evening of the day Adolf Eichmann was captured?" Buddy Silverman, editor of *The Jewish Athletes Hall of Fame*, asks breathlessly. He is referring to May 23, 1960, when Koufax threw his first one-hitter. "Before that, his record was twenty-eight and thirty-one. From that point on, one thirty-seven and fifty-six! Whether it was a swelling of pride, I don't know. Is that crazy? What do you think?"

Koufax remains a touchstone for measuring the progress of the Chosen People in the New World. When Senator Joseph Lieberman became the first Jewish American to be named to a national political ticket in 2000, a columnist in the *New York Times* dubbed him "the Sandy Koufax of politics." As filmmaker Aviva Kempner traveled the country promoting her loving film tribute, *The Life and Times of Hank Greenberg*, the question she was asked most often was "What about Sandy?"

He could not have calculated the effect his reflexive decision would have on his private life or what it would mean to others. Strangers in steak houses, delicatessens, public rest rooms, and funeral homes wanted to thank him, touch him. A couple of years ago, Koufax and his friend Tom Villante attended the funeral of Herbie Scharfman, the old Dodger photographer, in Fort Lauderdale. "This lady grabs his right hand," Villante recalled. "She's saying, 'I can't believe I'm with Sandy Koufax. All the things you've done.' I said, 'Lady, you ought to take his other hand. He's done more with that.'"

Until October 6, 1965, he was "a ballplayer, a terrific ballplayer," Villante said. "When that happened, he transcended being a player and became a symbol." A symbol who understands better than anyone else Portnoy's anguished complaint in Philip Roth's novel: "Oh, to be a center fielder, a center fielder—and nothing more! But I am something more, or so they tell me. A Jew."

Among the cognoscenti, and there are many of them, there is general agreement that there are 140 to 150 Jews to be found in the fine print of the *Baseball Encyclopedia*. It depends whether you count converts and when they converted. Standards vary. There were four Cohens (Alta, Andy, Hy, and Sid) who kept their last name and at least three others who changed it. Jesse Eugene Baker was born Michael Myron Silverman. There was a Rabbi of Swat and even a Chosen catcher—Harry Chozen, who caught one game for the Cincinnati Reds in 1937.

Koufax set no precedents as did Lipman Pike, the first Jewish major leaguer, who was also among the first ballplayers to be paid for his craft, accepting twenty dollars a week from the Philadelphia Athletics in 1876. Or Barney Dreyfuss, owner of the Pittsburgh Pirates, and father of the modern world series. Or the tunesmith who coauthored "Take Me Out to the Ballgame"—who had never been to one. Nor was Koufax the first prominent Jewish player to confront the dilemma posed by the High Holidays, which annually conflict with baseball's most important games.

In the World War II era, every home run Hank Greenberg hit for the Detroit Tigers was a potent retort to the image of Jews passively accepting Hitler's chosen fate for them. When, in the midst of the 1934 pennant race, Greenberg played on Rosh Hashanah and hit two home runs, he was saluted by the *Detroit Free Press* in a front-page encomium: "And, so to you, Mr. Greenberg, the Tiger fans say, 'Leshono tovo tikosayvu!' which means 'Happy New Year.'" No one objected when he chose not to play a week later on Yom Kippur, the more solemn day of observance.

Harry Eisenstat, a Brooklyn boy, who pitched for the Dodgers the year Koufax was born, roomed with Greenberg in Detroit. He and Koufax have never met. "The closest I ever got to him was Bensonhurst," Eisenstat says. "I was very proud we didn't play on Yom Kippur. For Rosh Hashanah we got a special dispensation from the rabbi. It was a case of letting the team down and not putting one individual player's interests above the other twenty-four. Because it involved twenty-four other players, the rabbi felt it was okay."

On Rosh Hashanah in 1936, when Eisenstat was still with the Dodgers, he was in uniform but not expecting to pitch. Turned out his teammates needed him more than God. Summoned to the mound, he gave up a grand slam on the first pitch. Harry inferred no displeasure from above. "Nah," he said. "I should have made a better pitch."

Koufax and Greenberg, New York City boys born a generation apart, are linked symbolically and by the fact that neither was an observant Jew. (They met only once or twice; Greenberg drove in 170 runs the year Koufax was born.) Shawn Green, the young outfielder who invoked Koufax's example when he signed with the Dodgers in 1998, also grew up in an assimilated family (they dropped the "berg" from their last name two generations before). Shawn was an adult, a multimillionaire, a Dodger, before he learned that his father had a collection of Koufax memorabilia in the attic.

Nearly forty years after he retired, Koufax still resonates with the American Jewish community, inspiring artists like Deborah Kass to render his likeness in the pop art style of Andy Warhol—an iconic treatment reserved for the likes of Marilyn Monroe. (Kass also claims she is a distant cousin.) He endures in image and imagination far longer than he did as an athlete.

Because, Rabbi Lustig argues, in his quiet, assiduous, and thoroughly unintentional way, Koufax broke all the rules. "Think of the stereotype of the Jew in literature, the ugly avariciousness of Shylock," Lustig said. "He broke so many of them. Here was a good-looking Jew, a lefty, very powerful on the mound; a perfect player, an enigma, a man who didn't reach for fame or money. He broadened the concept of what a Jew is."

It had been a long season. With Tommy Davis hurt and Drysdale and Wills hurting, Koufax carried the 1965 Dodgers toward an improbable pennant on his fragile left arm. It did not go unnoticed, even by the squash-playing editors of *Time* magazine, who assigned Bill McWhirter, a young staffer in the L.A. bureau, to report a cover story on Koufax. McWhirter was an odd choice, given his rawness as a reporter and his disinclination for baseball. Baseball was part of the old East Coast establishment culture he had come west to forget. California was happening. Baseball was not. Still, it was a cover story, his first.

McWhirter remembers:

"Things were simple then. There was no go-between, no agents, no such thing as p.r. I went to the Dodgers and asked them about it. They said, 'There's Koufax, go ask him.' I was so new, so young, I didn't know enough to be awed by Koufax. It wasn't like my knees were shaking. I was more impressed that *Time* wanted to do a cover on Koufax than I was by Koufax himself. I went up to him and he said, 'No, I don't think that's a very good idea. I really don't think I want to do it.'

"There was no negotiation, no second appeal. I was stopped in my tracks. Then he said, 'Of course, if you want to do it, go ahead.' He gave me a few names, including the Berles, who were friends, and some women he had dated. I couldn't imagine anyone turning down a cover."

McWhirter interviewed the women (he remembers them as "bit-part babes") and the friends and came away with the distinct impression that none of them had a clue who Koufax was. Wills, a clubhouse confidant, says even now: "There was so much depth there, and complexity too. He's still a mystery to a lot of us."

The conventions of news weekly journalism, as practiced in the mid-1960s, made no allowance for a subject this elusive, this multidimensional. "I knew I had an incredible story about an incredible guy who wasn't going to talk to me," McWhirter said. "It was almost like he vaporized after games. When he put on the uniform he was Sandy Koufax. When he took it off, he was a shadow man."

In the received wisdom of the time, Koufax was sublime but unhappy, the tortured artist of the pitching mound. "A captive of baseball, trapped by his talent and his instincts," Jim Murray wrote in the *Los Angeles Times*. Of course, he *was* tortured, but not in ways he ever acknowledged. Even his teammates had no idea the pain he was in. But, that wasn't the writerly implication. Koufax was tortured with a gift of a miraculous left arm that compelled him to do something he really didn't like. He would have been happier as a doctor, a lawyer. He was a nice Jewish boy. In a word, different.

The novelist E. L. Doctorow has written: "Of all the varieties of anti-Semitism, this is perhaps the most discreetly structural in form— the lingering widespread assumption of the irreducible otherness of someone of the Jewish faith."

The pigeonholing of Koufax began early. In a column written the day Koufax signed with the Dodgers, Jimmy Cannon lamented his lack of exuberance, describing him as "courteous and aloof." A spring training story written by Bill Roeder of the *New York Herald Tribune* on March 4, 1955, bore the headline "Koufax, Unorthodox, Reads Books," and mentioned that he might go back to school and study architecture if baseball didn't work out. Two weeks later, the *New York Post* reiterated the refrain, describing him as having "both feet on the ground, except he reads books and stuff like that." That theme and expectation followed him throughout his career. Thus: "Sandy Koufax belongs in baseball about the way Albert Schweitzer belongs in a twist joint," Murray wrote in 1963.

That which made him different became subject to interpretation and reinterpretation. Oh, sure, he played golf like everyone else. But he invested his money in real estate and in a radio station, KNJO, 92.7 on your dial, the first station built for stereo in Southern California. He admitted to reading *The Rise and Fall of the Third Reich* and listening to classical music—and regretted it because no one seemed to believe he also read best-sellers; that he listened to Sinatra as well as Beethoven.

He avoided Baseball Annies and compromising positions. ("He wants a wife, not a fan," Murray wrote.) He lived alone. He hated talking on the telephone, so much so, it was said, he hid the phone in the oven or had the ringer removed. It was also reported that the Dodger front office had to send telegrams when they wanted to get in touch with him. Though he was a heavy smoker and the surgeon general's report on tobacco hadn't yet been released, he would not be photographed smoking a cigarette. In an era when caution labels were not yet required reading, he refused to endorse either tobacco or alcohol. He did a sweater ad. He owned a piece of a motel on the Sunset Strip, Sandy Koufax's Tropicana Inn.

Once, in 1963, he vented his frustration publicly to Milton Gross, a sports columnist for the *New York Post:* "I'm just a normal twenty-seven-year-old bachelor who happens to be of the Jewish faith. I like nice clothes. I like comfort. I like to read a book and listen to music and I'd like to meet the girl I'd want to marry. That's normal, isn't it?

"You know the old stuff they keep writing about, that I read Huxley and Thomas Mann. I'm supposed to be an egghead. I may have read Huxley once in my life, but if I did, frankly, I don't remember. I like to read the latest fiction, nonfiction."

On the mound, he was different too. *Koufax don't throw at nobody. He don't need to throw at nobody.* That was the refrain. He wasn't one of the guys Brooks Robinson had in mind when he said: "Your heart's in it but your rear end isn't." Gibson, Marichal, and Drysdale left .300 hitters sleep-deprived. Hitters didn't fear Koufax; they feared being embarrassed by him. "Nobody could undress you the way Sandy could," Gene Mauch liked to say.

Koufax was a purist. "Too nice to be so great," Wills always said. Unlike Drysdale, who glowered for effect and exploited his reputation for all it was worth, Koufax burned inwardly. Jeff Torborg thought his eyes might just burn right through his head.

More than one of his African-American peers attributed Koufax's rectitude and reticence to his being a minority. "Stayin' right in his own house," as Lou Johnson put it, knowing he would be held to a higher standard. Perhaps Johnson was projecting. But if Koufax had been a White Anglo-Saxon Protestant who played clean and kept his nose clean, he'd have been proclaimed the second coming of Jack Armstrong. But he was a Jew. So he was moody, aloof, curt, intellectual, different.

His portrait hangs in the L.A. County Museum. The painting, by the esteemed Jewish artist R. B. Kitaj, is striking for several reasons: Among them it does not attempt to make him beautiful. The artist chose to illuminate duress, that portion of his delivery when his chest preceded his lower body and his elbow, cocked to a breaking point, trailed behind him like the tail of a kite. The squinched eyes, pursed lips, and skin drawn taut by effort, even the distorted maw of his glove make palpable his exertion. The artist's palette is equally thought-provoking. Hues of muted peach inform the fabric of his uniform; his cap and arm a fiery orange. They leap from the pastel blue background of the sky. The choice of color is eclectic and disconcerting. It is not the color of baseball, decidedly not Dodger blue. It is, in fact, a perfect rendering of his Otherness. What baseball executive Dick Cecil calls "the mysterious Hebrew."

At the heart of any bias lies inchoate assumptions, the stereotypes to which we unconsciously yield. Thus: Jewish men are nebbishes or wise men, shylocks or scholars, concave-chested specimens with two left feet who walked to Hitler's ovens rather than resist their fate. The stereotype is expressed in seventeenth-century European monographs and twenty-first-century on-line Haiku. "Seven-foot Jews/in the NBA slam-dunking!/My alarm clock rings." Early-twentieth-century Zionist leaders advocated a new "muscular Judaism" to counter such bias. This did not deter Henry Ford, America's best-known anti-Semite, who declared in 1921: "Jews are not sportsmen. Whether this is due to their physical lethargy, their dislike of unnecessary physical action, or their serious cast of mind, others may decide. . . . It may be a defect in their character, or it may not; it is nevertheless a fact which discriminating Jews unhesitatingly acknowledge."

In this regard, two incidents from the 1965 season are particularly revealing. On May 26, Koufax faced the Cardinals and his nemesis, Lou Brock, in Los Angeles. In the first inning, Brock led off with a bunt single, stole second, stole third, and scored on a sacrifice fly. In the dugout, Drysdale told rookie Jim Lefebvre: "Frenchie, I feel sorry for that man."

When Brock came up again in the third, Koufax hit him hard and with intent. "So darned hard that the ball went in and spun around in the meat for a while and then dropped," catcher Jeff Torborg said.

It was the first time, the only time, Koufax threw at a batter purposefully. He didn't brag about it. He didn't tell anyone he was going to do it. He didn't acknowledge it until long after his career had ended. "I don't regret it," he told fans more than a quarter century later. "I do regret that I allowed myself to get so mad."

You could hear it all over the stadium. In the Cardinals' dugout, it sounded like "a thud that had a crack in it," outfielder Mike Shannon said. Other Cardinal players insist Brock was hurt doing the limbo prior to the game. Drysdale would remember, wrongly, Brock collapsing in the base path and being carried off the field, a story he loved to tell because for once Koufax wasn't perfect. In fact, Brock stayed in the game and promptly stole second. The morning papers reported the incident in passing, noting that Brock left in the fifth inning and that X rays were negative. He appeared only once in the next five days, as a pinch runner.

Three months later, the simmering violence of a savage summer erupted in Candlestick Park. Koufax was pitching for the Dodgers; Marichal for the Giants. It had been a season of enmity between the two teams, a series fraught with knockdown pitches and threats. On August 22, bad blood turned to spilled blood. Marichal, practiced in the art of intimidation, had already decked Fairly and Wills. Roseboro was equally adept in the subtleties of retribution. When Marichal came to the plate, Roseboro purposefully allowed Koufax's 1-and-2 pitch to drop at his feet, whizzing the return throw just east of Marichal's ear.

Marichal raised the stakes when he lifted his bat and cracked it over Roseboro's head, leaving a two-inch gash in his skull and an enduring dent in baseball's beatific reputation. Koufax and Mays rushed to intervene. Koufax tried to grab the bat. The anguish was visible on his face as he raised his hand to prevent another blow. Mays dragged Roseboro away, stanching the blood and the violence, assuring him the wound wasn't as bad as it seemed. Shag Crawford, the home plate umpire, still refuses to talk about it. (Roseboro sued Marichal for $110,000, yet another unwelcome harbinger of the modern age. Nine years later, the suit was settled out of court and later still they became friends. Roseboro was one of the first people Marichal called when he was elected to the Hall of Fame.)

In the telling and retelling of the tale, Koufax, the pacifist, allows Roseboro, the tough black enforcer, to take care of business. "We had talked about it on the bench," Roseboro said. "I told him, 'I'll take care of it, knock him down behind the plate.' " Which is true as far as it goes. What Roseboro's account leaves out, others who heard the dugout conversation say, is that Koufax prefaced his remarks with the pertinent question: "Who do you want me to get?" Also, the dugouts had been warned by Crawford. A knockdown would have resulted in Koufax's suspension in the middle of the pennant race.

The legend, as handed down, reinforced the already established notion that Koufax wouldn't knock anyone on his ass, wouldn't protect his players. In the machismo-driven world of professional athletics, this was not a compliment. It also wasn't true. Koufax believed in protecting his players; he just didn't believe in throwing at someone he couldn't get out. In 1962, when Bill Skowron was still a Yankee, he made Marichal look bad in the world series. Next season, Moose was a Dodger. "First time up, he low-bridged me," Skowron said. "I'm hitting like two-twenty. I go back to first base. Willie Mays comes up. Sandy threw one up tight and Willie's cap flew off. They said Sandy didn't throw at anyone, but he protected his players. I blew him a kiss."

Nor did he disdain throwing inside. "The art of pitching is instilling fear," he always said. Wise batsmen avoided crowding his plate. Shannon still regrets a game-winning two-run home run he hit off Koufax in 1966—and the inside fastball he saw next time up. "I think you pissed the big Jew off," Roseboro told him.

When order was restored at Candlestick Park on Sunday, August 22, 1965, a rattled Koufax walked the next two batters he faced and gave up a three-run home run to Mays. "The only time I ever beat him with one," Mays said.

Koufax was stuck with a loss and a reputation. "Everybody else was a competitor," he would lament to friends. Perhaps that explained the gleeful, uninhibited smile that came over his face when he was asked years later about hitting Brock intentionally. "I didn't nail him in the shoulder," he said. "It was in the ribs."

When, on September 9, 1965, Major League Baseball announced that the world series would open on October 6 in the American League city, it wasn't at all clear that the Dodgers would be in it. But as they won eighteen of their last twenty-two games, headlines began to appear: "Koufax Problem: Jewish Holiday." Koufax told reporters, lightly, "I'm praying for rain." He also said he would consult the rabbis (as Greenberg had done) to discuss a dispensation. He was joking. He never intended to pitch on Yom Kippur. He never had.

In the early Brooklyn days, management encouraged him to take off on Jewish holidays. It was a demonstration of good faith to their heavily Jewish fan base. And, given how much he was contributing, Koufax later said, "They were probably glad I was gone."

Alan Dershowitz, who knew him as a neighborhood legend, recalls the scene outside one Brooklyn synagogue when Koufax showed up for services with his father. He remembers people cheering and rumors spreading that Koufax had been called to the Torah. When they met in later life, Koufax told him it never happened.

Twice, in the fall of 1960 and 1961, manager Walter Alston scheduled him to pitch on Jewish holidays. An hour after sundown marks the end of holiday observances in the Jewish faith. On September 20, 1961, after sundown, Koufax went to the mound and beat the Cubs 3–2 in thirteen innings, striking out fifteen. Soon after, a fan sent Alston a 1962 calendar marked with all the Jewish holidays. From then on, the manager made sure to consult Danny Goodman, director of advertising and novelties, before making out his starting rotation.

Far from being distraught over Koufax's willingness to pitch that evening—even if it meant missing afternoon services—Jewish authors of present-day on-line encomiums salute his toughness. Imagine pitching thirteen innings without eating or drinking! His observance of the fast is assumed without a shred of documentary evidence.

Koufax was presumptively devout. Teammates still testify to the strength of his faith. "Like Muhammad Ali's," Lou Johnson said. "His Jewish belief was bigger than the game." How else could they understand his decision not to pitch on Yom Kippur except as a reflection of compelling belief? Why else would anyone voluntarily skip the world series? Others needled him about getting religion only after he got famous. "I used to jokingly say that Sandy didn't become Jewish until he had his first great years," Stan Williams said.

Their assumptions were rooted in ignorance. In fact, like Greenberg, Koufax was neither a devout nor a practicing Jew. "His Jewishness has nothing to do with whether he wears a yarmulke every day," Fred Wilpon said. "And I will tell you this—he is very Jewish. He is a Jewish being. And unlike most of us who aren't very religious, he is very Jewish in his thinking because he's very New York in his thinking and his background."

It's a sensibility. To wit: One night in Philadelphia, Koufax and the Sherry brothers went out for Chinese food. They got in a cab and told the driver to take them to a good place. Norm Sherry remembers: "The cab pulls up at a restaurant and Koufax says, 'This is not where I want to eat.'" So, the cabbie takes them to another and another and another. "Finally, Koufax says, 'This is okay.' Larry says, 'What the hell is the difference?' Koufax says, 'You don't go to a Chinese restaurant unless it has an awning like they have in New York. It's gotta have an awning.'"

The Jewish boys from Southern California didn't get the humor.

He never spoke publicly about religion except to acknowledge his Jewishness, no small fact. After years of traveling with Koufax, Phil Collier could not recall a single conversation on the subject until one day at Los Angeles International Airport when a fan interrupted Koufax at a urinal to ask, "Would you mind settling an argument for me?"

"Sandy said, 'No, I don't mind.'

"The guy waited until we washed up. I swear to God, we walked halfway across the terminal. He introduces us to five or six people. He says to Sandy, 'Are you Jewish? I bet money you're Jewish.'

"I wanted to knock the guy on his ass, dragging him across the airport for that. Sandy couldn't have been nicer about it. He said, 'Yes, I am. It was nice to meet all of you. I hope you'll forgive us. We have a plane to catch.'"

Yom Kippur is a day of denial. It is why Jews fast. In fact, Koufax's sacrifice was greater than his teammates knew. Rabbi Hillel Silverman, who annually invoked Koufax's name in his Yom Kippur sermon, spoke with him about it once. "He said to me, 'I'm Jewish. I'm a role model. I want them to understand they have to have pride.' Not being observant and feeling a connection with his people, it's an even greater sacrifice."

The morning of the opening game of the 1965 World Series, the *St. Paul Pioneer Press* carried the following dispatch:

Sandy Notes Holy Day

Dodger pitcher Sandy Koufax left the team's Hotel St. Paul quarters Tuesday evening to begin the 24 hour observance of Yom Kippur, the Jewish Day of Atonement. He planned to spend the night with friends in suburban Minneapolis, will attend services today and rejoin the team tonight for his starting assignment in Thursday's second game of the world series. He was asked whether he would view today's game on television or listen to radio accounts. "No," he said. "I don't think that's possible."

He was apocryphally seen at synagogues throughout the Twin Cities—and even in Los Angeles. Bonnie Goldstein, now a private investigator in Washington, D.C., was a young congregant at the Temple of Aaron in St. Paul, the synagogue closest to the ballpark. The crowd was strictly standing room only and unusually devout that day in deference to Koufax. "Everyone was in their chairs," she said. "None of the usual restlessness. There was so much speculation. Is that him? People who weren't Sandy Koufax were getting a lot of attention.

"Everyone agrees he was at the early service. Nobody got up and left. I was much more interested in boys than Sandy Koufax. But the boys were more interested in Sandy Koufax so I was a little interested."

The rabbi, Bernard Raskas, waited until afternoon services to address the issue, affirming to the congregation that Koufax had been there, seated in back, near an exit. In Raskas's recollection, they nodded to each other, the rabbi noting the pitcher's nice head of hair. He did not want to infringe on the pitcher's privacy. Nor did he want to make an example of him. After all, Koufax wasn't so observant.

In fact, Koufax did not attend services there that day or anywhere else. A friend may well have made arrangements for Koufax to attend as Raskas was led to believe. But friends say he chose to stay alone in his hotel room. Raskas could not have seen him unless he was the room service waiter at midnight. Koufax never publicly contradicted the stories. He never commented at all—except for a mild written rebuke, in his autobiography, to Minnesota sports columnist Dan Riley, who wrote that the Twins were looking forward to eating matzo balls when Koufax pitched the next day.

Choosing not to work on Yom Kippur was not a difficult decision. It's what Jews do. His roommate, Tracewski, doesn't remember him agonizing over it. "It was a given with him." So, you pitch a day late. Big schmeer. And, as Osteen said, "It wasn't a real bad choice having Drysdale."

Drysdale started in his place and got hammered. The score was 7–1 when Alston came to the mound to relieve him. "Hey, skip, bet you wish I was Jewish today, too," Drysdale said. For Jews, the loss was a win. If Big D could joke about being one of the Chosen People, that was already something, a tacit acknowledgment of their acceptance into the mainstream. *Shtetl*, farewell.

Koufax started and lost game two. The flight back to Los Angeles was difficult, especially for Osteen, who was scheduled to start game three. He sat on the aisle and every coach and player walking by made sure to touch his left shoulder. With each reassuring pat and each pat rejoinder—"You'll get 'em!"—his shoulder got tighter. Koufax and Drysdale loosened everyone up with humor. "Don looks at Sandy and goes, 'Well, we sure got ourselves in a hell of a mess, didn't we?'" Jim Lefebvre said. "And they started laughing."

The Dodgers won three straight in Los Angeles—Osteen, Drysdale, and Koufax outdid themselves and each other. In the final home game of the series, Koufax shut out the Twins, 7–0. After the game, Koufax cheerfully told Scully, "I feel like I'm a hundred years old."

The Dodgers needed only one more win but they needed to go back to Minnesota to get it. They were confident. Lou Johnson packed enough clothes for a one-day business trip. The Dodgers checked out of the team hotel the morning before game six was played. Osteen lost, forcing management to scramble for rooms and Alston to make a difficult decision. Parker, the first baseman, went into the bathroom and cried. Alston summoned his coaches—Preston Gomez, Danny Ozark, Lefty Phillips—to a gloomy tribunal. Drysdale was the logical choice to pitch game seven. It was his turn in the rotation. He would be pitching on a full three days' rest; Koufax on two.

The players were showering; no one had popped a beer. All three coaches put their heads between their knees when Alston broached the question. Ozark recalled the scene. "'Jeez,' Lefty Phillips says, 'Koufax does real well against them, maybe he can go.' Alston says, 'Who's gonna ask him?' Everyone got laryngitis. Me, the big dumb Polack says, 'I'll do it.' I find out later on that there were differences between him and Alston. They may have been going back to '57. I don't think he could overlook what happened. It was his career. They held him back."

His teammates knew how he felt. "He felt he always had something to prove with Walter Alston," Ron Perranoski said. "He wasn't used when he was young and when he was used he wasn't trusted. He always had this thing in the back of his mind about the way he was treated, that he didn't get a chance. He knew what he was made of, what he was capable of."

Those feelings endured. In 1985, thirty years after his rookie season, twenty years after his world series triumph, there was a celebration in Vero Beach. "Buzzie was there and they were telling stories and Buzzie's laughing," Tom Villante recalled. "And then Sandy starts with Buzzie about why the hell didn't Alston pitch me. Buzzie was giving him some double talk but Sandy was getting mad all over again. I'll never forget it. Sandy was transformed into this nineteen-year-old kid again, puzzled why the hell Alston didn't pitch him."

When Ozark approached him at his locker at Metropolitan Stadium on the eve of the seventh game of the 1965 World Series, Koufax told him, "I'm okay for tomorrow." It would be his third start in eight days. "He didn't want to be known as a person who couldn't have the strength and the ability to take the ball on two days' rest," Wilpon said. He did so eight times in his career, winning six; three were complete-game wins with a combined total of thirty-five strikeouts. He never lasted less than seven innings. How much, if at all, this represented for him a refutation of stereotype is unknowable. How much it represented a retort to early doubters is easier to guess. But it spoke volumes to the Jewish community.

Alston told Mel Durslag, the Los Angeles writer, it was the hardest decision he ever made as a manager. Drysdale subsequently made it easier by volunteering to go to the bullpen. "He was worried about Drysdale's feelings and afraid of saying something anti-Semitic," Durslag recalled. "He was an uptight guy, not a loose guy. People intimated—he was a farmer from the middle of Ohio—that he might have been anti-Semitic. Maybe he felt if he didn't give it to Koufax, he'd look anti-Semitic."

The heart of bias is as intangible as it is corrosive. When he was interviewed by Charley Steiner for ESPN's *Sports Century* series, Koufax was asked, off camera, whether he believed anti-Semitism played a part in the way he was used early in his career. "I don't even want to think about that," Koufax replied. It violates his code of honor to argue with the dead or the past. He has never addressed the issue publicly and he won't. But as Steiner, now the voice of the Yankees, says, "When he says he hasn't thought about something, you know he's thought about it a lot."

Others have, too. Eddie Liberatore, the late Dodger scout, said before he died in 2001, "One story I don't like to tell, there were certain guys in the organization who referred to him as 'a gutless Jew' because he was wild. When he got control and began to be a big winner, he was probably the most idolized pitcher of this time. They all jumped on his bandwagon, these same critics."

Among his black teammates a degree of bias was presumed. Like Ozark, they noticed who pitched on Opening Day, whose face appeared on yearbooks and press guides and newspapers. "Don was blond and blue-eyed and more marketable as far as being the Dodger image," Wills said. "Sandy was second fiddle. All the black players felt that. Don was the poster boy: it was always Don and Sandy. We knew it was Sandy and Don."

Rumors started flying on the bus on the way back to the hotel. Coaches, rookies, other members of the pitching staff all weighed in. Opinion was unanimous. "You don't have to ask our ball club, 'Who do you want to see pitch?'" said Gomez. "The whole world is going to say, 'Give the ball to the Jew.'"

Wills: "We might not have gone on the field if he hadn't."

Koufax and Drysdale arrived at the ballpark the next morning unshaved—a signal that neither knew the skipper's decision. In fact, it was a ruse. Koufax knew but wasn't supposed to tell anyone, not even his roommate, Trixie. Alston announced his decision at a team meeting before the game, explaining with soothing if impersonal logic why he had chosen Koufax. "He says, 'We're going to start the left-hander,'" Tracewski remembered. "'After that we have Drysdale in the bullpen and if we need it we'll finish off with Perranoski. And if that's not good enough, we are in trouble.'

"It was a very quiet meeting and it was a very quick meeting and Sandy said, 'He called me the left-hander,'" Tracewski said. "He felt he should have called him by his name."

Watching the videotape of the seventh game of the 1965 World Series is like looking at a piece of American folk art. There is an innocence about the broadcast as primitive as the production values. There were marching bands and decorous cheerleaders, skinny ties and vendors selling straw boaters to polite Minnesota fans. "Not a smokestack crowd," as infielder Frank Quilici described them. "Nice." The Twins' front office sat Dodger wives behind home plate. In Los Angeles, the Twins' wives were given seats way out in right field. Between innings, go-go dancers did a decorous frug; and Gillette hawked a new super stainless-steel blade with Miracle Edges to a clean-shaven nation. Harry Coyle, the director, had only a couple of cameras to work with, and a batboy who kept wandering into the frame. The narration is uncluttered and understated, so quiet you can hear the sound of an airplane buzzing the outfield. On the pregame show, Vin Scully and Ray Scott talked about the pitching matchup: Sandy Koufax and Jim Kaat for the third time. No one mentioned Yom Kippur. Today, ESPN would be doing man-on-the-street interviews at the Wailing Wall.

The broadcast is a staple of *Classic Sports* television. Sam Mele, the Twins' manager, has seen it nine, maybe ten times. "Lost every goddamn game," he says. He, too, remembers the quiet. "They normally weren't *that* quiet," Mele said. "I think everybody could sense—even my bench and me—that it's Koufax out there. You know what I mean? You can't get too excited because this guy's going to knock the jubilance out of you, you know?"

That morning a thunderstorm of biblical proportions inundated the Twin Cities. Helicopters were brought in to dry the field. By game time, the skies had cleared. Temperatures were in the fifties. Osteen, who had lost game six, went down to the bullpen to see if he could help out, standing in an imaginary batter's box so that Koufax would have someone to throw to. Osteen had never seen his curve from that vantage point before. He remembers thinking, So that's why they can't hit it.

As they walked in from the bullpen, Koufax stopped to say hello to Joe Nossek, the Twins' rookie outfielder, playing in his first world series. Nossek thought, "Cloud number nine just got a little more elevated." Neither Nossek nor Osteen had any intimation of how much of himself Koufax had left in the bullpen. Though they might have gotten a scent of it, as Kaat had before game one, when the opposing pitchers met on the field for the ritual pregame handshake. Kaat's eyes began to water, then tear, then burn. Kaat fled as soon as baseball etiquette allowed, driven away by the smell of Capsolin. "It was like walking into a steam room with camphor," he said.

Koufax was pitching on fumes. When he walked two batters in the first inning, Drysdale got up in the bullpen. He was a two-pitch pitcher without a second pitch. Roseboro kept calling for the curve; Koufax kept shaking him off. Finally, Roseboro went to the mound for a conversation. For the first time, Koufax acknowledged how bad his elbow was. "He said, 'Rosie, my arm's not right. My arm's sore.' I said, 'What'll we do, kid?' He said, 'Fuck it, we'll blow 'em away.'"

The game was scoreless when Johnson came to bat in the fourth inning. He had called his mother before the game, vowing, "I'm going to do something today, Ma. I told Sandy I was gonna get him a run."

He kept his promise, hitting Kaat's fastball long and deep to left field. It was curving foul when the foul pole got in its way. Home run! Johnson applauded as he rounded the bases. The rest of the stadium was so quiet Tracewski could hear Johnson's footsteps as he came around third. "So quiet," Johnson said, "you could hear a cat pissing on cotton."

The crowd remained nicely catatonic until the bottom of the fifth. Quilici, the Twins' second baseman, doubled, and the next batter walked. With one out, Zoilo Versailles hit a ball hard down the third base line. It was past Junior Gilliam when he realized it was in his glove. Somehow he beat Quilici to the bag. In the press box, the game was officially declared over.

The afternoon sun waned. Koufax pitched from the shadows. His royal blue sweatshirt appeared navy; his beard darkened inning by inning. His mouth hung open after every pitch. Drysdale got up in the bullpen again. Scully wondered aloud how far a man could go with only one pitch. "Everybody sat there with their mouths open," Ozark said. "He pitched like it was going to be his last breath."

In the ninth inning, the 360th of his season, Koufax faced the heart of the Minnesota order: Tony Oliva, Harmon Killebrew, Earl Battey, and Bob Allison, a two-time batting champion, a six-time home-run leader, a four-time All-Star, and a onetime Rookie of the Year. With one out, Killebrew singled sharply to left, the Twins' third hit of the game. Battey came to the plate. One swing, he thought, and I could be the world series MVP! By the time the words formed a sentence in his brain, the umpire had signaled, "Strike three."

Up to the plate strode Allison, a formidable slugger whose two-run home run off Osteen had forced the seventh game. He fouled off the first pitch and looked at two others for balls and then swung at the next. "It's two and two," announcer Ray Scott informed the television audience. "Koufax is reaching back. Every time he's had to reach back, he's found what he needed."

Killebrew watched from first base as Allison swung through strike three for the final out of the series. "I told Bob, 'If you'd have swung at the ball as hard as you swung at the ground after you struck out, you might have hit it.'"

The orderly Minnesota fans exited Metropolitan Stadium, taking all the air with them. The scoreboard congratulated them for being the best fans in the world. The Dodgers were almost as low-key. Parker, the young first baseman, wasn't sure what to do with himself. "I'd been dreaming about this my whole life. I was ready to go nuts. I'm running toward the mound and there's no noise. I'm wondering if someone called time. But no, the Minnesota fans were filing out. I looked at Sandy. Sandy wasn't doing anything. He didn't pump a fist or jump in the air. He was just walking toward Roseboro."

It was his second shutout in four days, his twenty-ninth complete game of the season. The locker room was joyously subdued, partly because a phalanx of sportswriters had gotten stuck between floors in the press elevator and partly because everyone was so drained. Scully wrapped an arm protectively around Koufax, the bright light of live television highlighting his fatigue. "Here's the fella who gave the Dodgers the championship. Sandy, in Los Angeles, when you pitched a seven-nothing shutout, you were quoted as saying, 'I feel like I'm a hundred years old.' So today, Sandy, how do you feel?'"

Koufax was too tired to do anything but smile and tell the truth. Viewers at home saw a grin so wide his dimples threatened to implode. "Well, Vinnie, I feel like I'm a hundred and one. I'm just glad it's over and I don't have to do this again for four whole months."

Time devoted a page in its next issue to baseball, a cut-and-paste story cobbled together from series coverage, recycled quotes, and McWhirter's unused file. The tone was decidedly "cool"—grudgingly appreciative at best. It got right to the point: "Just because a man does his job better than anybody else doesn't mean that he has to take it seriously—or even like it."

And it continued:

> Alone among ballplayers, Koufax is an anti-athlete who suffers so little from pride that he does not even possess a photograph of himself. TV and radio interviewers have learned to be careful with personal questions—or risk a string of billingsgate designed to ruin their tapes. . . .

> To his teammates, even to his few close friends, Koufax's aloofness is often downright annoying. "Imagine," says Dodger catcher John Roseboro, "being good-looking, well-off, single—and still be so cool. I know guys who would be raising all kinds of hell on those stakes." Dodger vice president Fresco Thompson considers him a heretic. "I don't think he likes baseball," mutters Thompson. "What kind of a line is he drawing anyway—between himself and the world, between himself and the team?"

In the fall of 1965, you'd have to have been decidedly square to miss Roseboro's meaning. Cool as in hip. What had been intended as a compliment was construed as evidence of a "taciturn" personality. What Koufax had said to Scully in a moment of utter depletion was interpreted as further evidence of his dislike for baseball. In the great American fiction known as the World of Sports, Our Hero is a selfless, square-jawed exemplar of uncommon grace and modesty, who always plays for the Love of the Game, no matter how much he earns. Thus, to say he doesn't love it is to deny him the status of Our Hero. To label Koufax as an "anti-athlete" was to damn him forever for being different. It is what author Roger Kahn calls "a genteel form of anti-Semitism."

After the series, Ed Linn, newly hired as the ghostwriter for Koufax's proposed autobiography, went to Hawaii to meet him. Koufax was staying by himself on the beach on a remote part of the Big Island. Bill Hayes, Koufax's lawyer and business manager, gave Linn explicit directions: "You will pass two dirt roads very close together, a little variety store in between. You take the second dirt road; if you pass it and miss it, you'll never find it. Go to the end. There will be a link fence. There's a door that will be open. Sandy's there. He will be in a beach house."

"I found it without any difficulty. I get to this fence. There's no open door. There's a chain lock. There's a half dozen workmen. I say, 'Have you seen Sandy Koufax?'

"One said, 'You talking about Sandy Koufax, the ballplayer? Boy, are you lost. He's three thousand miles away.' Just at that moment, out of this little shack comes Koufax in bathing trunks. I said to the guy, 'No, he's maybe fifty yards that way.'"

After Linn climbed the fence and they began to talk, he learned how hurtful the *Time* magazine story was, particularly the perception of aloofness for a man who was a consummate team player. So when he sat down to write, Linn composed an impassioned fourteen-page protest, in Koufax's voice, aimed at the editors of *Time* magazine and all other reductionist thinkers.

> I have nothing against myths. But there is one myth that has been building through the years that I would just as soon bury without any particular honors: the myth of Sandy Koufax, the anti-athlete. The way this fantasy goes, I am really a sort of dreamy intellectual who was lured out of college by a bonus in the flush of my youth and have forever after regretted—and even resented—the life of fame and fortune that has been forced upon me.

Mordecai Richler reviewed the book in the November 1966 issue of *Commentary* magazine. The fact of the review by the distinguished Jewish author in the distinguished journal of Jewish thought was testimony to Koufax's standing among his people, especially the literary intelligentsia. The review was scathing, damning the effort as a "very bush-league performance, thin, cliché-ridden." In short, a typical ghost-written sports autobiography. (Had Richler read more closely he might have heard an authentic voice in the opening cri de coeur.)

Getting to the heart of the matter, Richler wrote: "Anti-Semitism takes many subtle shapes and the deprecating story one reads again and again, most memorably recorded in *Time*, is that Sandy Koufax is actually something of an intellectual. He doesn't mix. Though he is the highest paid player in the history of the game, improving enormously on Lipman E. Pike's $20 a week, he considers himself above it."

Then he goes further: "In fact, looked at one way, Koufax's autobiography can be seen as a sad effort at self-vindication, a forced attempt to prove once and for all that he is the same as anybody else. Possibly, Koufax protests too much." In denying his putative intellectualism, Richler seemed to be saying, Koufax was denying an essential part of his Jewishness. Which no doubt accounted for the deluge of letters to *Commentary*'s editors accusing Richler of being anti-Semitic.

Having held himself to a higher standard, Koufax was then impaled upon it. To wit: The Minnesota rabbi, who still insists that Koufax was in his synagogue, said nothing at the time because he wasn't too thrilled with Koufax's lack of piety. "That's why I couldn't build him up," Raskas said. "He's not such a good Jew because he didn't marry a Jewish girl. So I don't get too excited about it."

The significance of Koufax's decision has been debated ever since in synagogues and at dinner tables, by Talmudic scholars and baseball players. How much did he change the way Jews are perceived? How much did he change the way Jews perceive themselves? "He gave little Jewish boys some hope," said pitcher Steve Stone, who was one of them. "The series went seven games instead of four," said general manager Buzzie Bavasi. "I always told him, 'You made Walter O'Malley a million dollars.'"

Four decades after the fact, two best-selling Jewish authors, Scott Turow and Mitch Albom, engaged in a heated polemic about the significance of a ham sandwich Koufax allegedly was seen eating in the hotel elevator in Minnesota that week. Albom's friend, a rabbi's son still a young man in 1965, was apparently still devastated at having seen pork touch Koufax's pitching hand. Turow responded indignantly: "Who's to say what is Jewish enough? Who's to say what a Jew is?" Except that Jew himself.

Peter Levine, author of *Ellis Island to Ebbets Field: Sports and the American Jewish Experience*, argues that Koufax's symbolic potency was attenuated by world events. Who needs Koufax when you have Henry Kissinger playing realpolitik? "However tough and strong a pitcher Koufax was," Levine wrote, "he clearly was no match for Moishe Dayan and his legions of commandos when it came time to search for heroes and deeds symbolic of the contemporary Jewish experience—far more relevant than anything Koufax offered."

Rabbi Lustig, who as a boy wired a transistor radio to his seven-year-old person and took the world series into the synagogue, understands why Koufax is hardwired into the psyche of the American Jewish community and his congregation—why grown men are transformed by putting on Koufax's jersey. The decision not to pitch was a transforming event, providing the catalyst for an unknown number of lawyers and Little Leaguers to acknowledge and honor their religion in like kind. Koufax made them brave. By refusing to pitch, he both reinforced Jewish pride and enhanced the sense of belonging—a feat as prodigious as any he accomplished on the field.

"The Six-Day War was important to Zionism," Lustig said. "It changed the image of the Jew in the world. He could be a true soldier. The world series was important to the whole community. What could be so American? We had finally made it. We had earned the right to be as interested in baseball as in our Jewish identity."

The discussion and debate proceeds without any comment from him. Some have attributed his silence to modesty; others to the realization that nothing he could say would improve upon what he did. But this too is true. It's embarrassing being a religious icon, especially an inadvertent one. Later, friends say, he would become a reader of Holocaust literature and quit driving German cars. He came to appreciate the significance his decision had for others. After the old lady at Herbie Scharfman's funeral finally let go of Koufax's right arm, Tom Villante said to him, "You know, Sandy, in my lifetime there's three guys I've known who have transcended their sports and become a symbol for their race or nationality: Jackie with the blacks, Joe D. with the Italians, and you with the Jews."

"He said, 'I know it.' And he said it as if he knew it and accepted it. This is something he carries around with him. And he is very proud of it."

Koufax refused to be a Jew's Jew or a gentile's Jew. He may have been different but he refused to be anything other than himself. In the Talmud, it is written that some attain eternal life with a single act. On Yom Kippur, 5726, a baseball immortal became a Jewish icon.

Chapter 18

THE EIGHTH INNING

ALONE AMONG THE PRINCIPALS ON THE FIELD, Ed Vargo was oblivious. The year before in Philadelphia, he knew Koufax had a no-hitter. Philly fans always let you know what's going on. This time he was too invested in calling a perfect game to notice that it was one. Koufax knew; and he knew something else too. Never before had he thrown a baseball with equal measures of control and velocity. It was a confluence of experience and opportunity, muscle memory and kinetic understanding, reflex and thought. Quite unexpectedly, in the eighth inning of his 349th major league game, everything he had learned about the physics of pitching and everything his own physiology enabled him to do was at his disposal. He thought, It's as total as it has ever been.

Everyone in the stands knew. Spines stiffened in club seats and up the middle of the diamond. Last call came and went. No one went for another Blatz Beer or another Dodger Dog. No one went anywhere at all. Except to get up for every pitch. "One step to the left, one step to the right," Bill DeLury noticed from his seat high above third base. "And on every pitch, a roar."

In the dugouts, stasis reigned. In the seventh, they move a little, DeLury thought. In the eighth, they don't move, they don't talk at all.

Everyone was accountable. Just being there carried a measure of responsibility. Nate Oliver, the utility man known as "Pee Wee" to everyone but Koufax, who called him "Brute," felt as if he were carrying the Empire State Building on his back. "Nobody wants to be the one to mess up by getting a beer or soda. *You're* responsible. You don't want your neighbor or relative or spouse to say later, 'You should have kept your butt where you were.'"

If the Dodgers were muted by superstition, the Cubs were silenced by embarrassment. Our guy is pitching a one-hitter and losing! Ken Holtzman thought. On an error, an overthrow! He glanced down the bench. Everyone was feeling the same thing: Terrible for Hendley and helpless against Sandy.

Scully introduced the late-inning defensive changes and speculated about the butterflies in John Kennedy's stomach. "The big boys are coming up," he added. "Santo, Banks, and Byron Browne."

Koufax wanted the no-hitter but he wanted the win even more. With the Dodgers leading 1–0, he needed to keep the ball in the ballpark and away from their power. The first pitch to Santo was a fastball away; the next two he swung at and missed. There was no chance his bat was going to get in the way of them. The guy threw ninety-five mph without thinking about it; a hundred mph when he put his mind to it. Santo had never seen him throw this hard before. I was waiting for the fastball and he threw it right past me, Santo thought.

By the time he quit thinking about it, he'd been caught looking at a vindictive curve.

"All right," Scully said. "Sandy Koufax needs five more outs as Ernie Banks steps in at the plate."

Two previous strikeouts had done nothing to compromise his determined optimism, nor would a third. After which he headed back to the dugout, considering what he would say to his twin sons when he got home. *What happened last night, Dad? Was that a no-hitter, Dad? What did you do?*

He would tell them: "I failed to make contact."

Koufax felt looser than he had all season, more in control than he had been all year. The fastball and the curve were on their best behavior. "One going up, one going down, both hard," Hendley murmured to himself, a solitary sentinel standing watch at the corner of the dugout, spitting seeds. (He never chewed.)

It's not fair, Torborg thought.

Byron Browne agreed. Walking to the plate felt like walking the plank. Browne hoped it would be quick. He swung through a curve for strike one, then watched a fastball sail high. It was the only lapse in Koufax's form or composure. "The first time I saw him force himself tonight," Scully noted. "He wanted oh and two."

The next pitch produced a futile swing. "Oh, doctor," Scully said.

One ball and two strikes. What Browne would remember was how the number 32 appeared after the pitch, like a child peeking around the corner. That's how complete Koufax's delivery was. Al Campanis, the old scout, kept a photograph in his office demonstrating how Koufax finished a pitch—a reminder to others seeking a raise. "I can't see the number on your back," Campanis would say, dismissing them.

Koufax tried to shake off the weight of the moment. "Koufax standing in back of the rubber, tugging at the bill of his cap, pulls at his belt, pushes up his sleeves, goes to the rosin bag," Scully reported. "Normally, he's not a fidgeter. Now he toes the rubber. Byron Browne waiting. Curveball got him swinging!"

As he trudged back to the dugout, Browne thought, At least he didn't get me three times—like Ernie.

Hendley was torn. One instinct was to marvel, the other was to hope. He was looking at something he had never seen before and would never see again. But to savor it was to accept its inevitability and he wasn't ready to do that. He tugged on the brim of his cap and headed back to the mound, reminding himself, You're only down a run.

Due up for the Dodgers: Lefebvre, Parker, and Torborg. Scully urged his listeners to pick up the phone and call their friends and neighbors. "If you're listening and you have a neighbor who is a red-hot baseball fan, it would be a good idea to give him a ring just to make sure he's at the other end of this thing tonight."

Immediately, the phone rang in the home of one such fan who was curled up in a fetal position on the living room floor beside his father trying to stave off anxiety. He hung up on his best friend, fearful that the call violated the taboo against talking about a no-hitter. Father and son resumed the fetal position, communicating by hand signals in order to preserve the karma.

The Dodgers went quickly in the bottom of the eighth, three up and three down. Torborg was the last hitter to face Hendley. Scully encouraged his listeners to give "the kid at the other end of eight perfect innings a hand." The stadium responded with pitch and volume. Torborg responded by driving a ball to the left-field wall. God, I hit a home run on the night Sandy's gonna pitch a perfect game! Torborg thought. But the wind caught it and then so did Browne, his back against the bullpen gate. Behind him relievers were jockeying for position to witness the top of the ninth.

"Sandy Koufax is slowly walking out to the mound for a meeting with destiny," Scully said, as Hendley took his leave.

He received a standing ovation: the first and last of his major league career.

Chapter 19

WARNING SHOT

FRED WILPON'S OFFICE HOVERS FORTY FLOORS ABOVE New York's Fifth Avenue. It is well appointed and well located, filled with objets d'art deserving of museum-quality lighting and a desk large enough to measure in wingspan. It is a trophy office, calculated to impress. Most impressive is the panorama: South and west in New York Harbor is the Statue of Liberty. And, two blocks north, the art deco terraces of Rockefeller Center, that most elegant monument to capitalist zeal. This is the one place Wilpon never expected to be: eye-level with the captains of industry.

On a clear day (and with a little imagination), he can see all the way back to Brooklyn and the boyhood he shared with Koufax. As a pitching prospect, Wilpon peaked too soon. There was no hidden speed behind the curve. As Koufax would later observe, "Fred hasn't lost anything off the fastball he had then." Word in the neighborhood was he turned down a $4,000 offer from the Dodgers to stay in college.

After graduating from the University of Michigan, Wilpon returned to New York, looking for a future. It was the fifties. The anti-Semitism he encountered was latent but patent. Looking up at the skyscrapers of Manhattan he saw names painted on the walls, Jewish names: Rudin and Tishman. He went to the New York City Public Library and studied their careers. Real estate is where he would make his name, where he would earn the money to acquire a 50 percent stake in the New York Mets and a view worthy of the Rockefellers.

It is from this unique vantage point, as boyhood friend and owner of the New York Mets, that Wilpon views what may have been the most underestimated event in Koufax's career: the Great Koufax-Drysdale Holdout of 1966. By bargaining collectively, they not only challenged the owners' omnipotent domain, they forcibly dragged the industry into the twentieth century. "It was radical because it was the two of them," Wilpon said. "They were unionists."

"It was a small union," Koufax likes to say, "a union of two. But it *was* a union."

In the spring of 1966, baseball was as insular as the round, cookie-cutter ballparks that would soon dominate the landscape. All over America authority was under siege. Dr. Timothy Leary was exhorting Americans to "turn on, tune in, drop out." Everyone was mobilizing, sitting in and walking out, even Frankie's kid, Nancy Sinatra, who topped the charts with "These Boots Are Made for Walkin'." (Stiletto-heeled white "go-go" boots became an immediate fashion imperative, though not at political demonstrations.) Black was beautiful. Women were abandoning their stays. But baseball was still run as a plantation. "Everybody was speaking out then from all places and all walks of life, protesting, outside, inside," Lou Johnson said. "Sports had always been in a different category."

Players were owned in perpetuity, tethered for life to the clubs that signed them by the Reserve Clause in the Uniform Players Contract, a legal oddity which allowed owners to interpret each year's contract as infinitely renewable. Players had no bargaining power, and no one to argue on their behalf. Absent the right to sell themselves to the highest bidder, they resorted to empty threats. On the morning of September 9, 1965, the *Los Angeles Times* reported Drysdale's sudden interest in Japanese baseball: "$500,000 Offer Tempts Drysdale!"

The Players Association had no leverage at all. The director was appointed by—and paid by—management. As was legal counsel. The owners put forth that noted labor activist former vice president Richard M. Nixon as their new candidate for the job. Agents were for actresses. When Roger Maris tried to take his brother, the businessman, with him to talk money after hitting 61 home runs, the Yankee brass kicked him out. Contract negotiations were, in fact, not negotiations at all. "Negotiation by ultimatum," Koufax called it.

Salary talks were often comic monologues. Like the time Phil Regan went to see general manager Buzzie Bavasi after winning fourteen games and saving twenty-one in 1966. Before Regan could even state his case for a $40,000 salary, Bavasi had trumped him, writing figures on five pieces of paper, wadding them up into balls, and throwing them across the table. "Pick one," he said. By chance, Regan picked the highest, $37,000. "My bad day," Bavasi said.

Another time, Tommy Davis went to see Bavasi and found Maury Wills's contract for the coming season lying on his desk. When Davis saw how low the numbers were he figured he better take whatever he was offered. The contract was a fraud. Bavasi had left it out intentionally.

Ploys like these left a bitter aftertaste. Players would mutter under their collective breath, but that was the limit of collectivism. There had been attempts to organize, to create rival leagues in hopes of forging a competitive market for their services. All had failed or been rebuffed.

In the mid-1940s, two Mexican brothers tried to lure players south of the border with promises of big money. In 1946, Robert F. Murphy, a lawyer for the National Labor Relations Board, quit his job to form the American Baseball Guild, an attempt at an effective players' union. He demanded and got a minimum salary ($5,000), a pension plan, and a spring training allowance—still known as Murphy money. When Pittsburgh management refused to discuss player grievances, the Pirates authorized a strike vote. Baseball Commissioner Happy Chandler got the word via pitcher Rip Sewell and quickly organized a team of scabs—including seventy-two-year-old Honus Wagner. The uprising was put down. Sewell happily accepted a gold watch from the commissioner.

In the early fifties, Yankee minor leaguer George Toolson challenged the reserve clause in a case that went to the U.S. Supreme Court before the justices reaffirmed Justice Oliver Wendell Holmes's 1922 decision exempting baseball from antitrust laws. Robin Roberts, an early union activist among players, remembers a proposal made to the owners at winter meetings in the mid-1950s which would have allowed limited free agency after six years. Then the player would be tied to his new club for six years. "For the owners, it would have been a chance to loosen up on control," Roberts said. "They didn't give us any satisfaction. It was shortsighted on their part. It would have really made sense because they do spend a lot of money developing guys in the minors. But they were so used to having complete control, they were out of control."

In the spring of 1966 to say of a man *he'd a played for nuthin'* was the ultimate accolade and the ultimate fiction. They played for money, just a lot less of it. The conceit of mercenary selflessness is a fin de siècle construct, a gauzy, revisionist mythology which allowed fans to think better of their heroes and owners to keep salaries down. When spring training camps opened that February, the minimum player salary was $7,000—one thousand dollars more than it was when Koufax signed with the Dodgers in 1955. Winning mattered. World series checks weren't just latte money.

That spring, two events altered forever the balance of power in baseball. Jim Bunning and Robin Roberts put forth Marvin Miller, a seasoned trade unionist, as their candidate to lead the new Major League Baseball Players Association. And Koufax and Drysdale held out in tandem. In challenging Walter O'Malley, the power behind the commissioner's throne, they were taking on not just the Dodgers but the Institution of Baseball. No one else could have done it; no one else had their standing or the irrefutable attendance figures to assert their value. The Dodgers acknowledged they drew an additional ten thousand fans every time Koufax started and three thousand when Drysdale pitched.

They were the *Big Two, K & D, 1 and 1A.* "The dynamic duo," Orel Hershiser called them, "Batman and Robin."

Their closeness was one of proximity and shared experience rather than personality. They were amicable rather than intimate. They were two very different people who came from two very different worlds and, in the words of Drysdale's second wife, Anne Meyers Drysdale, "they shared an unbelievable moment in time." With Drysdale what you saw was what you got: Big D, California large and California handsome. Koufax was 3D—his essence elusive. A posed photo from the era, much circulated, showed them side by side on the mound, leaning in for the sign, gaze unwavering and intent. It underscored the impression that they were joined at the hip. In fact, everything about them was antithetical except their purpose. They were perfect foils, if not perfect friends. "They were so different," she said. "That's why they were so good together."

They were teenagers when they met. Koufax came to the Dodgers first but Drysdale came to prominence earlier. By 1957, he was the ace. Koufax was still worrying about whether he would be sent down to the minor leagues. They spent that last winter as Brooklyn Dodgers in basic training at Fort Dix, New Jersey. They lived on base and visited Koufax's parents in Brooklyn on weekend leave. It was there that Koufax taught Drysdale how to walk on snow; there that they heard the news about Roy Campanella's accident on an icy stretch of Long Island macadam. Campy's paralysis seemed to seal the Dodgers' fate. There was nothing left for them in New York.

Drysdale took Koufax home to meet his parents in California, where his father, Scotty, now lives out his life "battling my eyes." Scott remembers Koufax as a nice boy. Nobody said Don Drysdale was nice until he was dead.

He was the Ultimate Boy. "He was a marching band," Scully said. "Where you saw Don, you saw at least a half dozen other players." Drysdale tended bar at Club 53, the joint he named for his uniform number, and hung out at the racetrack with Bavasi. Koufax hung with utility guys and also-rans, players as marginal as he had once been—

Doug Camilli, John Werhas, Dick Tracewski. They called themselves The Three Stooges, though it was hard to think of Koufax as a stooge. He'd been to college. "He was the kind of guy who'd have one drink, throw some money in the kitty, and go home," pitcher Johnny Podres said.

Not one of the boys, reporters concluded.

"Don was so gregarious I think about him in the present tense," Hershiser said. "A man's man, larger than life. He understood his position in baseball and in public, and he capitalized on it but not in a slimy way. He treated the clubhouse kid and the president of the ball club the same.

"Sandy was somebody when you walked in a room and saw he was there, you approached Sandy with more of an aura of respect. It's like the difference between walking onto public links as opposed to Augusta. You take your clubs out a little different."

Always they were a driving force for each other. They tried to outdo each other and in so doing outdid everyone else. The Dodgers promoted and profited from their rivalry, playing them off against each other in salary negotiations. Ten years after Drysdale's death Bavasi was *still* at it, saying, "I told him one hundred times, if I told him once, 'You're getting paid to pitch innings, Donald, he's getting paid to break the records.' Donald knew that. Drysdale had to battle for it. I think he was the one that was on Sandy's coattails."

No doubt, this is what Wills was getting at when he said, "The Dodgers didn't do anything to help the relationship. It was not a competition between them. The Dodgers used Don against Sandy in contract negotiations. They lied to him."

One night in the winter of 1965 after Koufax had gone in to discuss his 1966 contract with Bavasi, he met Drysdale for dinner. Drysdale knew immediately that something was bothering him. He reconstructed their conversation in his autobiography, *Once a Bum, Always a Dodger:*

> "You walk in there and give them a figure that you want to earn," Sandy said, "and they tell you, 'How come you want that much when Drysdale only wants this much?'"

"I'll be damned," I replied. "I went in to talk to them yesterday for the first time and they told me the same story.
Buzzie wondered how I could possibly want as much as I was
asking when you were asking for only this."

Koufax harbored ill feelings dating back to the "negotiations" for his
1964 contract when his alleged demand for $90,000 was leaked to Los
Angeles newspapers. The only problem with the story was he hadn't
asked for $90,000. He had asked for $75,000 and said he would settle for
$70,000. The story was calculated to make the Dodgers look good and
generous and wise and make Koufax look bad. And he resented it.
Drysdale was equally tired of Bavasi's act. Between them they had won
fifty-two games in 1965. It was Drysdale's first wife, Ginger, who came
up with the revolutionary proposal to join forces: "If Buzzie is going to
compare the two of you, why don't you just walk in there together?"

Whatever residual differences or jealousies there may have been stem-
ming from the 1965 World Series, they were in complete solidarity on this.
They went to see Bavasi and told him that neither would sign unless both
were happy. What would make them happy was $1 million to be divided
equally over the next three years, or $167,000 each for the next three sea-
sons. In 1966 dollars, Drysdale said later, "It was like asking for the moon."

Bavasi replied: " 'No way.' I said, 'Sandy, you know O'Malley, he
works on a budget. He gives me x dollars and that's it.' He looked me
right in the eye and he said, 'Buzzie, budgets are made to be broken.' "

Everyone in baseball knew the unwritten law: There was a $100,000
salary ceiling. Only a few superstars, Musial, Mantle, Mays, DiMaggio,
Williams, had reached that—and always under the table. The precedent
of paying pitchers $100,000 was not one Bavasi wanted to set. Even
more troubling to management, they were asking for a three-year, no-
cut contract, unheard of at the time. But it wasn't only the money that
worried organized baseball.

Koufax was represented by an entertainment lawyer, J. William
Hayes, in his business dealings outside of baseball. Drysdale had gone
to him for advice when his own lawyer had a conflict of interest. Now

Hayes began to advise them on their collective negotiations. This was, perhaps, the most dangerous precedent of all. "It was a radical step and it got more radical as it went," Marvin Miller said.

When the Dodger plane left for Vero Beach on February 26, Koufax and Drysdale weren't on it. A great public relations battle ensued, which Bavasi casts in a rosy retrospective hue. "I loved it, absolutely *loved* it," he said. "We couldn't buy those headlines."

> Bavasi Raps Stars Demands, Calls $500,000 Pacts Ridiculous
> K & D Spurn Offer
> Koufax-Drysdale Trade Looms, Bavasi Fed Up
> K-D Contract War Has Mates Uneasy
> Friends Say Sandy Is Hopping Mad
> K and D Making Other Plans
> K and D Will Wow 'em in Show Biz

The name of the film was *Warning Shot.* The pitchers were photographed lounging on the set, their names inscribed on their director's chairs. People noticed how much Koufax looked like David Janssen, the leading man. Drysdale was to play a TV commentator. Koufax was to play a detective sergeant. In the sports pages, they were cast as villains. O'Malley milked it for all it was worth, playing to the conservative Southern California audience, branding them as communists.

He was a master at playing the local sporting press, many of whom were condescendingly referred to by Eastern reporters as "house men." It wasn't hard to get them to play this tune. He would direct Bavasi to leave messages at Drysdale's home, knowing the pitcher wasn't there, and then when the call was returned, tell the press, "See, they're getting anxious. They called me yesterday."

Red Smith, the revered sports columnist who always referred to himself as "a working stiff," presented a rare dissenting opinion:

> Koufax and Drysdale defiled the name of the game by trying to bargain collectively and by bringing a lawyer to talk for

them. Under the law, coal miners may bargain collectively but not ball players. Under the law, a rape-murderer must have legal counsel but not a ball player.

Their resolve did not crack, even when management began leaking stories alleging dissension between K and D, trying to drive a wedge between them. That spring, Miller made his first tour of spring training camps, introducing himself to the players prior to the election that would make him executive director of the Players Association. Wherever he went, he was asked about Koufax and Drysdale.

As a trade unionist, Miller viewed their holdout as an argument for collective bargaining, telling players: "You can be the two best pitchers on the planet and still not get what's coming to you if there's only two of you." He cited DiMaggio's famous holdout. "Even if you were the number one player in the game, playing for the number one organization, they could tell you to take their offer or go fishing in San Francisco."

The day after Miller visited Dodgertown, Bavasi spoke to the players, Jim Lefebvre recalled. "Bavasi said, 'We can't have this guy. This means strike. Strike means no money, no food to feed your family.' We all looked at each other and said, 'He's in.' Anybody Buzzie was that scared of had to be good for you."

Still, the mood in Dodgertown was bleak. "It was a scary thing," said Lefebvre. "Without them, where are we going to go?"

"Without them, we were naked," said first baseman Wes Parker.

From the outset, Hayes told his clients that their gambit would work only if they were truly prepared to walk away. Koufax was. What had begun for him as an irresistible opportunity to tweak Dodger management had become a cause. Hadn't his grandfather, Max Lichtenstein, an immigrant, walked away from a good job at Consolidated Edison? His first day of work at New York's vast power company, Max watched the huge iron gates close behind the men on his shift. This was not why he came to America. "I came to get away from locked gates," Max said. At the end of the shift, he walked back through those gates and never returned.

"The greatest hero in Sandy's life was his grandfather," Wilpon said.

"And his grandfather was a socialist with high intellectual values and goals and ideals. And I think Sandy learned from that. Baseball players at that time were chattel. He didn't think that was right. Not only because it was occurring to him, not only because there was money involved.

"Now, today, when you look back on that, everybody will tell you, 'Oh, I don't think that was right.' But there was nobody who did anything about it. So with the background from Max, he felt he had to right the situation. He loved to challenge the system."

Besides, he had already decided that the 1966 season would be his last. Drysdale had neither his independence nor his fragility. Koufax had no wife or children to provide for. Drysdale had no arthritis in his elbow. One morning, four weeks into the holdout, Drysdale appeared on the front page of the *Times* sports section in uniform, working out at Pierce College in Woodland Hills. With publication of the photograph, their leverage disappeared. It was over. Koufax gave Drysdale the go-ahead to negotiate new deals for the two of them.

The impasse was quickly resolved through an unlikely labor mediator, Chuck Connors, the onetime Dodger better known as *The Rifleman*. "Walter told me the highest I could go was two hundred twenty-five thousand dollars," Bavasi said. "That's all I could do. Well, I know that Sandy had to get the hundred twenty-five thousand dollars he wanted. I mean, there's a young man who brings people to the ballpark. So I settled with Sandy for a hundred twenty-five thousand and with Donald for a hundred thousand. Now we get back to the office and I said to my secretary Edith, 'I want you to make out a contract for a hundred twenty-five thousand dollars for Sandy and a hundred thousand for Donald.'

"And Sandy said, 'I thought we're supposed to get the same thing.'

"I said, 'No, we agreed to this. I'll tell you what I'll do. Edith,' I said, 'make the Drysdale contract for a hundred ten thousand dollars.' Well, that's ten thousand more than O'Malley told me I could spend. So they were both happy and they both signed. Now we won the pennant that year. Donald had a mediocre year but Sandy had the best year of his life. And Walter promised me an increase in salary if we won the pennant. So I got a nice note from Walter at the end of the season after we won the pennant: 'Dear Buzzie, too bad you gave your bonus to Drysdale.' I had to pay for Drysdale's ten thousand."

When the signing was announced aboard the team plane en route to the West Coast, everyone cheered. Bavasi joked that he was left holding a bloody cashbox.

The pitchers joined the team in Arizona for the last weekend of exhibition games. In his first appearance, Koufax went six innings without giving up a hit. The next day, Drysdale pitched six scoreless innings and was booed.

In the history of baseball's labor revolution, this early experiment in sweaty solidarity is generally given short shrift. It pales next to Curt Flood's landmark refusal in 1969 to accept a trade from St. Louis to Philadelphia. The 1975 decision by arbitrator Peter Seitz liberating Andy Messersmith and Dave McNally from their contracts was baseball's Emancipation Proclamation. But revolutions begin with baby steps. When Koufax and Drysdale withheld their services together, they made it possible for Flood to run. "Baseball players today owe a lot to Curt Flood and Andy Messersmith and Dave McNally," former Dodger Don Sutton said. "But Flood, Messersmith, and McNally owed a lot to Koufax and Drysdale. Because they were the first guys who really took a stand. This was the first challenge to the structure of baseball."

The establishment view is that O'Malley reeled them in like a couple of shiny trout swimming upstream. He *played* them, reporters said. They didn't get the money they asked for; therefore, they caved. In fact, the dollars they asked for and the dollars they received were not nearly as important as the demand to be reckoned with. They had lured O'Malley into turbulent waters, the vast undercurrent of players' rights.

Peter O'Malley, who inherited the team from his father, says the prospect of player agents didn't daunt the old man. By then, O'Malley was wise in the ways of Hollywood. Everybody had an agent there. But they didn't have agents in Kansas City and St. Louis and other so-called major league towns where the men who ran baseball were accustomed to running deals down the throats of players whose best arguments for themselves were never verbal. The idea that crotch-scratching, tobacco-chewing ballplayers, proud wielders of the tools of ignorance, would be on equal footing was untenable, which is why Bavasi still denies having negotiated with Hayes. Talked to him once, maybe. Negotiated, never.

In these "discussions," Hayes never directly challenged the Reserve Clause. But, he had instructed a young lawyer working in his office to research the topic. Richard Hume discovered a 1944 case brought on behalf of the actress Olivia de Havilland, against Warner Brothers Pictures, in which she argued that any personal services contract binding her to the studio for longer than seven years was illegal. The California Appellate Court agreed, ruling:

> A contract to render personal service, other than a contract of apprenticeship . . . cannot be enforced against the employee beyond the term of seven years from the commencement of service under it.

This case was cited three years later, when basketball player Rick Barry challenged the validity of his contract with the San Francisco Warriors. The law went straight to the heart of free agency. Hume says O'Malley became aware of this potentially explosive legal doctrine through his Hollywood friend Mervyn LeRoy. "I'll never know whether Buzzie folded because of the work we did or because he was missing his two best pitchers," Hume said. "But we had the case law."

The full impact of the Great Holdout would not be realized for another decade. In 1976, after Seitz had sanctioned free agency, Miller began the arduous process of negotiating the players' new rights. Time and again, perhaps even fifty times, Miller says, management cited Koufax and Drysdale as their worst nightmare, invoking the plaintive words of Braves manager Bobby Bragan: "What if my entire infield holds out?"

Since his interest was in negotiating for individual rights, Miller was only too happy to agree and insisted that ownership draft the language. "Lee MacPhail, who was doing most of the writing, came in with language that prevented another Koufax and Drysdale. It said nothing about what the clubs were prevented from doing. I said, 'We agree in principle with what you are saying but what's good for the goose is good for the gander.' With no argument and no delay, they agreed to language that said, 'And no club shall have the right to act in conjunction with any other club.' "

That language would come back to haunt them. By 1985, Miller and the Players Association had revolutionized not only how players were paid but how professional athletes were perceived. The owners, under the leadership of commissioner Peter V. Ueberroth, tired of consistent defeats at the bargaining table and escalating salaries, agreed among themselves not to sign any free agents. In legal terms, that's called collusion. Two arbitrators ruled that ownership had violated the provision they had sought in the 1976 Basic Agreement. Settlement talks ensued. As an indirect result of their abiding fear of Koufax and Drysdale, the owners agreed in 1985 to pay $280 million to players disadvantaged by the collusion. "We have Koufax and Drysdale and Bobby Bragan's imaginary infield to thank," Miller said.

By then, the Great Holdout was an asterisk in the avalanche of money and benefits coming down on players' heads. Koufax and Drysdale, needing to make a living, had begun second careers. Both became sports broadcasters. Drysdale thrived in the public role, filling the small screen with his big personality. Koufax shriveled when the red light came on.

Drysdale remarried and had a new family with Anne Meyers, the former UCLA basketball star. When Koufax visited their ranch for a week in the early 1990s, she was surprised at how well they got along, given everything she had heard and read. "It was always 'Don and Koufax didn't get along.' The media played them against each other. All those guys did was laugh. They had such a special connection."

Koufax is not, as many former teammates believe, the godfather of Drysdale's children. But they do call him Koo-foo, the name their father gave him. Drysdale died of a heart attack in 1993 at the age of fifty-six, alone in a hotel room in Montreal, where he had gone to broadcast a Dodger game. By then, Koufax had left television, as well as his career as an itinerant pitching coach in the Dodgers' minor league system. When asked years later why he had quit TV, Koufax replied, "I didn't want to die in a cheap motel."

Chapter 20

THE NINTH INNING

For ONCE, NO ONE TRIED TO BEAT THE TRAFFIC. Ears pressed to transistor radios, thirty thousand static souls listened to Scully render the events unfolding before them. His words punctuated a vast communal hush, reaching into every part of the city and the stadium. He was no longer simply the voice of the Dodgers. He was the narrator of a collective aspiration.

> *Three times in his sensational career has Sandy Koufax walked out to the mound to pitch a fateful ninth where he turned in a no-hitter. But tonight, September the ninth, nineteen hundred and sixty-five, he made the toughest walk of his career, I'm sure, because through eight innings he has pitched a perfect game. He has struck out eleven, he has retired twenty-four consecutive batters, and the first man he will look at is catcher Chris Krug.*

Dusting off home plate, Ed Vargo looked up at the scoreboard for the first time, and murmured to himself, "Whew, we got something going here." Koufax conferred with Dick Tracewski on the infield grass between the mound and second base and confided in his roommate, "I could do this."

Scully was at Ebbets Field the day Koufax tried out, when he was a raw young kid without a trucker's tan and no idea how to pitch. As Koufax stepped to the rubber in search of his fourth no-hitter, Scully took a moment to call downstairs to the truck and tell the radio technicians to turn on the tape recorder. Whenever a pitcher had a chance for a no-hitter, be it a Dodger or a member of the visiting club, Scully would have the final inning recorded just in case. I've already done three for him, Scully thought. What can I do to make this a little extra special?

Baseball is distinguished by its lack of temporal imperatives. Nine innings take what they take. Scully intuitively understood that locating the game in time would attest to its timelessness. Always, he gave the date. This time, he decided to give the time on the clock, too, so that Koufax would remember the exact moment he made history.

Krug was the batter Torborg feared most—"a big right-handed batter," Scully noted—"flied out to center, grounded to short." Krug had motive and now the opportunity to atone for the run he had allowed. But not for long. Quickly, too quickly—no one had ever seen Koufax throw *this* hard—he found himself behind in the count, 0 and 2.

> *You can almost taste the pressure now. Koufax lifted his cap, ran his fingers through his black hair, then pulled the cap back down, clutching at the bill. Krug must feel it, too, as he backs out, heaves a sigh, took off his helmet, put it back on, and steps back up to the plate.*

Krug restrained himself long enough to allow Vargo to call the next pitch a ball. But in the Canoga section of Los Angeles, eleven-year-old Kevin Kennedy could restrain himself no more. He slipped out of bed and went to find his father, hoping that parental reprobation would be subverted by the news he brought: "It's finally happening, Sandy's throwing a perfect game."

One and two, the count on Chris Krug. It is 9:41 P.M. on September ninth, the one-two pitch on the way.

As Krug gamely fouled off one pitch and then another, Kennedy's father joined his son on the edge of the bed for the denouement.

The Dodgers defensively, in this spine-tingling moment: Sandy Koufax, and Jeff Torborg; and the boys who will try to stop anything hit their way, Wes Parker, Dick Tracewski, Maury Wills, John Kennedy, and the outfield of Lou Johnson, Willie Davis, and Ron Fairly. There are 29,000 people in the ballpark and a million butterflies.

No one wanted to touch the ball. No one wanted to make a mistake. Everyone was implicated in the result. In the Dodger dugout, the tension was compounded by the unstated fact of Koufax's fragility. Koufax may not have been thinking, This is it, it's almost over, but others were. Nate Oliver, who had the locker beside his, knew, the arm was getting worse. Who could say if Koufax would ever get this chance again?

Koufax into the windup. Fastball fouled back and out of play. In the Dodger dugout, Al Ferrara gets up and walks down near the runway. And it begins to be tough to be a teammate and sit in the dugout and have to watch.

Tougher still to be Krug's best friend. When the next pitch arrived wide of the plate, extending the drama and the count to 2 and 2, Krug and Vargo were inundated with a cacophony of boos. Scully scolded the crowd for calling pitches with their hearts. Gary Adams held his breath as Koufax delivered yet another fastball, the one he knew Krug was hoping for. Like so many batters before and after him, Krug had the sensation that the pitch was an offering. *It was there for him.* It looked like a big balloon, in and down, just where he liked it. He took what felt like the best swing of his career. He thought he was on it.

> *Fastball got him swinging! Sandy Koufax has struck out twelve. He is two outs away from a perfect game.*

Adams wondered what in God's name to say to him later. Amalfitano, waiting on deck to pinch-hit for Kessinger, had as good an answer as any: "What the hell? He's famous."

Three times this season, he had pinch-hit against Koufax, getting on base twice. "He hit my bat two times," Amalfitano liked to say. He had been replaying those at-bats since the seventh inning, trying to outthink Koufax. "He knows I'm a first-ball, fastball hitter," Amalfitano reminded himself. "First pitch gotta be a curveball."

A 100 mph fastball refuted that logic. "That ball sounded inside," Amalfitano told Vargo and the umpire laughed. "Holy go to hell, Eddie, this guy is really throwing the damn ball."

Watching from the sanctuary of the dugout, Kessinger thought: If he doesn't have it tonight, I ain't playing next time.

Koufax could win without his curve if he had to; with it, he rarely lost at all. Sometimes in the late innings he didn't bother throwing it. When people asked why, he would reply, "Because I didn't have to." Now Torborg called for the curve. But even as he gave the sign, he regretted it. If he loses his perfect game 'cause I made a dumb call . . .

The thought trailed off as Amalfitano's swing produced a foul in the dirt. Torborg pounced on it like a writer on a perfect simile.

> *And Amalfitano walks away, and shakes himself a little bit and swings the bat. And Koufax with a new ball takes a hitch at his belt and walks behind the mound. I would think that the mound at Dodger Stadium right now is the loneliest place in the world.*

Resolutely, Joey A. stepped back up to the plate. The count was 0 and 2. He was not optimistic. "Here comes the third pitch. I swing. I go after it. It was a low pitch but it had enough zip on it that it moved up and went away from me."

"Strike three!" Vargo said.

He is one out away from the promised land!

As Amalfitano retreated to the dugout, Harvey Kuenn, who had come out on deck to pinch-hit for Hendley, asked, "How's he throwing, Joe?"

"You better be ready because it's getting up there real good," Amalfitano replied.

"Wait for me," Kuenn said. "I'll be right back."

Kuenn was a lifetime .300 hitter, the 1959 American League batting champion, a man with nearly 7,000 major league at-bats. What are the odds that twice he would be the last man to face Sandy Koufax in the ninth inning of a no-hit game? And that twice Amalfitano would bat ahead of him in the inning? "Harvey, you're back," Torborg started to say, and then thought better of it.

The time on the scoreboard is 9:44, the date, September the ninth, 1965. And Koufax working on veteran Harvey Kuenn.

Kuenn took the first pitch, a fastball, for strike one. Scully pointed out that Koufax had struck out five consecutive batters. "A fact that has gone unnoticed." The next ball was thrown so hard and soared so high it nearly yanked Torborg's shoulder from its socket. He couldn't feel the bones inside his mitt at all.

He really forced that one. That's only the second time tonight where I have had the feeling that Sandy threw instead of pitched, trying to get that little extra. And that time, he tried so hard his hat fell off. He took an extremely long stride toward the plate and Torborg had to go up to get it.

Hendley watched, passively, from the end of the Cubs' bench, keeping his thoughts to himself; his hopes were long gone. Now his teammates joined him on the dugout steps, in solidarity and awe. They saw what he saw: "A guy literally coming out from under his hat, just blowing people away."

Another high fastball gave Kuenn a momentary reprieve, 2 and 1.

> *You can't blame a man for pushing just a little bit now. Sandy backs off, mops his forehead, runs his left index finger along his forehead, dries it off on his left pants leg, all the while Kuenn just waiting. Here's the pitch.*

Swung on and missed! "By a foot!" Torborg estimated. It was the greatest margin of error he had ever seen on a major league baseball field. As he threw the ball back to Koufax (remembering not to throw too hard), he thought back to the first inning. The game paralleled the arc of Koufax's career. Nine innings: from nothing special to never better.

> *It is 9:46 P.M. Two and two to Harvey Kuenn. One strike away.*

One more time, Koufax wedged his back foot into the pitching rubber. His front leg reared up. His torso turned like a matador evading a charging bull. His eyes never left Torborg's target. His arm came forward and the ball headed toward home like an eighteen-wheeler appearing down the highway out of a mirage.

> *Sandy into his windup. Here's the pitch! Swung on and missed! A perfect game!*

For the next thirty-eight seconds, Scully allowed the crowd to have its say. The sky rained Dodger blue, seat cushions cascading down from the upper reaches of Blue Heaven. People in the stands were jumping up and down, hugging people they didn't know. Santo had a word with his chagrined roomie, Beckert. "You don't know shit about this game."

*On the scoreboard in right field, it is 9:46 P.M. in the City of the
Angels, Los Angeles, California, and a crowd of 29,139 just sitting
in to see the only pitcher in baseball history to hurl four no-hit, no-run
games. He has done it four straight years. And now he capped it. On
his fourth no-hitter, he made it a perfect game.*

Torborg leaped into Koufax's arms, an embrace he wouldn't remember until he saw the photograph. The rest of the team followed, piling on top of the man who had carried them all season. Koufax saved a special hug for Lou Johnson and a special word for John Kennedy. "When I looked over and saw you there," Koufax told him, "I was gonna make sure nobody hit the ball."

Then he disappeared into the dugout. Summoned for a curtain call, he came out, tipped his cap, and disappeared again. The stands and the dugouts emptied. Krug sat alone on the visitors' bench for half an hour contemplating the irrefutable numerals on the scoreboard. "They left that thing up there a long time," he told Adams later.

When finally he went inside he couldn't bring himself to speak to Hendley. What do you say? "Nice game, tough luck." That's what the veteran catcher Bailey had to say. Probably it was the only thing to say.

Having lost, the Cubs cheerfully allowed themselves to enjoy being part of history. Banks sought out the shell-shocked rookies, Browne and Young, wanting to know, "You sure you guys want to play in the National League?"

At his locker, Kuenn was surrounded by reporters. Amalfitano was surprised to see such a crowd; he figured they'd all be over in the Dodger clubhouse. When the writers left, Amalfitano asked, "What the hell are they doing here?"

"They asked me about the difference between this game and the San Francisco game," Kuenn replied.

"What did you tell 'em?"

"About two years," Kuenn said.

The Cubs packed up quickly. They had a late flight to San Francisco. There was little time for sleep, less for reflection. Later, Hendley would conclude, "You can't say all is lost. If I'm remembered in baseball, I'm remembered for that." But it was too soon for that.

On the postgame show—"The Sandy Koufax Scoreboard," Scully called it—Koufax offered his sympathy. In the background, Elsie the Cow, the sponsor's emissary, mooed contentedly. "It's a shame that you have to get beat that way," Koufax said. "But I'm glad we got the run or we might have been here all night."

In the ebullient Dodger locker room, a bottle of chilled champagne was waiting at his stall. *Baseball* champagne, an unworthy and undrinkable vintage. Koufax gave it to the clubhouse guys to put in the refrigerator, but gladly accepted Walter O'Malley's giddy embrace. The old man hadn't seen a perfect game since Don Larsen beat his boys back in the 1956 World Series. "I hope I can slip Koufax an extra five hundred before Bavasi gets back," the owner said with disingenuous largesse. "He might fire me."

At his locker, Koufax was surrounded by reporters, photographers, and smiles, none bigger than his own. He posed with two baseballs in either hand, each indelibly marked with a fat, black zero, one for each of the no-hitters he had thrown. "A zero is at once the perfect emptiness and the most complete sense of possibility," the poet Joseph Brodsky wrote. Koufax was still sweating, his fingernails caked with the mound's dirt. His satin warm-up jacket shimmered in the sodium glare of the camera's flash. Four no-hitters, four consecutive years, each better than the last. "Do you think they'll take the uniform off him before they bronze it?" Drysdale wondered aloud. "Or will they leave him in it?"

Reporters had other questions. *Was there any pitch he wanted back?* There was one in the third inning, he allowed, to Byron Browne. "I didn't want it back as soon as I threw it," he said. "I wanted it back as soon as he hit it."

What had he thrown to Kuenn? the reporters asked.

"Everything I had left," Koufax said.

Who had given him the most trouble?

"Torborg," Koufax replied, referring to the young catcher waiting eagerly for an autograph.

Not everyone got the joke.

Yosh Kawano, Nobe's brother, brought Ken Holtzman over from the Cubs' locker room to get an autograph for his mother. Richard Hume, the young lawyer working for Bill Hayes, came in and got his scorecard signed. Koufax autographed the official lineup card for Alston, who gave it to his grandson, and had his picture taken with Torborg and Uncle Miltie. When the sycophants and the deadline guys cleared out, Koufax went to the umpire's dressing room to congratulate Vargo. "He had a perfect game, too," Hendley said.

"Except for getting hit by a foul ball," Koufax said, just as he had in 1964.

"Thanks for a second great game, Eddie," Koufax wrote on the sweet spot of a game ball.

"The game called itself," Vargo replied.

Then Koufax retreated to the trainer's room to ice his arm in thirty-five-degree water. That's where Claude Osteen found him, sitting alone, sipping a beer, one of three Buhler had left behind in the tub. Half an hour earlier, Osteen had been lying right there on the training table when Drysdale ordered him to get up for history. He wanted to pay his respects as Drysdale had done. But the only words that came to mind were banalities. So he offered his congratulations and headed home.

Osteen wasn't alone in his loss for words. At the *Los Angeles Times*, a headline writer on the sports desk was busy setting type for the morning paper: "Koufax Pleased."

Chapter 21

SWEET SORROW

THE MASTERMINDS BEHIND "Major League Baseball's Team of the Century" broadcast had thought of every contingency. Roadies in black T-shirts had established a temporary beachhead in the infield at Atlanta's Turner Field. Arrangements had been made to hoist Ted Williams's wheelchair to the stage. The honorees had been instructed what to wear. Koufax, ever the team player, came in the suggested uniform: blue blazer, gray slacks, and shoes so highly shined they glowed in the TV lights. Mark McGwire showed up in jeans and sneakers.

The script called for each of the greats to mount the dugout steps when his name was called and then climb a second set of stairs to the stage. Koufax was announced just ahead of the other lefty on the exalted, imaginary squad, Warren Spahn. When Koufax was selected as the left-hander of the last one hundred years, he told reporters that any Team of the Century without Spahn was a joke. A special panel was convened and Spahn was added to the roster. Koufax had a special affinity for

Spahn—they shared a skewed left-handed view of the game—and respect for his twenty-one years in the majors. Spahn did the one thing Koufax couldn't do—endure. But with Spahn, the old adage "the legs go first" applied. He needed help getting up the dugout steps at an event he needed help getting invited to. Not wanting to see Spahn left behind, Koufax waited at the lip of the dugout and offered him an arm, guiding the old lefty to the stage where he belonged.

Age marks everyone differently. Spahn had a rubber arm and pitched until he was forty-three. Koufax had a golden arm much older than its years. One April morning in 1966, soon after he and Drysdale ended their spring job action, Koufax was examined by Dr. Robert Kerlan, the team physician. Kerlan was Buzzie Bavasi's racetrack pal, a gambler. But he knew when to cut his losses and he had promised to tell Koufax when the odds of permanent disability became prohibitive. "I just told your pitcher to retire," he informed Bavasi.

Koufax had already put his future at risk by pitching the 1965 season without missing a turn. The damage was no longer parenthetical, like his arm, or hypothetical—he was beginning to drop things, everyday things like screwdrivers. The fingers on his left hand tingled and occasionally went numb. Buttons and hair combs presented a challenge.

Koufax kept the pain—and Kerlan's advice—to himself. He began the '66 season as he had ended the last, taking the ball every four days. By season's end he had accumulated 323 innings of work, again without missing a start. His astonishing record, 27 and 9 with a 1.73 ERA, and astonishing consistency camouflaged the extent of his injury. Even other Dodger pitchers, privy to training room secrets, were unaware of how bad it had become. Later, Phil Regan could recall only one instance when it was even intimated that Koufax might not be able to pitch— trainer Bill Buhler whispering sotto voce, *Koufax says he might not be able to go.* "He minimized how bad it was," said pitcher Joe Moeller. "So people said, 'He can't be hurting that bad.'"

Fame wore on him equally. In Hollywood, he was "Sandy baby." "Bigger even than Sinatra," his roommate Dick Tracewski said. So big you could walk down the street on Balboa Island, not exactly a Jewish enclave, and never miss a pitch. When Koufax was starting, every house had the radio on. California wasn't so different from Brooklyn after all.

When the Dodgers made their first visit to Atlanta to play the newly relocated Braves, fans stood in line all night to get tickets. "They sold standing room only behind the fence on the field for a dollar a ticket," Regan remembered. "I've never seen it before or since."

People didn't come to see whether he won or lost but to be able to say they saw him. Every game was an event accompanied by hoopla and subtext. An arm has only so many pitches to give, and with any one of those not yet delivered, Koufax's could come unhinged. That was the irony. The more unassailable he appeared, the more vulnerable he became. As the pitch counts and the innings and the strikeouts and the victories and the accolades mounted, so did his awareness of how tenuous it all was. His elbow reminded him with every pitch. Chapter 1 of his autobiography, published that spring, ended with an intimation: "An athletic existence is a self-liquidating life."

Sports autobiography is a peculiar genre: ghostwritten fiction masquerading as fact. In the literature of sports, the truth has always been easier to tell in fiction—Pete Gent's *North Dallas Forty* and Dan Jenkins's *Semi-Tough* are among the best examples. It wasn't until Jim Brosnan's *The Long Season* and Jim Bouton's *Ball Four* that a semirealistic view of the baseball locker room emerged between hard covers. The authorized life stories of America's greatest athletes form an oeuvre of mythology. What are myths if not as-told-to stories? Occasionally, and inadvertently, the putative author actually makes an appearance in his own book. Such is the case on page 160 of *Koufax:*

"Late success is quieter."

It's a quiet sentence, audibly Koufax. You can hear his voice in the syntax and the sentiment. It's also true. Late success *is* quieter, and perhaps a bit untrustworthy. Its vagaries were as palpable to him as its demands. For the first six years of his career, he toiled—when he toiled at all—for respect amid muted expectations. Then he became suddenly and reluctantly famous. He viewed his success through the scrim of early failure, which tempered his view of center stage. He knew how chimerical it all could be.

After all those years at the margins, the swift appropriation of self did not come easily or naturally. Some personalities—Tommy Lasorda and Larry King come to mind—embrace celebrity and crave proximity to it, make careers of it, basking in belated recognition. For others, it's like wearing a dress shirt whose collar is too tight. Koufax is one of those. "It's almost like he ran away from popularity," his teammate Tommy Davis said.

Celebrity is as old as Homer, but he lacked the technology to exploit it fully. Koufax had the cathode appeal and the Hollywood connections to become a star, but lacked the instinct and the desire for it. He was the product of a more sedate and modest time, an unconscious era in baseball (see Billy Martin and Mickey Mantle circa 1957 at the Copacabana) when there was no mass media. There was only "the press"—and the press of attention that came with daily baseball reportage was gentle compared to a dimly perceived future of 24/7 coverage, microphoned managers, catcher-cams, satellite dishes, and perpetual news cycles. When, in the small hours of a 1964 summer night, his roommate, Doug Camilli, arrived at the team's New York hotel after catching Koufax's third no-hitter, he was astonished to find the corridor staked out by reporters. TV lights blazed a hot path to their door. It was Camilli's first encounter with a new American phenomenon: the media event.

This technology-fueled notoriety mandated a new sensibility on the part of the famous. Larry Sherry, a holdover from the Naughty Fifties, thought Koufax was "image-conscious before it was popular." While Bo Belinsky and Dean Chance, the playboy pitchers, were lighting up Los Angeles, Koufax was developing the internal radar required of modern celebrity. One night, he asked John Kennedy and Ron Perranoski if he could tag along with them to a local bar. By the time they placed their order, the first floozy had made her approach. "Sandy said, 'Let's get outta here,'" Kennedy said. "We didn't even have the drink. He didn't want to be in the wrong place if there was trouble."

When he was expected at a place, management invariably stationed a valet outside with a camera. Little wonder his roommates came to know him as a room service guy. "We'd be on a long road trip," Tracewski said. "I'd say, 'C'mon, Sandy, let's go to the movies or out to dinner.' He'd say, 'No, you go.' He'd be sitting on the bed in that white shirt he always wore and his underwear. And when I came back he'd still be sitting on the bed in his underwear, smoking cigarettes."

He gave up golf and basketball. He didn't go out the night before he pitched. "I think he was very hard on himself," said Wes Parker. "He kind of reminds me of Heifetz, the violinist. There was a story in *Life* magazine about him and the caption said, 'He sacrificed his humanity in the attainment of perfection.' Sandy didn't sacrifice all his humanity but he definitely sacrificed some of his humanity in his ability to be comfortable with people. I purchased a stereo. I told Sandy. He said, 'Let me tell you about my stereo.' He had to be better. He didn't say, 'I'm glad for you.' He had to be number one. His stereo had to be better than mine. I was happy with what I had."

Gene Mauch remembers watching from the Philadelphia dugout as Koufax warmed up before his 1964 no-hitter. "The man threw a hundred and fourteen pitches!" Mauch said. "Warming up! One hundred and fourteen pitches! For about eighty-five or ninety or maybe close to a hundred of those pitches, he was scowling and grimacing and shaking his head, just really down. He couldn't find anything. He couldn't find his release point or his rhythm. Something was bothering the hell out of him. But he was gonna stay out there until he got things the way he wanted it.

"So after about ninety-five or so pitches, he started nodding his head and smiling. Sandy Koufax didn't smile. But now he's smiling at his catcher, who had his back to me. He started nodding his head, and I said, 'Oh my God, I'm in for it.'"

It was a given that he would pitch every four days and that every four days he would win, regardless of how many errors the Dodgers made or runs they didn't score. His career record in 1–0 games was 11 and 3. His record in his last two Septembers was 14 and 3 (16 and 3 if you count October). In those last two seasons, he struck out 699 men in 658⅔ innings, an average of 9.6 per game. Once after Koufax struck out Rico Carty of the Braves three times, Carty went to him, demanding, "You mad at me, Koufax?" Koufax replied, "Young man, I don't even know you, but as long as you're hitting in front of Henry Aaron, you're going to have a tough time with me."

The Dodgers not only counted on him to win, they counted on him to make them all better, to infuse even the most modest among them with his quiet bravado. If he was bullet-proof, so were they. He wasn't exaggerating when he told Ron Fairly late in the season, referring to rookie Jim Barbieri, "If I pitch well from here on out, I can double the man's income." And when a television network offered him $25,000 to film a documentary on a day in his life, he said he would do it for $35,000—and only if $1,000 was given to every member of the team and coaching staff.

His teammates recognized their indebtedness to him. Wills tells the story of an otherwise meaningless ground ball hit to him in the ninth inning of a lopsided shutout. There was one out with a man on third. The correct play was to go to first for the sure out. Wills threw home instead. It was hard to say who was more surprised—Roseboro or Koufax. "I just knew that he had pitched his heart out, like he's done so many times," Wills said. "He deserved a shutout." Afterward, in the locker room, Wills told him: "I only owe you three now."

Though Wills remembers it as if it were yesterday, baseball statisticians can find no record of any game that resembles this scenario. In baseball, stories like these acquire a life of their own. They become an inheritance. Thirty years later, in September 1996, when Roger Clemens had twelve days left in his Boston Red Sox career and a chance to tie Cy Young's record of thirty-eight shutouts, manager Kevin Kennedy promised him that if the situation arose, he would play the infield in to preserve the shutout, invoking the legend of Koufax and Wills.

The Dodgers relied on Koufax more than ever in 1966. Missing spring training may have worked to Koufax's benefit but Drysdale struggled all season. And the Dodger offense was no juggernaut, "piling up runs," Jim Murray wrote, "at a rate of one every nine innings." At the end of May, the world champions were two and a half games out of first place. At the All-Star break, they were in third place, five games behind the Giants. Koufax had already won fifteen games.

Alston named him to start the All-Star Game in St. Louis—the first time he had been so honored. On two days' rest! Jim Bunning was warming up in the bullpen when Koufax threw his first pitch. "I couldn't figure out why Walter Alston would do that except that Koufax was hurting," Bunning said.

The day was a scorcher, 105 degrees in the stands and ten degrees hotter on the field. "NBC packed its cameras in ice," Bunning recalled, "and the little metal disks on the seats were burning people."

Marvin Miller, newly installed as executive director of the Major League Baseball Players Association, lasted one inning longer than Koufax before retreating to the air-conditioned sanctuary of the clubhouse. "The only one in the locker room was Sandy," Miller said. "He was sitting with his entire arm and shoulder in a bucket of ice, with his back to me. He turned around to see who was there and raised his arm. I've never seen an arm swollen like that in my life. He saw that look of horror and he said, 'Don't worry, it goes down. This happens every time I pitch.' He only pitched three innings! We didn't discuss the future. With an arm that looked like that, there wasn't much to talk about. It was as big as a basketball."

Koufax was still icing his arm when Bunning joined them, having completed his two innings of work. "My God, how can you be hurting and throw the ball a hundred miles an hour?" he asked. "Some of us are not hurting and we can only throw it ninety."

In fact, Koufax could throw as hard as ever—just not as often. One National League umpire told Regan at the end of the season, "If he loses as much next year as what he's lost from '65 to '66, he'll be an ordinary pitcher." He began experimenting with new pitches. "He tried a slider but that hurt his elbow," said Joe Torre, who caught him at the 1966 All-Star Game. "He tried a forkball but it didn't work for him physically. Then he started cutting the fastball toward the end, which was tough on a right-handed hitter because normally when you faced Koufax he threw the fastball and the curve."

After all those early years of disuse and misuse, Koufax wasn't about to complain about overuse. Besides, he knew it was the last time around. On July 27, he and Bunning faced each other in a brilliant scoreless duel, the first-ever meeting of perfect-game winners.

There were 45,000 at Dodger Stadium that Wednesday night, among them Ira Green, a Koufax fan from Chicago. Growing up, Ira was a lefty pitcher who threw hard but not quite hard enough. As a teenager, he walked four miles to Wrigley Field to see Koufax. Money was almost as scarce as Jewish major-leaguers. Ira would buy a sixty-cent ticket for a grandstand seat and volunteer to help clean up after the game. "You'd work a half an hour," he said. "If you were real lucky, you'd get to work on the field and pick up hot-dog wrappers. Each kid had a row. We'd race each other, flipping the seats up. If you lifted up a whole row, they'd give you a free pass to the next game. Those were our season tickets."

That was the only way he could afford to see Koufax. But he paid his way into Dodger Stadium for the game against Bunning, sitting in seats so high behind home plate he could barely make out the form on the mound. It didn't matter. He could say he was there. Later, Ira played semipro ball and had a son, Shawn, who also loved baseball. It wasn't until after Shawn signed an $84 million contract with the Dodgers in 1998 that his father told him about seeing that game. "*You* saw Sandy pitch at Dodger Stadium?" Shawn said.

"Yeah," Ira replied sheepishly.

"Wow," his son, the multimillionaire, said.

Bunning struck out eleven, Koufax sixteen. It was tied 1–1 after eleven innings, when both left the game. The Dodgers won in the bottom of the twelfth—Koufax got a no-decision. Regan came in to get the win. That was the day Koufax nicknamed him "the Vulture."

The second week of August 1966, there was a rematch between Koufax and Atlanta pitcher Denny Lemaster, whom he'd beaten 2–1 earlier in the year. Slugger Eddie Mathews, who was nearing the end of his run with the Braves, struck out in his first three times at bat. The game was delayed endlessly by rain. It was two o'clock in the morning when Mathews came to bat again in the ninth. "They've had Sandy in the ballgame, sitting down during the rain delay, back in the ballgame, sitting down during the rain delay, back in the ballgame," Mathews said. "Never in the world did I understand why they did that to Sandy. But at two A.M. I hit a home run off him to beat him. I've never seen a pitcher abused like that in my life."

"Alston never took him out," infielder John Kennedy said. "It could be ten to two, ten to four, ten to five, ten to six. Alston wouldn't take him out unless it was tied. He was afraid to take him out of there."

As summer ceded to fall and the season wound to a close, Koufax went to Alston and told him, "Use me any way you want, as often as you want." He did not explain his reasoning. The manager took him at his word. In the last twenty-six days of the season, Koufax started seven games, completed six, and won five, giving up just a fraction over one run per game. He had almost as many cortisone shots as complete-game wins.

Doctors were injecting steroids directly into the elbow joint. Once he had an adverse reaction. He was lying on the training table when infielder Jim Lefebvre walked in. "His arm, it was, like, twice the size," Lefebvre said. "It was like a boil. I looked at him and I said, 'Oh, my God, your season's over.' He looked at me and he goes, 'No, no, Frenchie, it's too late in the season. I won't miss my start.' And he didn't."

It was a gut-wrenching, three-way pennant race between Los Angeles, Pittsburgh, and San Francisco. On September 11, the Dodgers seized first place on the strength of Koufax's fortieth—and last—career shutout. Five days later, he beat the Pirates 5–1 for his twenty-fourth win. The numbers were more impressive than his stuff. Noting his unusually low number of strikeouts (five), Bob Bailey said, "Compared with the way he usually throws, he had nothing."

Roberto Clemente thought otherwise. After the game, he sounded off to Phil Collier: "When my back hurts, they call me a goldbrick. Koufax says his elbow hurts and they make him national hero. Sore arm my foot. He threw as hard tonight as he ever has. He can't have a sore elbow and throw like that. I know. I had bone chips in my elbow once and I had to throw underhand.

"What does he think the National League is, a joke? Last year he wins twenty-six games and this year he wins twenty-four, and all I hear about is how much pain he has in his elbow. What does he want people to believe? That he could win fifty games a year if his elbow isn't sore?"

Clemente had made the incalculable error of underestimating Koufax, questioning not only his toughness but also, implicitly, his integrity. Koufax hated being doubted as much as he had loathed being misjudged early in his career. He rarely got angry. As former teammate Ed Palmquist said, "He was a gentleman, with all the social graces that ballplayers don't have."

The next day behind the batting cage, there he was, on the dead run, going after Clemente, with Drysdale right behind him. "Wow," Torborg said. "He must really be hurting." When he faced the Cardinals on September 29, the Dodgers had a two-game lead with four games left to play. It was presumably his last start before the world series. The St. Louis fans gave him a standing ovation when he struck out Curt Flood in the fourth, becoming the first pitcher ever to strike out 300 men in each of three seasons. Flood's home run in the seventh accounted for the Cardinals' only run. When he doubled with two outs in the ninth, a sickening feeling permeated the Dodger dugout. Alston banished Barbieri from the bench after the rookie literally got sick to his stomach. "You just knew we were going down to the final game of the season," Regan said.

The Dodgers headed to Philadelphia for the last three games of the season. The second-place Pirates were playing the third-place Giants in Pittsburgh. All the Dodgers needed was one win, one Pittsburgh loss. It should have been easy. But fate had a more operatic denouement in mind. On Friday, the Dodgers and the Pirates lost. On Saturday, the Dodgers lost a game to rain, and the Pirates just plain lost. Suddenly, there was a pennant race again.

When the final day of the regular season dawned, the Dodgers held a tenuous one-and-a-half-game lead over the Giants. It was decided that the rain-out would be played as part of a Sunday doubleheader but only if needed to determine the pennant; if it was necessary, Koufax would pitch. Not that anyone wanted that: He was supposed to open the world series against the Orioles three days later.

It was baseball's best version of improvisational theater: four teams in two disparate cities trading leads back and forth. Scoreboard watching was raised to high art. Everyone within radio frequency was tuned to events at either end of Pennsylvania. Veteran Dick Stuart wore headphones on the Dodger bench, updating the game in Pittsburgh. Sportswriters across town covering the Eagles game at Franklin Field watched the action with bifurcated vision—wondering whether to hurry over to Connie Mack Stadium. By the end of the afternoon, pro golfer Bob Rosburg was so nervous he forgot to sign his scorecard at the end of his round at the Canadian Open.

Drysdale pitched "the lid-lifter" and lasted less than three innings. The Dodgers rallied to take a lead but so did the Pirates in Pittsburgh. The Dodgers clung to their one-run lead until the eighth inning. "Suddenly, the bases were drunk with no outs and Koufax leaped up out of the dugout and ran down to the bullpen," said Doug Harvey, who was umpiring at first base. "Everybody in the ballpark saw him run down there. They knew what he was trying to do. They needed one ballgame. He was going to try to save it knowing that he would have to pitch the second game if they lost."

The Phillies tied the game on an error and took the lead on another one just as the scoreboard flashed the word: They were all tied up in the ninth in Pittsburgh. When the game ended, the Dodgers had a one-game lead over the Giants. They retired to the clubhouse to await their fate. "You could hear a pin drop," Lefebvre said. "It was the most draining year I've ever had in my life 'cause you never had momentum. One day it was the Pirates, one day it was the Giants, one day it was us. It just kept switching back and forth. So finally we're sitting there and Sandy stands up and says, 'The hell with it.'"

And he went out to warm up. Torborg caught him while tethered to a headset. Twice the Pirates loaded the bases. Twice they failed to score. In the umpires' dressing room, Harvey ordered the clubhouse man to turn off the radio. "I told him, 'Jim, just shut that off if you don't mind.' 'Cause I'm in my fifth year and believe me it's a lot of pressure knowing that you've gotta go behind the plate and work the game."

In the Phillies' locker room, Dick Groat decided not to shower and bit into a sandwich he never would have had if he thought he might be playing another game. By the time he finished it, Mauch had penciled him into the starting lineup. "I walked up the runway just in time to hear the announcer on the PA system in Philadelphia say that Willie McCovey had just hit a home run off Steve Blass in Forbes Field to win the game for the Giants," Groat said. "And all of a sudden, the Dodgers have to win to clinch it."

The game took two hours and thirty-four minutes to play but a lifetime to develop. Looking into the Phillies' dugout, Koufax saw Groat, now well fed and unshowered, who was at Forbes Field in 1954 when Koufax tried out for Branch Rickey; and at second base in 1962 when Koufax got jammed trying to hit left-handed and almost lost his index finger. Groat even fielded the infield single that resulted from it.

He saw Bill White, who was batting against him in the spring of 1964 when the accumulated adhesions in his arm cut loose and his vulnerability was first publicly exposed. He saw Bobby Wine, Tony Taylor, and Richie Allen, all of whom were in the lineup when he held the Phillies hitless two months later. Opposing him was Bunning, whose path Koufax first crossed in Cincinnati when he was playing freshman basketball and Bunning was the opposing coach. In the Philadelphia bullpen was Ed Roebuck, an old teammate, who was at Lennie's that night in 1961 when Kenny Myers helped Koufax find his release point with a dead cigar. And, starting in left field in his last major league game: Harvey Kuenn.

In his own dugout, Koufax saw Drysdale, bat in hand, ready to pinch-hit if necessary; Al Ferrara, a graduate of Lafayette High in Brooklyn; and Wes Covington, who played winter ball with him in Puerto Rico in 1956. In the Dodger clubhouse, Don Newcombe was visiting with "Doc" Anderson and Bill Buhler. In the press box, *New York Post* columnist Larry Merchant, who once tried to recruit him to play football for Lafayette, had just arrived from Franklin Field. Catching his breath, Merchant thought, Practically the only games that matter for Koufax are ones like these.

It was a year to the day since Koufax had clinched the 1965 pennant. Then, too, he was working on two days' rest. But, in 1965, there was another game to be played in the season and another season left in his career. This time, he went to the mound knowing not just that he had to win but that if he didn't it would be the last time he ever pitched.

There comes a point when statistics are no longer a sufficient gauge of greatness, and Koufax had reached it. A more accurate measure was the way he altered and enhanced memory, how teammates and spectators defined themselves in relation to him. So, a utility infielder like Nate Oliver, who never had the career he wanted or expected, would take solace in middle age from the nickname Koufax gave him and from the honed memory of fielding a sharply hit ground ball to save Koufax's second no-hitter.

So, an impressionable young baseball fan, Glenn Waggoner, would swear he saw Koufax carry a no-hitter into the sixth inning on a sultry summer night when baseball was still played outdoors in Houston. In his memory, mosquitoes swooned and fans collapsed but Koufax stayed in the game, soaking through a parade of woolen jerseys, until the first hit was allowed. In fact, Koufax won the game, an otherwise meaningless July contest, but it wasn't close to being a no-hitter.

Myth-making is a collaborative process, a collusion between recollection and fact. It requires the consensus that there is a larger truth to be told than the one found in a box score. The last game of the 1966 season has long since morphed into myth. Two umpires, Crawford and Harvey, insist Koufax struck out Allen with the bases loaded in the bottom of the ninth to win the game and the pennant. And that prior to the final swing Allen vowed "to air-condition" the stadium, telling Harvey, "It's his ass or mine."

In fact, Allen struck out three times but not in the ninth inning. The first time, in the bottom of the first inning, there were two on and two out. Koufax would say later that the fastball that got Allen was the most essential pitch of the day, not just because of what could have happened but because of what it revealed about his own stuff. Heat was all he had to offer. "After one and one-third innings, Roseboro looked at me and said, 'Sit back, kid,'" Harvey said. "I said, 'What do you mean?' He said, 'Koufax said he can't get his curve over. He's gonna go with the heater, the fastball.'

"That's all he threw, the fastball, the rest of the game. He threw seven and two-thirds innings with nothing but a fastball. And they knew what was coming. And he still won the game for them, and the pennant. It was the greatest exhibition of baseball I've ever seen in my life."

What Harvey did not know was what transpired between innings. Pitching to Gary Sutherland in the fifth, Koufax felt something pop in his back. Retreating to the clubhouse, he called for more Capsolin from the trainers. Newcombe, who first introduced Koufax to the hot stuff, watched Buhler smear his arm, his back, his side. When he was done, Newcombe and Anderson tried to help Buhler pop that something in his back into place by pulling Koufax in opposite directions. "I pulled on his legs and they held his shoulder," Newcombe said. "We tried to stretch him out. I remember he kept taking the pills. Every inning, he'd come in and holler for the trainer, 'Give me some more.'"

The Dodgers held a 6–0 lead going into the bottom of the ninth. Koufax had given up three infield hits and one solid double to White. But he still had to face Allen, Kuenn, and Taylor and he was spent. Allen was the only man to reach base in the 1964 no-hitter, on a 3-and-2 walk. This time, he reached on a gift by second baseman Lefebvre. Kuenn stepped to the plate for his 6,913th and last major league at-bat. The baseball gods had given him one last chance to atone for those two no-hit ninth-inning failures. Seeking redemption, Kuenn settled for a single.

Next up: Taylor. He, too, singled, driving in the Phillies' first run. White waited in the on-deck circle while Alston paid a visit to the mound, not to remove Koufax, as he had so often in the early years, but to remind him not to fall into the young pitcher's trap, reaching back for too much. What else could he do? Nothing else was left.

White admired Koufax as much as anyone in baseball admired adversaries in 1966. Later, they would become good friends. "Sandy, he didn't cry and bitch about anything," White said. "That's why I liked him."

White hit an unsentimental double off the scoreboard, driving in two more runs. Dodgers 6, Phillies 3. And still no one out. Koufax struck out Bob Uecker for the first out. Mauch summoned Wine to pinch-hit, just as he had in the bottom of the ninth of the no-hitter in

1964. This time, Wine grounded out on a ball Maury Wills almost threw away. Out number two.

Jackie Brandt approached the plate. "Koufax reared back and threw three balls by him," Lefebvre said. "He had no chance. From somewhere, he got enough energy to blow him away. It reminded me of the intensity he had in the perfect game. Now, the game is over and the pennant won. I said, 'Wow, man, where did that come from?' He says, 'I thought that was the tying run at the plate.'"

In the hurly-burly of the locker room, Koufax pointed to the spot behind his left shoulder where the problem was while Covington doused him with champagne and shaving cream. "It doesn't hurt when I *drink* champagne," Koufax told the equally drenched reporters, pointedly.

Umpires don't ask for autographs. They collect memories, not memorabilia. In thirty-one years, Harvey made one exception to the rule. After he retired, he purchased an autographed picture of Sandy Koufax at an auction. "I have as much respect for Sandy Koufax as for any man I've ever met in my life," Harvey said. "It was a privilege to work that game."

The anticlimactic world series opened two days later. Bookies made the depleted Dodgers 8–5 favorites to defeat the Baltimore Orioles. Los Angeles newspapers were already speculating about who would start game five—if the series went that far. The Orioles' advance scout, Jim Russo, took three hours at a team meeting to describe the infallibility of Dodger pitching. Finally, manager Hank Bauer growled, "If these guys are that good, we got no chance. Meeting over."

Drysdale faltered in game one, outpitched by an unheralded reliever, Moe Drabowsky. In game two, Koufax was opposed by baby-faced Jim Palmer. It was his third start in eight days. Frank Robinson, who knew Koufax well from the National League, offered his new teammates this cogent advice: "If it starts at the belt, take it because it's going to choke you."

Neither Palmer nor his young catcher, Andy Etchebarren, had ever seen anything like it. For four innings, Koufax was everything Robinson said. "The first time up, I'm hitting eighth, Palmer is in the on-deck circle," Etchebarren said. "I take two strikes, swing at the third, the three hardest fastballs I've ever seen. When I was walking back, Jimmy Palmer looks at me and said, 'You had no chance.' You just say, 'Shit and god-damn, I ain't never seen anything come up here that quick.' "

But by the second time through the batting order, it was apparent to Robinson that Koufax wasn't the same pitcher he had known. "I couldn't tell he was hurting," Robinson said. "Sandy will never let on. But you knew he didn't have the real good fastball. It was down in the low nineties, where before it was right about ninety-eight."

The game was easily summarized for the morning papers. "In the fifth inning, Willie Davis dropped two fly balls in center field," Palmer reported. "And after the world knew he had trouble fielding, he threw a ball into the dugout trying to show he had a great arm."

No outfielder in world series history had ever made three errors in one inning before. Thanks to Davis, the Orioles scored three unearned runs, ending Koufax's streak of twenty-two scoreless innings in world series play. When the third out was recorded, Davis headed for the end of the bench and so did Koufax. Teammates, misconstruing his purpose, stepped in his path. They should have known better. Koufax draped an arm over Davis's shoulder and said, "Don't let them get you down."

The next morning, the *New York Post* printed an exclusive interview with Koufax's genetic father, Jack Braun, and the snapshots he had given the editors of a young boy in a shirt and tie, socks pulled high, trying to hit one over the fence in a distant New York playground. The story spoke of Braun's ordeal as he watched his biological son betrayed by team-mates on television. "He pitched his heart out and they do this to him."

The last hit Koufax surrendered was an opposite-field bloop single to Davey Johnson. "I only had three at-bats against him lifetime, and hit three hundred," Johnson said. "I think I should be in the Hall of Fame." He told Koufax as much the next spring when they ran into each other at Dodgertown. "Sandy had retired but he was in uniform. I said, 'Hey, Sandy, I guess you know who hit the last hit off you.' He said, 'Davey, that's why I knew I was washed up.' "

Decades later, riding a bus to an old-timers game, Boog Powell sat with Koufax and reminisced about that game. "He said, 'If I had one thing to do over in my life, I'd love to pitch that game again.' I'm sure he regretted it. I think what he was saying was, 'You guys didn't see the best I had.' What he had was pretty good. He might have been hurtin' but he was bringin'."

In Baltimore, Koufax warmed up on the sideline for a start he would never make, wincing with every delivery. Surrounded by photographers, he told Norm Sherry, his old catcher, "Get them away. If they're here, I'm not throwing."

When Ed Linn, his coauthor, saw him in the locker room after the Orioles completed the unexpected four-game sweep, Koufax didn't seem dejected. "When he came over, he put his arm around me and said, 'Hey, collaborator, hey, pal, how come you left me to do the signings alone?' I came back and said, 'He's through.' There was a sense, 'Okay, I climbed the mountain and now I can go on.'"

On the flight back to Los Angeles, Koufax told Collier he was going to announce his retirement on the plane. "Shit, don't do that," Collier replied. "You'll screw every A.M. paper in America. There's no hurry. Wait a couple of weeks."

Koufax reluctantly agreed. A few minutes later, Drysdale came down the aisle. "Sandy turned to me and said, 'He'd quit too if he could afford it,'" Collier remembered. "I thought, What a strange thing to say. But Sandy was at that point proud that he was able to get out at thirty, at the top."

The unhappy former world champions, minus Koufax and Drysdale, set off on an exhibition tour of Japan. Midway through the trip, Wills bolted from the team. It was an omen and a precursor. Back on the West Coast, Koufax was doing his best to avoid phone calls from reporters, all of whom wanted to know his plans and many of whom he considered his friends. On the evening of November 17, while Collier and his wife were at the Ice Capades, their baby-sitter took a message from Mr. Koufax.

Collier didn't require an explanation. When he got Koufax on the phone, Koufax told him, "When I get up in the morning I'm going to call the wire services and tell them I'm holding a press conference at the Beverly Wilshire at twelve P.M. Do you need anything?"

Having honored his commitment not to write what he had known for fourteen months, Collier was honored with the scoop. "I said, 'Sandy, I wrote the story six, seven, eight months ago.' I had it in the drawer. He said, 'Why don't you come up and go with me?' They played that thing on page one, across the top, in the kind of type you'd use for the end of World War Two. The guys in L.A., the other writers, they were so pissed off. They said, 'How the hell could you sit on that for fourteen months?'"

That night Koufax also called Bavasi. *Wait until O'Malley returns from Japan*, he pleaded. *Wait until the winter meetings*. Koufax demurred. Bavasi was worried about leverage and trading options; Koufax was worried about his integrity. He told Bavasi he was going ahead with the announcement. He didn't want to lie anymore. Ask Bavasi now what made Koufax different from everyone else, he'll tell you, "I don't think Sandy ever told a lie in his life." Bavasi told the wire services the announcement would do the team "irreparable harm." (And, by the way, thanks for the memories.)

The next day, one hundred reporters in dark suits and thin ties dutifully scribbled Koufax's words as a single ray of light, slanting through the ballroom window, illuminated his face. Women, none of them carrying press cards, cried. Hard-boiled baseball writers crafted open letters to their sons imploring them to grow up to be like Sandy Koufax. No one from Dodger management attended.

Fifteen microphones amplified his words as he read a short written statement acknowledging his request to be placed on the voluntary retired list. "Why, Sandy?" a reporter asked.

Koufax repeated the question slowly. "The question is, 'Why?' I don't know if cortisone is good for you or not. But to take a shot every other ballgame is more than I wanted to do and to walk around with a constant upset stomach because of the pills and to be high half the time during a ballgame because you're taking painkillers, I don't want to have to do that."

"What about the money?" someone asked.

"Well, the loss of income . . ." He paused. He said he'd rather have full use of his arm—bend it, for example. "If there was a man who did not have the use of one of his arms and you told him it would cost a lot of money if he could buy back that use, he'd give every dime he had, I believe. I don't regret one minute of the last twelve years but I think I would regret one year that was too many."

When Trixie tracked him down by phone the next day, Koufax picked up after one ring, as if anticipating the call. All Tracewski could say was "Sandy." Koufax replied, "Well, all of my sport coats have two different arms in them. I can't go on doing this medication thing and pitching. It's going to kill me."

In later years, he reiterated the notion, time and again, saying he never regretted the decision; he regretted having to make it. Still, there were disbelievers because, as Tom Boswell, the baseball bard, said in the *Washington Post*, "He wasn't at his peak, he was above it." His record for the last five years of his career was 111 and 34. His earned run average was 1.95, more than one and a half runs less than the rest of the National League average.

His retirement was invariably described as shocking. No one should have been surprised, certainly not Bavasi. The handwriting was not only on the wall, it was in print. Back issues of sports magazines and deadline newspaper stories from 1964 on reveal endless speculation over how long and how effectively he could pitch.

No, what was disconcerting, revolutionary even, was the idea. Athletes don't quit, certainly not after their best season. They don't walk away. They limp away. They play until the joints play out, until bone rubs against bone, until they are shown the door. Those who retire on their own terms are few and legend: Jim Brown, Rocky Marciano, Gene Tunney. Bill Bradley soldiered on in the NBA deliberately past his prime, choosing to experience the inevitable downward arc of his athletic career so he wouldn't be tempted later to find out how much air was left in the jump shot. "Koufax quit when he had to, when he wanted to, when he needed to," Newcombe said.

The shock that greeted his announcement was rooted in the assumption that athletes need to play in order to be complete. Koufax needed to quit in order to be whole. It was an act of imagination to see himself as something other than just a ballplayer, an asset to be depreciated on someone else's books. "He had a real sense of what life really is," his friend Dave Wallace would say years later. "And baseball's a game. We hold on to it until we find out it has held on to us."

Which explains his hold on fans such as Al Meyers, who wasn't born until after Koufax retired. "It's that he put his health ahead of being a figurehead," Meyers said. "He didn't need baseball to be Sandy Koufax."

In the coming days, months, and even years, tabloid conjecture was at a lather. *Would he come back? Could he come back? Should he have gone on? Could he have gone on?* "Probably," he says now, but at what level and at what cost? His arm? His sanity? That, too, was questioned.

Quitting was the sanest thing to do. It took him six years to become the pitcher some believed he would never become; to *devise* Sandy Koufax. He wasn't about to sully that, to compromise, subject himself to renewed doubt. "He went from the shithouse to the castle," Wallace said. "It was 'I'm not going back to where I was. I'm walking away with my head held high.'"

"He expected so much of himself all the time," Mauch said. "I think part of the reason he retired as early as he did (after having the two best years I could imagine a pitcher having) is that he expected that of himself and he knew that every time he went out there, if he pitched a seven-hitter and won 5–3, that wasn't gonna please anybody. And I honestly thought that just wore on him, just wore him down. The expectancy on the part of everybody of him doing something super every time he went to the mound." Perhaps that's what Koufax meant when he confided to a friend years after he retired, "Maybe I was just tired of being me."

The jolly pink cover of the 1967 Dodger yearbook featured a goofy caricature of a Dodger juggling four world series crowns. The cartoon was meant to convey an abundance of postseason riches. It could just as easily be interpreted as an image of the franchise reeling under the weight of Koufax's departure. No mention was made of his retirement or of the trades that sent Wills to Pittsburgh and Tommy Davis to the Mets. Billy Hitchcock, manager of the Atlanta Braves, offered the definitive epitaph: "The Dodgers start twenty-seven games out."

His career ended, the rest of his life began. Koufax went for a walk on the beach, alone.

Epilogue

THE AFTERLIFE

On September 9, 1965, Dave Smith had to choose between hormones and baseball. His high school girlfriend was leaving for college in the morning. Sandy Koufax was pitching for the Dodgers at Chavez Ravine. Koufax was his favorite player on his favorite team. Dave was so devoted to the Dodgers that he charted twenty-five consecutive games every year, pitch by pitch, in his Peterson's ScoreMaster Scorebook. But he was also a teenage boy with other urges. Before leaving the house to meet his sweetheart, Dave set up a reel-to-reel tape recorder in his bedroom, which, in his hormonal zeal, he neglected to turn on. It was the bottom of the second inning when Dave's father, Hugh, wandered into his son's bedroom and flipped the switch, muttering under his breath to his wife—because he knew how much Dave would regret the missed innings—"If he doesn't like it he can just drop dead." As the reels began to turn, Scully was setting the scene: "One ball, one strike, one out, second inning, no score." And Hugh can be heard growling over the play-by-play: "Did you hear that, David? If you don't like it, you can drop dead."

Hugh Smith wasn't much of a baseball fan. It was his wife Nancy's passion for Duke Snider that ignited the son's flame. But when Dave returned from his date with the girl who would become his first wife, mother of his daughter, Sandy, Hugh was waiting for him at the front door. "He ushered me into my room, where he insisted that I sit down with him and listen to the game all the way through," Smith said. "I kept asking, 'Did he do it?' But my father just grinned. It was pretty obvious that the answer was yes or we wouldn't have been sitting there listening but he wouldn't tell me in advance. We went to bed about a quarter of two."

On September 9, 1965, Sandy Koufax and Bob Hendley pitched one of the best baseball games ever played. Hendley pitched a one-hitter, the game of his life, and lost on a young catcher's error. The only run scored on a walk, a sacrifice, a stolen base, and a bad throw. As Scully said, "The only hit, you almost couldn't dignify as one." Hendley's teammate, Ken Holtzman, calls it "the greatest loss in baseball history."

Koufax threw a perfect game, his fourth no-hitter, then a major league record. He never pitched better than he did those last three innings and rarely, if ever, has anyone pitched better than that. It was, he would say later, "As total as it's ever been."

Today, Dave Smith is a professor of microbiology at the University of Delaware, and the head of Retrosheet, a nonprofit, volunteer organization dedicated to the collection and publication of play-by-play accounts of every major league game played since 1901. According to his research, it is still the only game ever played to qualify as a true one-hitter and the only game with only one runner left on base. It still holds the record for the fewest base runners, two, both of whom happened to be Lou Johnson. The next lowest total is four. Dave keeps track of these things.

Yet, apart from the official scorecard and yellowed newspaper clippings, there was little known documentation of the game that came as close to perfection as baseball gets. The broadcasting industry may have been on the precipice of a technological revolution but radio station

KFI was still airing "re-creations" of out-of-town ballgames the way Ronald "Dutch" Reagan once did as the voice of the Chicago Cubs. Allan Roth, the statistician who kept pitch-by-pitch records of every Dodger game beginning in 1947, had left the team in August 1964. All that survived was Scully's memorable call of the top of the ninth inning. Pressed into vinyl, it acquired a life of its own. It was sold at stadium concession stands for the next twenty years, its cadence memorized and internalized by fervent fans, including Bob Costas.

Every September 9, Dodger broadcasters would observe the anniversary by pulling the tape from the vault and finding someone still in uniform who had been on the field that night. Finally, only Joey A. was left. Every year the radio guys asked the same question, and every year Amalfitano replied: "Let's change the script this time."

It *did* change. Absent the technological exactitude of the present, it was replayed in memory and reimagined. Guys who were there now swear that no one took a bat off a shoulder in the ninth, that Koufax struck out the side on nine pitches, every one a fastball, that his hat flew off with each vehement delivery. It wasn't enough that he struck out the last six men he faced, that he threw so hard his hat flew off at all. That he was perfect. Jeff Torborg still insists he called only one curve in the ninth inning. Ernie Banks is still convinced he homered off Koufax four days later (it was Billy Williams). Ron Santo still swears he never swung his bat in the second inning. *Whish, whish, whish.* "Are you sure?" he says. "I remember three fastballs. I remember taking all three. I thought it was Billy who popped up."

Then, one day, a videotape arrived in the mail from Major League Baseball Productions. It was an unedited highlight reel of Koufax's career, images spliced together, black and white, and leached of color, snippets without order or organizing principle.

Koufax smiling, dimples prominently displayed. Koufax talking without sound. Koufax signing autographs at Holman Stadium. Dugouts draped with bunting. Shadows creeping across distant fields. A sea of white broadcloth and skinny ties. Women wearing sunglasses as big as fantails. The Dodgers serenading Moose Skowron: "M-I-C-K-E-Y M-O-O-S-E." Ritual world series handshakes: Bob

Shaw (1959), Whitey Ford (1963), Jim Kaat (1965), and Jim Palmer (1966).
Koufax leaping. Koufax leaping again.

And then this:

> *Two minutes of black-and-white footage. In the distance, foul poles loom*
> *and a 410-foot outfield sign. A limber, young catcher crouches behind*
> *home plate, the number on his back obscured by the elastic bands of his*
> *chest protector. There is nothing whatsoever to verify the time or the*
> *place: no names stitched in satin, no advertisements on the outfield wall.*
> *The footage is raw and pure, disembodied and archetypal. It exists out*
> *of time and context. Only one thing is clear: the man on the mound*
> *with the number 32 on his back, tugging on his cap after each heave*
> *threatens to carry it away.*

Jeff Torborg knew what it was immediately. No longer a punk
receiver but a middle-aged former catcher squatting before a VCR, he
leaped from his crouch. "They told us nothing existed! They told us
there wasn't anything!"

Torborg had no guess as to the film's genesis or its whereabouts
since then. It was Koufax's suggestion to ask Bill Buhler, the retired
trainer. Buhler recognized his handiwork immediately. "Yup, that's
mine," he said almost shyly, his voice as thin as an old man's hair. "Don't
know who else it could have been."

He remembered the day and the dispute with the unctuous usher
and the Dodger vice president who had him removed from his spot
behind home plate, preventing him from recording the last three outs of
Koufax's perfect game. When it was over, Buhler turned the
unprocessed film over to the front office and never laid eyes on it again.
The identity of the club v.p. remains his training room secret.

Thanks to Buhler's raw cinematography and Dave Smith's reel-to-
reel recording of the broadcast on KFI, all nine innings can now be
revisited. The difference between what is seen and heard and what is
remembered offers a lesson in history and imagination, the human
impulse to perfect the former with the latter. That isn't the only revela-

tion. What leaps from the tape is the experience of surprise. So little was expected of Hendley and so much of Koufax. No one expected this. In history, it is The Perfect Game, a fait accompli. When Dave Smith's father turned on the tape recorder in his son's bedroom, it was just another Thursday night in September with no score at the end of two.

By the time Dave and his father listened all the way through, it was nearly 2:00 A.M. on September 10. The Cubs had just arrived in San Francisco, their short, late-night flight the culmination of a very long day. Nobody got much sleep. Reality didn't set in until breakfast. It greeted Hendley in the hotel coffee shop like the last cold cup from the urn. "You go down to eat, you know you've been through something," he said.

Krug didn't feel a whole lot better. Not only had his error cost Hendley the game but when he arrived at Candlestick Park, a local writer demanded to know whether he had thrown the ball away on purpose. "I just about went after him, it angered me so," Krug said.

He found Hendley shagging fly balls on the warning track and summoned the words of apology that had eluded him the night before. "Sorry I screwed it up for you," he said.

Hendley has no memory of the conversation, preferring instead to remember his next start, four days later, when he hooked up with Koufax again on a raw, windy Chicago afternoon. There were 6,000 people in the stands at Wrigley Field. He threw a four-hitter and beat Koufax 2–1. It was the last of their six major league encounters. Hendley won three and lost one; Koufax beat him only once, the night of the perfect game. "Krug didn't screw it up, I'm sure that's what I told him," Hendley said. "He threw the ball away at third. But he didn't put the guy on base. He didn't let him steal third. I didn't blame him. I didn't blame anybody. You didn't then. You probably do now."

He has no regrets about that night except that he lacked the foresight to keep a tangible reminder of it. Everyone else, it seemed, got something. Charlie Sheen, a six-day-old future actor with a passion for baseball memorabilia, got his lawyer's signed scorecard—the only game Richard Hume ever scored. Kevin Kennedy, the eleven-year-old who stayed up past his bedtime listening to the radio, got to be Koufax's friend. Jeff Torborg got to catch another two no-hitters. Harvey Kuenn got to heaven wth a .303 batting average. And Byron Browne got the satisfaction of knowing that Koufax would always remember his name. "It's a pleasure to be mentioned in the same sentence as Sandy Koufax," he says.

Krug got over it. He moved on, bought a car wash, using Scully's description of his leadoff at-bat in the ninth in a radio commercial: "Come to Chris Krug's car wash. Chris Krug won't strike out with you." He went back to school, got a degree in landscape architecture, and became a facilitator of aspirations. "This will shake your boots," he said. "You've seen my work." The Field of Dreams constructed for the movie based on W. P. Kinsella's novella is his. It is now the biggest tourist attraction in the state of Iowa.

Koufax got a $500 raise from Walter O'Malley, the maximum then allowed under baseball's unwritten law. Any more might have tempted a player to seek individual glory in lieu of team goals. Each of his teammates received a wooden plaque with a photograph commemorating the occasion. It is 9:46 P.M. in the City of the Angels. The count is 2 and 2 on Harvey Kuenn. Koufax stands on the precipice of perfection, delivering the 113th pitch of the game. A length of luminous zeroes is perched over his left shoulder, and the lineups, too, almost as if he is carrying them on his back. Only later, upon reflection, was it noted that the angle of the photograph is impossible. Someone had enhanced it, creating an impossible picture to document an implausible event. Like Koufax, it had to be perfect.

What did Hendley get? A new name, "One-Hit Hendley," and his picture on the front page of the newspaper, above the fold. "Almost Perfect," the caption in the September 10 edition of the *Chicago Tribune* said. He looked like a man with a bad blister, which in fact he had the day the picture was taken.

He got another two seasons out of his left arm. In 1967, he was a short relief man with the Mets, which was all his elbow had left to give. There were bone chips floating around inside the joint. "I would throw a pitch and my elbow would lock up," he said. "The chip would slip down in the elbow joint. It felt like a pea in there. I'd walk off the mound, pull on it, and throw again."

After that season, he went home to Macon, Georgia, and finished college—"Enrolled in '57 and graduated in 1970." The same year Koufax was named Athlete of the Decade by the Associated Press. Two years later, Koufax became the youngest man ever elected to the Hall of Fame. By then, Hendley had gotten his teaching degree. He never did get elected to the Georgia State Hall of Fame, though he did donate a few items to their collection: a Braves equipment bag and an auto-graphed ball.

Hendley got a job at a nearby private school teaching physical edu-cation and coaching baseball, throwing the ball every day. "I haven't left baseball," he liked to say. "I just haven't made money at it." When he retired at the end of the 2001 school year, the Stratford Academy renamed the baseball field in his honor. Some of the boys had his base-ball card. Almost none of them knew about the perfect game. He never talked about it until one kid showed him a card from a Trivial Pursuit game, asking, "Who was the other pitcher in Sandy Koufax's perfect game?"

"The fact that I played major league baseball doesn't have anything to do with my purpose. My purpose is to teach the fundamentals of baseball, right and wrong. There are other things, lots of values outside of winning and losing, to offer them. My players know that I played. I think that's enough. I don't live by what I did but by what I do."

One day, back in the early eighties, the local paper sent a reporter to interview him. They ran their story with a picture of him striking out Sandy Koufax. Hendley's son, Bart, the youngest, cut out the article and sent it to Koufax, who sent it back, signed, with a note: "Say hello to your father." It was the first time their paths had crossed since September 1965.

"I'd have loved to have done better," Hendley said, "but I wouldn't want to be famous. I wouldn't want to be Sandy Koufax. I'd want to be me. I am who I am. I'm from where I'm from. I understand he has a problem wherever he goes, he's swarmed. I don't want to switch places. If roles were reversed? I'd still be who I am now."

Still, it would be nice to have a signed ball, something to pass on to his children and grandchildren. "I doubt that's going to happen," he said. "I know how he is about those things."

People think they know how he is. What they know is the public perception of the greatest lefty of all time, who walked away from baseball at age thirty and kept walking. Who allegedly valued his privacy so much the Dodgers had to send telegrams to his house when they wanted to reach him. Who said he was tired of all the hotel rooms and the travel but has wandered the globe ever since, moving so many times friends say they don't know where the hell he is. Who showed up at Turner Field for the Team of the Century ceremonies in 1999, took one look at the press mob gathered around him, and announced: "I'd almost rather have root canal." The quote was solemnly reported and recycled, absent context and humor.

One thing for sure, Koufax wasn't going to be another old ballplayer, hanging on, hanging around, trying to cram his former self into a pair of too-tight double-knits. "Baseball was what you did until you grew up," he always said. "A way station in life."

He had no master plan for life after baseball except to live in the present tense. Asked once what he was doing to keep busy in retirement, Hank Aaron replied, "I'm *being* Hank Aaron." It is the career choice of former greats. But Koufax didn't want to grow old being Sandy Koufax. So his choices were limited.

It came as no surprise to those closest to him that the woman he fell in love with and married didn't know who Sandy Koufax was. "It was probably the first thing that attracted him," said his old friend Trixie.

Anne Widmark is the daughter of the movie star, Richard, the product of a star system even bigger than that of the L.A. Dodgers. They met on the beach and married in 1969. They bought an old house that needed lots of renovating, Wimkumpaugh Farm in Ellsworth, Maine, and went to work on it. It was during this period that he remained largely out of public view and earned the reputation of a recluse. Roger Angell, the great baseball writer for the *New Yorker* magazine, a summer resident of Maine, invited him to go sailing one time. After accepting the invitation, Koufax abruptly declined. Strange guy, Angell thought. He wasn't alone.

Don Sutton regards him as a "clinical introvert," someone who knows and values the difference between solitude and loneliness. Red Adams, the old Dodger pitching coach, concurs: "Sometimes people are misunderstood for being aloof when they're really just quiet."

He had signed a ten-year contract with NBC for $1 million to do the Saturday Game of the Week. He looked male-model good in the blazer but was as stiff as the creases in his pants. All he had to do was look in the camera and be himself, which was the one thing he couldn't do. Sports video geeks at the Classic Sports Network still cite a live 1971 World Series interview he conducted as one of the most painful moments in the history of broadcast sports. His partner, Joe Garagiola, tried to coach him through it, prompting. "Sandy, you've been there, lots of years."

"Definitely," Koufax said.

"You've been through it, the seventh game of the world series. You have anything to add?"

"I don't think you can add anything to what they said," Koufax replied.

He quit before the 1973 season, telling NBC execs to keep their money, and went home to Maine. In the received wisdom, he disappeared. Unlike the Yankee Clipper, a.k.a. Mr. Coffee, to whom he is so often compared, Koufax refused to cannibalize himself for profit. "What people don't understand is Sandy doesn't cash in because Sandy feels he *did* cash in," said Jerry Della Femina, the advertising maven from Lafayatte High.

The year after he retired, he turned down an offer from Gillette to market an updated paperback edition of his autobiography as a world series giveaway. He told his disappointed coauthor Ed Linn, "My giving them that is just giving them an endorsement. I've already turned that down."

"More evidence," Sutton says, "of an ethical life."

His lack of commercial visibility reinforced the notion of his reclusiveness. In another culture, it might have been viewed for what it was—a lack of venality. "He wasn't driven by money, he wasn't driven by fame," said Fred Wilpon. "He has enough resources to be comfortable and happy. Possessions aren't the gospel. He will often tell you, 'The less possessions the better.'"

"A minimalist," Scully calls him. "To say the least."

Those who've known him longest say he hasn't changed at all. Bill DeLury is a slight man with black horn-rimmed glasses and a Brooklyn accent that hasn't faded with the years. He isn't slick or smooth. He's a throwback, a *Brooklyn* Dodger, who worked his way up in the organization from the ticket office to traveling secretary. "From the day Koufax came up to the day he left, he never changed. He's a perfect gentleman. Koufax don't need a Mercedes. Koufax don't need a Jaguar. Give him a golf club and a sandwich after the game and he's the happiest man in the world. We're two peas out of the same pod. Don't need publicity. Don't need fame."

And so the refrain caught on: He's just like DiMaggio—private, reclusive; the ghost of Dodgertown, Greta Garbo, and J. D. Salinger rolled into one. "There aren't many people that Sandy has let into his life in terms of really knowing him," said Wilpon. "But the degree to which he was more remote, the degree of being out of the public eye, has changed over the last forty years, depending on his circumstances. When he was married to Anne, that stage of his life, he was more remote."

The marriage didn't last but the reputation did. Andy Etchebarren, who cherishes the distinction of being the last batter ever to face him, met him in a bar at one of those old-timer boondoggles soon after he and Anne parted. "It was a sad thing," he said. "He stayed single a long time. He was really in love with this girl. He had just got divorced. He loved this girl something terrible. He was going from there to Indonesia. I remember sitting at the bar, knowing how down he was. I could see he was really hurting. He told me he loved her very much and it didn't work out. I thought, 'Jesus Christ, this guy's really a nice guy.' Not like everybody thought."

He is offended by the right things: a lack of civility, honesty, kindness. As Walter O'Malley once said of him: "Sandy gets a little disillusioned. He'd like a better world. He wants to see the best in everybody." And so is disappointed when organizers of a dinner honoring his old college coach promise he'll be just one of the guys and put his name on the awards program to sell tickets. Or when a rabbi asks him to sign yarmulkes for seventy-five bar mitzvahs and sells them. Or when Larry King, the talkmeister, goes around telling stories about how they were buddies back in high school. The story King tells most often is the Carvel story: an innocuous tale of high school joy-riding to New Haven, Connecticut, to buy Carvel ice cream, Koufax's favorite, for fifteen cents a scoop. The only problem with the story is it never happened. David Finkel, a reporter at the *Washington Post*, working on a profile about King, wanted to hear Koufax's version. A couple of days later "the recluse" returned his call, setting the record straight. "This is Sandy Koufax," he said. "I've never been to New Haven."

The story tells more about Koufax than it does about King or ice cream. "Larry's a publicist," says Richard Kaufman, who knew them back in Brooklyn. "Sandy's a privatist." Friends told him to let it go. It's just a story. So what if King improved it. What's the big schmeer? But it was a big schmeer to Koufax.

People are always placing themselves in the center of his orbit. The impulse is antithetical to him. He lacks the instinct or the appetite for self-aggrandizement. Because he chooses not to comment publicly on his life or to refute the collective impression of it, the assessment of him as aloof continues to solidify into hardened perception. When he was a no-show at the 1999 All-Star Game in Boston, his absence was cited as further evidence of his reclusive self. In fact, he never received an invitation. When he does show up, he is invariably asked about being a recluse. "My friends don't think I'm a recluse," he says frequently and pointedly.

In the last summer of the old millennium, after the editors of *Sports Illustrated* named him their favorite athlete of the century, fans sought his autograph on the cover that bore the headline: "The Incomparable and Mysterious Sandy Koufax." They were stunned to learn he hadn't read it. Nor had he watched ESPN's video profile for its series on the top fifty athletes of the century although he was the only pitcher named. "Don't believe all that crap," he told reporters. "I haven't disappeared, I'm not lost, and I'm not very mysterious."

The profile made mention of the fact that the house in Maine he had shared with Anne thirty years earlier had been donated by a subsequent owner to the local fire department. The firemen torched the place and used it to practice their fire-fighting technique. When they were done, memorabilia bounty hunters scoured the charred remains for a piece of him like vultures drawn to carrion.

To the extent that he removed himself from public view, it was not so much because he believed there are no second acts in American life as because he was determined to have one. He does not disavow who he was or what he accomplished. He is proud of it. He simply refuses to exist in cinders and ashes. He doesn't speak of himself in the third person, but he does think of "Sandy Koufax" as someone else, a persona separate from himself. If he was seeking refuge from anything, it was that. "He may be the most misunderstood man in baseball," his teammate John Kennedy said.

He is a good friend, he remembers birthdays, he has an open heart— as Bob Hendley learned one day thirty-five years after the fact when an unexpected package arrived at his door. Koufax had taken his time thinking of the perfect inscription to write on the ball he had enclosed. "What a game," he wrote, finally.

Typical understatement from a man who devoted all of a page to it in his autobiography, seven paragraphs of which were about Hendley. There was also a note. "We had a moment, a night, and a career. I hope life has been good to you—Sandy."

When Hendley showed the ball to his son, Bart said, "Dad, this ball is from that era."

A Rawlings ball, not used these days. Signed by Warren Giles, the long-dead National League president.

"I'd often been asked what it was like to be the other guy," Hendley said. "I wrote Sandy a note and I said I always responded, 'It's no disgrace to get beat by class.'"

* * *

"The thing I wonder is, what do you do all day?"

The question, posed by his former teammate Claude Osteen, is the one everybody asks. After all, he was a young man, just thirty, when he left the game. Dusty Baker, the former Dodger, asked him about his plans one day and received this idiosyncratic reply. "He said he's gonna just be a farmer someplace, have very few clothes on and ride a tractor around all day. I thought that was one of the coolest retirement plans I'd ever heard. He's one of the coolest dudes I've met, ever."

"People ask all the time, 'What's he done with his life?'" Sutton said. "He's *enjoyed* it."

"Tell 'em I'm having fun," Koufax invariably replies when asked the same question.

He has married and divorced twice. He never had children. He built a house and a golf swing. He learned to fly-fish and to fly, taking lessons in an old crop duster. He drove a tractor, ran marathons, and tried to learn how to speak Italian. "He's done a lot of things since baseball," Sutton says. "He takes up fly-fishing and masters it. He takes up golf and masters it. Whatever he does, he masters it. When he gets tired of it, then he goes on and finds something to challenge him. He has a vast and broad knowledge of a lot of things, from plays to symphonies to wine."

He educated himself, though not formally. He is as well traveled as he is well read. He used to carry a business card identifying himself as a Peregrination Expert. The novelist Philip Roth, whom some say he has come to resemble in late middle age, has an exacting standard for those he deems serious readers—people who think not only about what they read but about what they are going to read. The only subject matter that doesn't interest Koufax is himself.

"He wasn't just a jock," said Richard Kaufman, the Bensonhurst wrestler turned Washington economist. "He had a reflecting intelligence."

On March 27, 1979, Koufax showed up in uniform in the clubhouse at Dodgertown, the newest and most renowned minor league pitching

coach in baseball history. "Like a lot of people living on a fixed income,
I need the money," he told reporters. Rarely, they noted, had anyone
seemed so happy to be pedaling a stationary bike in a locker room.

In all the published ruminations about his removal from the public
scene, it never seemed to cross anyone's mind that his self-imposed exile
from baseball was a consequence of his love for the game, not his distaste for it. Koufax would admit as much years later, saying, "I really didn't
want to be around it for a while."

For nine years, he traveled the baseball boonies, eating pizza at midnight in some dive in Missoula, Montana, or getting dressed in a rinky-
dink minor league locker room while on assignment with the
Albuquerque Dukes. Kennedy, also a roving instructor, would look over
at him, not quite believing he was dressing next to Sandy Koufax. Maybe
it was the uniform. Koufax looked a little funny in those rainbow uniforms the Dukes used to wear.

He worked with some of the best arms in the Dodger system: Orel
Hershiser, Dave Stewart, John Franco, Bob Welch. Hershiser still
remembers the particulars of a twenty-five-year-old conversation that
took place on a bench in an instructional league dugout, listening as
Koufax articulated the intricacies of the game, the mechanics of pitching; pointing out how the field was playing and what the wind direction
was and why the pitch selection was wrong; why as you fatigue a certain
pitch becomes better. Angell contacted him again, wanting to write a
piece about Koufax, the pitching coach. Again, after initial enthusiasm,
he was rebuffed. Again, Angell thought, Strange guy.

Just staying beneath the radar, friends explained. But not exactly off
the screen. At a Cracker Jack old-timers game in Buffalo, a reporter followed him into the shower. "He came up to me laughing," promoter
Dick Cecil said. "He said, 'I was doing this interview. It was late. I'm
heading for the shower. I get in the water and he's in there with me.' The
guy was just so happy to be talking to Sandy Koufax he'd follow him
anywhere—which he did."

At another Cracker Jack game played at R.F.K. Stadium in
Washington, D.C., in the mid-1980s, Koufax took the mound for the

National League in the first inning, just throwing the ball over to let people hit it. "And then somebody from the American League started throwing hard, trying to pitch to us," Billy Williams recalled. "And Sandy said, 'I didn't know that they wanted us to pitch.' And the next inning, he went out there and he threw twelve pitches and struck out everybody."

Afterward, in the locker room, Williams was sitting with Lou Brock, Willie Stargell, and Willie McCovey when Joe Garagiola wandered by this quartet of fair hitters and wondered out loud how many home runs they had hit collectively off Koufax. "That's when Koufax appeared," Williams said. "Sandy, right away, says, 'I'll tell you.' So he pointed to me. 'You hit two, and you hit none, you hit none, and you hit one.' He *knew*. He could count 'em."

It was at one of those Dodger Fantasy Camps that he first met Dave Wallace. Wallace watched from the third base coaching box the transformation in the aging left-hander when his mettle was questioned. "He was in throwing shape because he had thrown batting practice in the summer for the minor league teams. And you're throwing the ball and having a little fun and some wise-ass fantasy camper walking up to the plate says, 'Goddamn, Koufax, is that all you've got?'

"I mean to tell you, his eyes changed like that. He threw four or five pitches there's no doubt in my mind were on the verge of ninety miles an hour. 'Take that, you smart-ass sonofabitch.'"

At the celebration of the thirtieth anniversary of the Dodgers' 1955 World Championship, Koufax prevailed upon his old teammate Roger Craig to teach him the new split-fingered fastball he had developed. Koufax figured he needed to know how to throw it if he was going to teach it. "He was throwing it pretty good," Craig said. "A couple of days later, he said, 'I could make a comeback.' He coulda got people out."

Terry Collins thought so, too. He was working for Buzzie Bavasi's son, Bill, at the time. "Bill said, 'Hey, Sandy, if I give you the hundred grand Buzzie wouldn't give you, would you give me three starts?'" Collins said. "Oh, God, I laughed. Shit, he was throwing bee-bees. I said, 'Sandy, God, get in shape.'"

He *was* in shape: thirty pounds lighter than his playing weight. His second wife, Kim, was an exercise enthusiast. He became a serious though paradoxical runner, a marathoner who smoked, competing in Europe, where he was least likely to be recognized. Year-round employees at Dodgertown became accustomed to finding him in the workout room in the morning before anyone else arrived. "I came in and there was a guy sitting in the dark on the Exercycle watching *Sports Center* at seven A.M.," said Grant Greisser, then general manager of the Vero Beach Dodgers. "I said, 'You mind if I turn on the light?' I turned on half the bank of lights. It was Koufax on the Exercycle. After forty-five minutes, he was still going at it. I didn't want to quit and look bad."

He resigned his position with the Dodgers in 1990, saying he wasn't earning his keep. Peter O'Malley says the fault was his for not giving Koufax enough to do. Friends, reading between published lines, blamed his estrangement from the organization on an uneasy relationship with manager Tommy Lasorda, who, Collins says, resented Koufax's work with his pitchers. There was also the slight matter of the farm director who questioned his expense reports.

Four years later, when Kennedy became manager of the Texas Rangers, he asked Koufax's wife if she thought he might like to work with his pitchers in spring training—among them Nolan Ryan. "She said, 'I'm sure he'd love it. All anybody ever had to do was ask and he'd be there. People never ask. Like everybody else he just wants to be wanted.'

"He called me back the same day. He said, 'Tell the owners, I don't want to be paid or employed. I won't wear a Rangers uniform.' He wore Ranger blue pants and a generic hat."

Osteen was in Texas with Koufax and Kennedy that spring, too. "One night riding back to the apartment, at the end of the day, he said to me, 'You know, I've really enjoyed this. I've kind of missed it—the camaraderie, the talk, as much as the on-the-field stuff.' I can't tell you how good that made me feel. I never thought I'd hear that from him."

Years later, when Ryan entered into the Hall of Fame, he spent the morning of his induction walk-through in the library at Cooperstown reviewing photos of *Koufax's* career, marveling at his form and demonstrating for the archivists how Koufax did what he did.

Now, he mentors informally—showing up at the Mets spring training camp in Port St. Lucie to help Wilpon's team and, of course, at Dodgertown, eschewing face-time for distant mounds where he works with young pitchers. In this way, Koufax is not unlike Milt Gold, Milt Laurie, and Milt "Pop" Secol, Brooklyn men, coaches, who volunteered their time to help other men's sons realize their potential. This is where he can be a baseball player again, Collins says—and a teacher. "You should be better," he told Al Leiter one day after observing him in spring training. "I know," Leiter replied.

A couple of days later, Wilpon passed on Koufax's telephone number and a message: "Call anytime." Leiter was honored and astonished, unsure what he had done to merit the attention. Unlike so many self-satisfied players, Leiter wanted to get better. As Koufax likes to say, *When a pupil is ready, a teacher will come.*

One night, not long after, Leiter returned home after pitching eight shutout innings to find a message from Koufax on his answering machine: "Way to go. Great job. But when you've got him set up for the outside corner, you gotta nail it." And then he hung up.

He shows up: a small phrase redolent with clubhouse meaning. Koufax shows up at charity banquets and charity golf tournaments and charity banquets at charity golf tournaments; at induction ceremonies and funerals; at the Final Four and high school basketball games. Occasionally, he shows up in the pages of glossy magazines, as he did a while back with Kevin Costner in *People* at a benefit for pediatric AIDS. Or on the front page of the *New York Times* with all the other Hall of Famers who were among President George W. Bush's first guests at the White House in March 2001. Or on a banquet dais demanding to know of a surprised Gene Oliver, "How did a putz like you hit .392 off me?" (Oliver's polished reply: "He thought I was Jewish and took care of me.")

He is in constant demand—and the demand is insatiable. He does perhaps one autograph show a year. The six-figure salary he held out for in 1966 he can make just signing his name in an afternoon. Once, Kennedy says, Koufax signed 10,000 bats in a single week—at ten dollars a pop. He doesn't hate the memorabilia industry—it's how he makes his living—but he loathes its seamy underside.

Every year, the board of directors of the Jewish Community House of Bensonhurst asks Pearl Kane, their head of development, why she can't get Koufax for their fund-raiser. "Because he doesn't want to be gotten," she finally told them. "People want his money, his autograph. You know what I want? I want him to come here and meet the fifty thousand Russian kids in Bensonhurst—they all know him—show them how to hold a baseball and tell them about his immigrant family and how they once came here and how baseball made him an American." As if 50,000 Russian émigré teenagers know from Sandy Koufax. He engenders hyperbole—particularly in fund-raisers. He would no doubt be appalled to learn that staffers at the "J" Xeroxed copies of his annual dues check and plastered it all over the building—just so they could have a copy *of a copy* of his signature.

He always shows up for teammates. He showed up at Rachel Robinson's side at Shea Stadium during ceremonies marking the fiftieth anniversary of her husband's major league debut. And at Cooperstown for Sutton's induction into the Hall of Fame. Sutton, the son of Alabama tenant farmers, wanted to thank Koufax publicly for teaching him how to tip in a restaurant and a clubhouse; how to tailor a suit and a mound; how to behave like a professional.

In Al Campanis's final years, when so many others in the Dodger family were distancing themselves from the old scout, who had embarrassed himself and the franchise with insensitive racial remarks on ABC's *Nightline*, Koufax called and said: "Don't let one incident ruin your life. We know how you are. You know how you are."

When Campanis died some years later, Koufax and Scully were among the mourners. "We need some young guys to pick up the front end of the casket," Al's son Jimmy would recall the funeral director saying. "Vin and Sandy start backing away. I said, 'Sandy, you and Vin *are* the young guys.' As they're carrying him out, Sandy starts laughing and Vin says, 'Your dad is probably turning over in his grave.'"

Linn always thought Koufax looked for occasions to laugh—and found them even in the darkest situations. Mark Reese, Pee Wee's son, remembers being with Koufax and his dad in an airport lounge at LAX after Drysdale's funeral. Koufax wore a green baseball cap with one of those long, faux ponytails then in fashion. They killed time reveling in the double takes he engendered.

His sister's death in 1997 marked another turning point. He was divorced from his second wife soon after. Life is too short for one to be pinned down to unhappiness. He has a loving relationship with a mature woman who is his equal and nieces and nephews to spoil. Friends say he's never been happier or more at ease with "Sandy Koufax." They also say he is a genuinely modest man who dismisses idolatry with a practiced throwaway line: "The older I get, the better I used to be."

In 1998, when the Dodgers retired Sutton's uniform number, an invitation to the festivities never reached Koufax. O'Malley assumed Koufax knew he was invited based on an earlier conversation and did not want a form letter to be sent to him. So Koufax paid his own way, showing up at the stadium unexpected. There was no mention of him in the pre-written script. After the ceremony, Sutton told Koufax how much it meant that he had come. "How could I not?" Koufax replied. "You're the only three-hundred-game winner I ever played with."

He had brought an old equipment bag with him and filled it with some of the trophies the Dodgers had been holding for him. O'Malley assured him they would always be safe at Dodger Stadium. But the franchise was passing into the corporate portfolio of Rupert Murdoch. It wasn't the Dodgers anymore.

On the flight home, he was seated beside Joe Pietro, an Avon Company executive, who grew up a Yankee fan but rooted for Koufax. "You *had* to root for Koufax," he said. Pietro waited until the plane took off to acknowledge the obvious. "I'm a big, big fan," he said.

"He got that boyish, sheepish grin. He said, 'Thanks, thanks a lot.' He nodded and smiled. He wasn't turned off. I said, 'One of the things

I remember was the seventh game of the 1965 World Series. You're pitching with two days' rest and one of your two pitches wasn't working.'

" 'Nothing was working that day,' he said. 'I don't know how I got through it.' There was a gleam in his eye—a little pride."

But he quickly turned the conversation around, wanting to know what Pietro did, where he came from. Pietro thought, He could be your next-door neighbor or your best friend. If only people would let him. When the plane landed, they shook hands and said good-bye. At the baggage claim, Pietro saw him sitting alone on the conveyor belt waiting for his belongings. He couldn't help but watch. He wanted to see Sandy Koufax pick up his bag. Inside were the trophies ransomed from Dodger Stadium. Later, he would dig a hole and bury some of them at an undisclosed location, other Dodgers would confide. It wasn't as if he was burying the past or running away from it. Just putting it in its place.

At the Baseball Assistance Team dinner in Manhattan, held annually to raise money for indigent ballplayers who came of age before free agency, organizers invariably station him in the farthest corner of the massive ballroom. The lines that form before him are always the longest. Over his left shoulder one year, an exit sign burned crimson: Occupancy of More Than 60 Is Considered Dangerous and Unlawful.

A security guard stood to his right, an impassive sentinel in a bad tan suit. People thrust balls at him, pennants, ticket stubs, magazine covers. No one said please or thank you. The monotony was relieved by occasional levity, as when one fan inquired, "How come no women, Sandy?"

"Too old, didn't make enough money."

Everyone laughed. The total Dodger payroll for the fifteen years Buzzie Bavasi was general manager equals Kevin Brown's $15 million annual salary. Someone asked the inevitable question. If, in the brave new world of baseball, Brown is worth $105 million to the Dodgers, what would they have had to offer Koufax? The answer, to paraphrase Garagiola: "Howdy, partner."

Joe Pignatano, another old catcher, a buddy from Brooklyn, eased himself onto an adjacent stool. "Hey, how come he gets to sit there?" a voice demanded.

"Roomie seat," Koufax said, smiling.

On the surface, Piggy is everything Koufax is not—paunchy and balding, indifferently dressed in the manner of baseball men who never had to decide what to wear when they got up in the morning, his accent Brooklyn thick. In fact, they are not so different. Piggy is who Koufax aspires to be—just another guy happy to be on this side of the grass.

Piggy's pals don't stand on line for his autograph. Koufax looked up to see a familiar face, Solly Hemus, the third base coach of the Mets who gave him such hell during his first no-hitter. "Solly!" he said, brightening, then blanched at the commemorative baseball in Hemus's hand. Another peer had become an acolyte.

After an hour and fifteen minutes, the ballroom lights flickered, signaling an end to the affair. The conga line dissolved into a voracious mob. Kids who already had one autograph ducked beneath the velvet ropes, unrestrained by parents or manners. Ten, twelve, maybe twenty baseballs were thrust at Koufax from every angle: low and away, high and tight, right down the middle. There was nowhere to go, no personal space, no exit. The security guard placed a meaty hand protectively on his shoulder and whispered urgently into a lapel microphone, "Table five is a madhouse."

What is this impulse, this need for a shred of greatness, a name scrawled on a sweet spot? Koufax doesn't get it. The need mystifies him; he is dubious about his ability to fill it. But he does the best he can, within the bounds of taste and decorum, bringing dignity to this most undignified pursuit—the sycophantic elevation of one human being over another and the exploitation of that difference for material gain.

Not long ago, he was a featured guest at a BAT event in Omaha. Bob Costas was the emcee. As he was making the introductions, he inadvertently skipped over Koufax. At first, the lapse seemed intentional—the biggest star in the room should be introduced last. But it wasn't. Costas smoothly ad-libbed his way out of his embarrassment. "And, of course, who could forget the great Sandy Koufax?"

Costas was mortified, having done just that. Koufax was delighted.

For once, he was an afterthought. "Bob! Bob!" he said, getting up from his seat. "K comes after R in the Jewish alphabet!"

As he stood, the white helium-infused balloon inscribed with his name jerked free of its mooring in the center of the table and drifted to the ballroom ceiling, floating above the fray. This is where he'd like to be. In American life, that makes him odd, enigmatic. An enigma defies understanding. Koufax does not. "He doesn't defy anything," Costas said later, "except the norm."

That, finally, is what makes him different. Not his religion or his taste in music or literature or even his gentleness. Players recognize and respect that which distinguishes him, and they are protective of it. At the 1985 All-Star Game in Minneapolis, he and Harmon Killebrew were named honorary captains of their respective teams. Twenty years had passed since they faced each other in the ninth inning of the seventh game of the 1965 World Series. Metropolitan Stadium was gone, replaced by an egregious indoor ballpark shaped like a pillow. Some hot-shot public relations guy decided it would be fun to put them in uniform and take them out to the river, where Koufax would throw a pitch and Killebrew would try to hit the sucker across the Mighty Mississippi.

The two Hall of Famers got in a limo and drove to the narrowest bend in the river, where a crowd of 5,000 fans—and one ten-year-old boy in full catcher's gear—were waiting for them. Killebrew took one look at the whole carny setup, the 800-foot width of the river, and told Koufax, "No fucking way." He wasn't about to help embarrass the greatest lefty in history. "Kid," he said, wrapping his arm around the disappointed boy. "You ain't catching Koufax today."

The first time I met Sandy Koufax, I assumed it would be the last. The bar in the players' lounge at Dodgertown was empty, the taps dry, the lunch crowd gone. The lounge belonged to ghosts and legends: Jackie and Pee Wee, Podres and The Duke, Branca, Hodges, and Koufax too. Their unlined faces peered down from larger-than-life photo murals, each one given over to a different era, another world series team. I placed myself beneath a montage from October 1963, when Koufax struck out fifteen Yankees at the Stadium. Above my head, he was leaping into Roseboro's arms, their fates and shadows intertwined; their teammates engulfing them in an embrace of conjoined elation.

Koufax let himself in through a side door, emerging out of the sunshine into the shadows of the dimly lit bar. Over his shoulder were fields of green and empty pitching mounds. Backlit against Field One, where he threw his first pitch as a Dodger, he appeared in silhouette and much as the *Los Angeles Times* had recently described him, "a cross between a Greek god and Gregory Peck." He introduced himself politely and unnecessarily. He did not look up.

Twice a year, the old naval base is turned over to Fantasy Campers, grown men who pay $5,000 to cram themselves into double-knits adorned with the numbers 14, 4, 42, and 32 and walk the fields where Gil and Duke and Jackie and Sandy once roamed. They say they come for the competition and the instruction. The truth is, they come because spikes make the same sound on gravel no matter who's wearing them. The highlight of their stay is the annual game between campers and old-timers played at Holman Stadium. Koufax wanted to go over and see some friends, some of those guys in the photographs above our heads.

His arrival at Holman Stadium was heralded by the crackle of walkie-talkies—"We got Sandy in the press box"—the static generating unwelcome attention. Not that he needed to be introduced. Hatless and dressed in a T-shirt and jeans, Koufax was immediately apparent. A uniform would have offered better cover. He would have been just another middle-aged guy wearing number 32.

When he walks across an empty stadium parking lot an hour after a night game no one knew he was planning to attend, people materialize like moths drawn to a flame. Here, they swarm. "You want security?" a stadium official asked.

"Nah," he said, accepting a beer and a pretzel on the house instead.

"For your aggravation," the concession man said.

"It's not enough," Koufax said with a grin.

As he bit into the pretzel, a billowing woman swathed in a lime sun dress bulldozed her way toward him. "I've been trying to *get* you since

1955," she said. There was hardness in her voice and in her phrase, an edgy voraciousness at odds with the soft breeze that whispered through the orange groves. Nobody knew who Koufax was in 1955.

The Fantasy Campers in their gray road uniforms were lined up spryly along the first base line waiting to be announced—to hear the echo of their names roll across the field where Koufax pitched. As word of his arrival spread, the line began to curl back across foul territory toward the press box until it formed a question mark. Grown men broke ranks and ran galloping up the concrete steps toward him. First among them was a camper wearing number 32, who squatted at Koufax's feet unable to speak, to move, or to leave. "Excuse me," Koufax said, finally, "I've got to go see my friends."

He made his way quickly through the sparse, disbelieving crowd, descending the rows toward the home dugout. He climbed over the chain link fence and disappeared into a profusion of crisp white uniforms. True, the bodies occupying them were not quite as crisp as they once had been. But there they were: Duke and Branca, Erskine and Labine, Reggie Smith, Rick Monday, Steve Yeager, Jerry Reuss, and Jeff Torborg, Dodgers all, teammates, converging upon him. Koufax was mobbed in the dugout again.

In the weeks before our rendezvous, I had lots of time to prepare my arguments, advance my cause for making this an exception to his self-imposed rule against personal retrospective. I hadn't expected to get this far. And I didn't expect ever to speak to him again. I thought about the one thing I needed to know, the one question I had to ask, in order to proceed.

As we walked back toward the clubhouse from the stadium, he talked about the way Vero Beach looked in 1955, how he preferred the rustic, raw simplicity of the past. Back inside the bar, we were surrounded by it. This time, he looked up, taking in the whole tableau—the fond pummeling by the dugout steps as his teammates engulfed him, yanking on his arm, knocking his cap askew like some dead-end kid. Like they couldn't get enough of him. "I absolutely loved it," he said. "How could you do the things I did and not love it?"

Appendix

INTERVIEWS WITH PLAYERS, COACHES, DODGER EMPLOYEES, FANS
AT DODGER STADIUM, SEPTEMBER 9, 1965

Gary Adams, spectator (later UCLA coach)
Red Adams, Dodger coach
Joe Amalfitano, Cubs pinch hitter
Ed Bailey, Cubs reserve catcher
Ernie Banks, Cubs first baseman
Buzzie Bavasi, Dodger general manager
Glenn Beckert, Cubs shortstop
Byron Browne, Cubs left fielder
Bill Buhler, Dodger trainer
Phil Collier, sportswriter, *San Diego Union* (deceased)
Tommy Davis, Dodger outfielder
Bill DeLury, Dodger front office
Ron Fairly, Dodger right fielder
Preston Gomez, Dodger coach
Bob Hendley, Cubs pitcher
Ken Holtzman, Cubs pitcher
Richard Hume, attorney for Koufax

Lou Johnson, Dodger left fielder

Nobe Kawano, Dodger clubhouse man

John Kennedy, Dodger utility infielder

Kevin Kennedy, fan listening on radio (later Dodger coach)

Don Kessinger, Cubs second baseman

Chris Krug, Cubs catcher

Jim "Frenchie" Lefebvre, Dodger second baseman

Joe Moeller, Dodger pitcher

Nate Oliver, Dodger utility infielder

Claude Osteen, Dodger pitcher

Danny Ozark, Dodger coach

Wes Parker, Dodger first baseman

Ron Perranoski, Dodger relief pitcher

Johnny Podres, Dodger pitcher

John Roseboro, Dodger catcher

Ron Santo, Cubs third baseman

Vin Scully, Dodger broadcaster

Bill Singer, Dodger pitcher

Dave Smith, fan listening on radio

Jeff Torborg, Dodger catcher

Dick Tracewski, Dodger utility infielder

Ed Vargo, home plate umpire

Tom Villante, broadcast coordinator

John Werhas, Dodger utility infielder

Billy Williams, Cubs outfielder

Maury Wills, Dodger shortstop

Sandy Koufax: Career Statistics*

	W	L	PCT	ERA	G	GS	CG	IP	H	BB	SO	ShO	Relief Pitching W	L	SV	BATTING AB	H	HR	BA
1955 BKN N	2	2	.500	3.02	12	5	2	41.2	33	28	30	2	0	1	0	12	0	0	.000
1956	2	4	.333	4.91	16	10	0	58.2	66	29	30	0	0	0	0	17	2	0	.118
1957	5	4	.556	3.88	34	13	2	104.1	83	51	122	0	1	0	0	26	0	0	.000
1958 LA N	11	11	.500	4.48	40	26	5	158.2	132	105	131	0	3	1	1	49	6	0	.122
1959	8	6	.571	4.05	35	23	6	153.1	136	92	173	1	0	0	2	54	6	0	.111
1960	8	13	.381	3.91	37	26	7	175	133	100	197	2	1	0	1	57	7	0	.123
1961	18	13	.581	3.52	42	35	15	255.2	212	96	269	2	1	0	1	77	5	0	.065
1962	14	7	.667	2.54	28	26	11	184.1	134	57	216	2	0	0	1	69	6	1	.087
1963	25	5	.833	1.88	40	40	20	311	214	58	306	11	0	0	0	110	7	1	.064
1964	19	5	.792	1.74	29	28	15	223	154	53	223	7	0	0	1	74	7	0	.095
1965	26	8	.765	2.04	43	41	27	335.2	216	71	382	8	0	0	2	113	20	0	.177
1966	27	9	.750	1.73	41	41	27	323	241	77	317	5	0	0	0	118	9	0	.076
12 yrs.	165	87	.655	2.76	397	314	137	2324.1	1754	817	2396	40	6	2	9	776	75	2	.097
WORLD SERIES																			
1959 LA N	0	1	.000	1.00	2	1	0	9	5	1	7	0	0	0	0	2	0	0	.000
1963	2	0	1.000	1.50	2	2	2	18	12	3	23	0	0	0	0	6	0	0	.000
1965	2	1	.667	0.38	3	3	2	24	13	5	29	2	0	0	0	9	1	0	.111
1966	0	1	.000	1.50	1	1	0	6	6	2	2	0	0	0	0	2	0	0	.000
4 yrs.	4	3	.571	0.95 5th	8	7	4	57	36	11	61 4th	2 4th	0	0	0	19	1	0	.053

*Adapted from Joseph L. Reichler, ed., *The Baseball Encyclopedia: The Complete and Official Record of Major League Baseball*, 7th ed. (New York: Macmillan Publishing Company, 1988).

Acknowledgments

I NEVER LIKED THE WORD *ACKNOWLEDGMENTS* mostly because I couldn't spell it. Now that I can spell it, the word seems woefully inadequate to the task at hand. Writing is a collaborative act between author and subject, fact and imagination, scribe and supporters, friends, family, and colleagues, who are the flying buttresses to ambition. A simple thank you, while polite and pertinent, does not convey a sufficient degree of indebtedness. Really what these people are is contributors, and they ought to be credited as such. Here is my list.

Michelangelo had his David; I have three—Hirshey, Kindred, and Black, each an original, each deserving of his own pedestal. First among them is David Hirshey, better known to me as Dr. D. In 1978, David guided me across the threshold of my first professional locker room. Three years ago, when he broached the idea for this book, he swept me off my feet with his enthusiasm, confidence, and conviction. In so doing, he ushered me across another threshold and back to a place I didn't know I had missed. My gratitude cannot be sufficiently measured, because it is endless. The Doctor is always in.

David Kindred, my former colleague at the *Washington Post* and abiding friend, offered succor and tolerance. Every writer needs someone to turn to in moments of abject neediness, when the mind and the screen go blank. Dave is that person. His good opinion means the world to me. I owe him big time.

David Black is not just my agent. He is the agent of this endeavor, having brought me together with HarperCollins. Fifteen years ago, give or take, David read my account of my parents' first date at Loehmann's in Brooklyn and called to offer his services. I had other representation at the time. "No problem," he said. "I'll wait." And he did—first for my allegiance, then for me to produce. This is the fruition of his belief.

Gentle readers are not what any writer needs. A writer needs truth gently wielded. It's no small job. I turned to four kind and uncompromising souls whose judgment is clearer and better than my own. Howard Norman brought to the manuscript a novelist's acute sense of human drama and his own very idiosyncratic take on all things Jewish, forcing me to think outside the batter's box. Carole Horn, editor and healer, kept me sane, kept me well, and kept me searching for a better word. George Vecsey, sports columnist for the *New York Times* and author of *The Baseball Life of Sandy Koufax,* a children's biography published in 1968, offered unique and invaluable perspective. Dave Smith, the newest Dave, proprietor of Retrosheet, inundated me with his statistical generosity, access to Roth's scoresheets, and abiding enthusiasm for the subject.

Plundering memory is what reporters do. Those belonging to Joey Amalfitano, Bob Hendley, Jeff Torborg, and Dick Tracewski were formative in reconstructing the night of September 9, 1965. I could not have done this without them. The late Phil Collier, also there that night, was a source of unending information and moral support. Rabbi M. Bruce Lustig, senior rabbi at the Washington Hebrew Congregation, made sure I didn't embarrass myself theologically. Mark Langill, publications editor for the Los Angeles Dodgers—my "rabbi" at Chavez Ravine— saved me with patience, humor, and archival knowledge of the home team. I am indebted to Fred Wilpon and Don Fehr for their insight and entree. Amy Engelsman, PT, MS, SCS, physical therapist extraordinaire, massaged my aching back and the biomechanical sections of the manuscript with TLC. John Labombarda of the Elias Sports Bureau was my statistical backstop, ensuring there would be as few errors as possible in the delivery of this story. Samantha Medford, associate producer of ESPN's *Athlete of the Century* profile of Koufax, generously shared her research and her impressions. Jason McCullough did months of legwork at the Library of Congress, tracking down game stories and box scores from long-forgotten contests. Charles Heller and his staff at Mail Boxes Etc. made sure that when it absolutely, positively had to get there, it did.

Behind every competent woman, there is another more competent one. Christine Maloney, indefatigable aide de camp, made it possible for me to do what I do by doing so much of what I was supposed to do. And behind her is Fatima Tarrinha, without whom I could not function.

To friends and allies at HarperCollins: Susan Weinberg, Jeff Kellogg, Elliott Beard, David Koral, Aimery Dunlap-Smith, Tom Cherwin, Camillo LoGiudice, and p.r. babe Tara Brown. At Black, Inc.: Gary Morris, Jason Sacher, and Leigh Anne Elisero. At the Hall of Fame: Tim Wiles, Greg Harris, Bill Burdick, Russell Wolinsky—I'm buying.

As of this writing, I have a few stalwart friends and relatives left who are still willing to hear about Sandy Koufax. Chief among them: Anita and Sheldon Isakoff, Harry Jaffe, Annette Leavy, Dick and Caren Lobo, Liz Ohlrich, Wendy and Steven Phillips, Robert Pinsky, Jon Rupp, Norman Steinberg, Sid and Diana Tabak, Ada Vaughn, and Hal and Marilyn Weiner. A special shout out to my all-star girl group who carry me and the tune: Dede McClure, Florence Nightingale of the hard drive, who ministered to frayed nerves and disabled software at all hours of the morning and the night; Jane Shore, who made me laugh and think; and Nell Minow, who made me think and laugh; and my own dear Ms. H, who told me once a long time ago when I was least inclined to believe it that I was entitled to my own voice and thus helped me find it.

My father, Mort "The Sport" Leavy, taught me how to throw (not like a girl) and to love baseball. He also provides the best literary lawyering any daughter ever had. My mother, who used to hate baseball, has given up and now roots for the Mets.

Peter is, and always will be, my go-to guy. Nick and Emma are the heart of my order.

—Jane Leavy, April 2002

Index

ATTENDANCE

VARGO- PELEKOUDAS - JACKOWSKI - PRYOR
UMPIRES

CHICAGO CUBS	POS.	1	2	3	4	5	6	7	8	9	10	11	12
23-YOUNG	8	4			F3			K					
18-BECKERT	4	K			9			9					
26-WILLIAMS	9	K			K			7					
10-SANTO	5		2		X	7		X	Kc				
14-BANKS	3		K			K			Ks				
29-BROWN	7		8			63			Ks				
25-KROG	2			8		X	63		X	Ks			
11-KESSINGER	6			9			53			Ks			
23-HENDLEY	1			K			K			Ks			